THE BOY
KINGDOM

EL REINO DE
LOS VARONES

TAMBIÉN POR ACHY OBEJAS

PROSA:

The Tower of the Antilles: Short Stories

Kimberle

Aguas y otros cuentos

Ruins

Days of Awe

Memory Mambo

We Came All the Way from Cuba
So You Could Dress Like This?

COMO EDITORA:

Immigrant Voices: 21st Century Stories
(with Megan Bayles)

Havana Noir

POESÍA:

Boomerang / Bumerán

Un cuento y once poemas

This Is What Happened in Our Other Life

THE BOY KINGDOM

POEMS

ACHY OBEJAS

RAISED VOICES

BEACON PRESS, BOSTON

EL REINO DE LOS VARONES

POEMAS

ACHY OBEJAS

VOCES ALZADAS

BEACON PRESS, BOSTON

BEACON PRESS
24 Farnsworth Street
Boston, Massachusetts
www.beacon.org

Beacon Press books
are published under the auspices of
the Unitarian Universalist Association of Congregations.

28 27 26 25   8 7 6 5 4 3 2 1

Raised Voices: a poetry series established in 2021 to raise
marginalized voices and perspectives, to publish poems that affirm
progressive values and are accessible to a wide readership, and to
celebrate poetry's ability to access truth in a way that no other form can.

Voces Alzadas: una serie de poesía establecida en 2021 para
potenciar voces y perspectivas marginadas, publicar textos que
afirmen valores progresistas, que sean accesibles para un gran público
y que celebren las posibilidades de este género para acceder a la
verdad como ninguna otra forma de arte ha conseguido hacerlo.

This book is printed on acid-free paper that meets the uncoated paper
ANSI/NISO specifications for permanence as revised in 1992.

Text design and composition by Kim Arney

*Library of Congress Cataloguing-in-Publication
Data is available for this title.*
Paperback ISBN: 978-0-8070-1753-1
E-book ISBN: 978-0-8070-1754-8

The authorized representative in the EU for product safety and
compliance is Easy Access System Europe 16879218, Mustamäe tee 50,
10621 Tallinn, Estonia: http://beacon.org/eu-contact

For/Para
Baba & Lalo

CONTENTS

ÍNDICE

It has been reported and received thousands of times that I share this weight with you. We carry it together, sometimes take turns. A ton of osmium, mercury. I've learned at the end of love, there's mercy. Sometimes I pray the wounds will deepen, sometimes to disappear the scars. My prayer for you will always bring you to me, me to you. ✍

Se ha informado y recibido mil veces que comparto este peso con ustedes. Lo llevamos juntos, a veces nos turnamos. Una tonelada de osmio, mercurio. He aprendido que al final del amor, espera el consuelo. A veces ruego para que las heridas se profundicen, a veces para que desaparezcan las cicatrices. Mi rezo siempre los traerá a mí, y me llevará a ustedes.

PART 1

PARTE 1

At the beginning of becoming, there's a little light outside my emptiness—just a little light, a barely flickering, a glance at May. Turn right, take a piece of fruit as token, turn left: an aria. The stairs unfold accordion-like from heaven (do you know heaven?), past Earth and then below, below, below that too. There's a black-eyed dog wailing on the shore tonight. I will be your gondolier and stir the waters. The new day will be yours if you pantomime a spring bride with pulus in her hair. She will give you the gift of being born all at once, and I will teach you how to navigate the tides so you can live forever. ✎

Al principio del devenir, hay una pequeña luz fuera de mi vacío—sólo una pequeñísima luz, apenas un parpadeo, una mirada a mayo. A la derecha, toma un pedazo de fruta como muestra, a la izquierda: un aria. Las escaleras se despliegan como acordeón desde el cielo (¿conoces el cielo?), pasando por la tierra y luego por debajo, debajo, muy por debajo de ella también. Esta noche, en la orilla, aúlla un perro de ojos negros. Seré tu gondolera y agitaré las aguas. El nuevo día será tuyo si haces la pantomima de una novia de primavera, con flores de pulus en el pelo. Ella te dará el don de nacer de una vez, y yo te enseñaré a navegar por las mareas para que puedas vivir para siempre. ✍

I met him when he was brand new to this earth, like a sea lion cub waiting to launch. We rubbed and rubbed the scraps of white vernix all over his purple skin until we felt his heart beat faster. Tell him to breathe now, the midwife advised, these water babies . . . Keep me from falling, he whispered to me. Keep me from loving too much, I whispered back. Do you have shelter to offer? he asked, directing his inquiry to me again, ignoring the wreck he'd set out from. This here is no bed of roses, I said, and I don't know tooth or tongue. He showed me bikes ignored, skateboards forgotten, the jungle gym razed, the art of air. We have the same eyebrows, he said, proudly ignoring our parallel DNA, the impossibility of resemblance now vanquished by his resolve. No one can confirm their personal destiny but he most definitely will. He sees me carelessly eating a mango and waves me over. Get up, he says, it's too bleak here, like trying to get out of a locked room with a shooter waiting outside. (I want to say: this is the world we brought you into, and then apologize, but he won't have it.) That day, he said he dreamed of us: Look, look in the mirror. Can you even tell us apart? ❧

Lo conocí cuando era un recién llegado a esta tierra, como
un cachorro de león marino a punto de lanzarse al mundo.
Frotamos y frotamos los restos de vérnix blanco por toda su
piel morada hasta que sentimos que su corazón latía más
deprisa. Dile que respire, me aconsejó la comadrona. Ay, estos
bebés que nacen en agua . . . No me dejes caer, él me susurró.
No me dejes amar demasiado, le susurré. ¿Tienes algún
refugio que ofrecerme? me preguntó, ignorando el naufragio
del que había partido. Esto no es un lecho de rosas, le dije,
y no conozco ni diente ni lengua. Me mostró unas bicicletas
abandonadas, monopatines olvidados, el gimnasio del parque
arrasado, el arte del aire. Tenemos las mismas cejas, dijo,
ignorando con orgullo nuestro ADN paralelo, la imposibilidad
del parecido ahora vencida por su resolución. Nadie puede
confirmar su destino personal, pero él sin duda lo hará. Me
ve comiendo un mango con descuido y me hace señas para
que me acerque. Levántate, dice, esto es demasiado sombrío,
como intentar salir de algún lugar cerrado con llave con un
tirador esperando afuera. (Quiero decir: este es el mundo
al que te hemos traído, y luego trato de disculparme, pero
él no me deja.) Ese día, dijo que soñaba con nosotros: mira,
míranos en el espejo. ¿Nos puedes distinguir siquiera? ❧

Language makes it seem like all is well, that it's okay to wait, that they'll learn when they grow up, that forgiveness brings happiness. Language always restricts. And responsibility itself is also a symbol of responsibility. Life depends on it. Here's a faithless explanation: Over time, the spinal canal will form. Cartilage. Blood. Currents will flow, a steady stream. Connections. Show them. They'll understand what they're meant to learn. Think of your brain—the Broca, the Wernicke—as a rock underfoot, and crush it. ✍

El lenguaje hace que parezca que todo está bien, que no pasa nada si esperamos, que aprenderán cuando crezcan, que el perdón trae la felicidad. El lenguaje siempre restringe. Y la propia responsabilidad es también un símbolo de responsabilidad. La vida depende de ello. He aquí una explicación infiel: con el tiempo, el canal espinal se formará. Cartílago. Sangre. Las corrientes fluirán en un flujo constante. Conexiones. Muéstrales. Entenderán lo que deben aprender. Piensa en el cerebro—el Broca, el Wernicke—como una roca bajo tus pies, y aplástalo. ❧

I have a son, my youngest, who can destroy the lakes and wetlands of Asia, who can summon earthquakes, tsunamis and landslides because they come from him, they rise in him, they often threaten to take him down and far away. I have a son who will punch Pythagoras on the playground, make Paul the Apostle cry for all the damage his adulthood will inflict on young and old for centuries untold. I wait all day for signs: the goats sprinting for the hills, the cats chasing their own tails, the hot hot rain on my head, the texts that say: Come and get him, come and get him; save us. It's normal to be born out of sorts and not know it, I tell him, but what he's noticed are the boats on the water, the boats equipped with smaller boats fleeing and even smaller smaller boats. I have a plan, though I know my options are limited. First, we need to do something about the receding seas, the exposed reefs, the sea bass, the bluefish and red mullets fluttering on the now unreliable shores.

When we brought him home, his progenitors had shared and divided, shared and divided, exchanged prisoners on either side, burned the fields. It was the best way for them to start again. We went to him with bare arms and looked: There was no clap of thunder, no spleen calling to spleen. We shrugged. I waved. He seemed about the length of my finger. No one declared: I'm your real mother. ❧

Tengo un hijo, el menor, que puede destruir los lagos y los humedales de Asia, que puede convocar terremotos, tsunamis y corrimientos de tierra porque vienen de él, surgen en él; amenazan a menudo con tragárselo y llevárselo lejos. Tengo un hijo que le dará un puñetazo a Pitágoras en el patio de recreo, que hará llorar al Apóstol Pablo por todo el daño que infligirá, de adulto, a jóvenes y mayores por siglos incalculables. Espero todo el día por las señas: las cabras huyendo hacia las colinas, los gatos corriendo atrás de sus propias colas, la lluvia caliente sobre mi cabeza, los textos que dicen: ven por él, ven por él. Sálvanos. Es normal nacer trastornado y no saberlo, le digo, pero lo que él sí ha notado son las barcas en el agua, las barcas equipadas con barcas más pequeñas huyendo con barcas aún más pequeñas. Tengo un plan, aunque sé que mis opciones son limitadas. En primer lugar, tenemos que hacer algo con los mares en retroceso, los arrecifes expuestos, las lubinas, las anjovas y los salmonetes que revolotean en las orillas, ahora poco fiables.

Cuando lo trajimos a casa, sus progenitores habían compartido, dividido, y repartido; habían intercambiado presos de ambos lados, y quemado los campos. Para ellos era la mejor forma de volver a empezar. Nos acercamos a él con los brazos desnudos y miramos: no hubo trueno, ningún bazo llamó a otro bazo. Nos encogimos de hombros. Lo saludé. Parecía tener la longitud de mi dedo. Nadie declaró: Soy tu verdadera madre. ✺

In late May, we dig in the garden, unearth a rusty toy truck about as big as his torso. A sharp metal flap slices his hand and he tries to hide the palmful of blood. At night, wild turkeys, coyotes and skunks come to visit. He's thinking of them when he digs a little hole with his good hand, the unblood hand, and he points the gusher to top the hole red. He will make them his when they drink it, especially the coyotes; he's already in tune with their high-pitched howling. He cries out the windows each night: I'm here, here. When his shadow finally falls on the bed, dejected, abandoned, I tell him the whole world can be his. But he is so angry now, and tired, and he barks and barks, and growls into his pillow.

Once—it must have been June—he entered a pool by raising his legs, his hands bound. Then he climbed up the sides and out and sat dripping in a chair and laughed. His eyes gleamed, his lips shone. I could make some more cool holes, he said, with a wave of his free and now-healed hand. ✌

A fin de mayo, cavamos en el jardín y desenterramos un camión de juguete oxidado del tamaño de su torso. Una aleta metálica afilada le corta la mano y él intenta esconder la palma llena de sangre. Por la noche, pavos salvajes, coyotes y mofetas vienen de visita. Piensa en ellos cuando cava un agujerito con su mano buena, la que no sangra, y apunta el borbotón de sangre para llenar de rojo el agujero. Los hará suyos cuando se lo beban, sobre todo los coyotes; ya está en sintonía con sus agudos aullidos. Grita por las ventanas cada noche: aquí estoy, aquí. Cuando por fin su sombra cae sobre la cama, abatida, abandonada, le digo que el mundo entero puede ser suyo. Pero ahora está tan encabronado y cansado que ladra y ladra, y gruñe en la almohada.

Una vez—debe haber sido en junio—entró en una piscina levantando las piernas, tenía las manos atadas. Luego trepó por los lados y salió, se sentó chorreando en una silla y se echó a reír. Le brillaban los ojos y los labios. Podría hacer más agujeros lindos, dijo, con un gesto de su mano libre y ahora sana. ❧

At a young age, I learned the moment when the voices quieted, when breathing slowed, when whatever had been riling the winds had calmed and I knew not to say a word. Time was lost from time to time. I always liked that, always thought I knew what was uncovered when clouds subsided. My youngest son holds a bouquet of white freesia bulbs and says: I love this beautiful flower; I love the sunset. My oldest says: I love the sea, I want my clouds colored, full, to burst with neon and mercury vapor. I will loll here, I will linger and gaze at the twirling stars while lying on the trampoline, a boy on each side. That must be a star, or a plane, or a comet, a UFO, a constellation, Andromeda. It's dark but not so dark. I can't see water from here, but I heed the inhalation of the boys, feel their velvet breaths on my neck coming in waves. ❧

A una edad temprana, aprendí el momento en que las voces se callaban, cuando la respiración se ralentizaba, cuando lo que fuera que había estado agitando los vientos se había calmado y sabía que no debía decir ni una palabra. De vez en cuando el tiempo se perdía. Siempre me gustó eso, siempre pensé que sabía lo que se revelaba cuando las nubes amainaban. Mi hijo menor sostiene un ramo de bulbos de fresias blancas y dice: me encanta esta hermosa flor, me encanta la puesta del sol. Mi hijo mayor dice: amo el mar, quiero mis nubes coloreadas, llenas, que estallen de neón y vapor de mercurio. Yo me tumbaré aquí, me quedaré contemplando las estrellas girando mientras estoy estirada en el trampolín, con un hijo a cada lado. Eso debe ser un astro, o un avión, un cometa, un ovni, una constelación, Andrómeda. Está oscuro pero no tanto. No puedo ver el agua desde aquí pero escucho la inhalación de los chamas, siento su aliento aterciopelado que llega a mi cuello en olas. ✍

When I talk in Spanish, my eldest boy looks at me as if I'm
dancing with the dead. We're both deaf then: Him to my
song, me to his slurry Rs, to all the things we both want
now, fast, forever. You have to have an attitude, a certain
insolence, I know, to curl a tongue, to click and snap, to
pierce and punctuate like this. My eldest son, my boy with
sea-green eyes, prefers to let precious stones tumble in his
mouth. His body refuses him what he needs to talk like me,
like my father and mother and all who came before us, and he
embraces that lack. My boy doesn't know what he's missing.
I want to take him to the places where they unearth those
precious stones, for example, the sapphire mines in Malawi,
Tanzania, Madagascar. I want him to find that Spanish
(which is not spoken in Malawi, Tanzania or Madagascar,
except by those plotting escape to Europe via Tarifa, where
it's *la calor* and *la mar*, and aspiration can result in post-
aspiration)—my shambolic whiplash Spanish—is also a riot,
abundance and pleasure, a stunning string of sapphires.   ☙

Cuando hablo en español, mi hijo mayor me mira como si bailara con los muertos. Entonces ninguno de los dos oímos: él, sordo ante mi canción; yo, ante sus Rs babosas; no existen las cosas que ambos queremos ahora, instantáneamente, para siempre. Hay que tener una actitud, una cierta insolencia, lo sé, para rizar la lengua, para chasquear y zumbar, para perforar y puntuar así. Mi hijo mayor, mi niño de ojos verdes marinos, prefiere dejar que las piedras preciosas den vueltas en su boca. Su cuerpo le niega lo que necesita para hablar como yo, como mi padre y mi madre y todos los que vinieron antes que nosotros, y él abraza esa carencia. Mi hijo no sabe lo que le falta. Quiero llevarlo a los lugares donde desentierran esas piedras preciosas, por ejemplo, las minas de zafiro de Malaui, Tanzania, Madagascar. Quiero que descubra que el español (que no se habla en Malaui, Tanzania o Madagascar, excepto por aquellos que planean escapar a Europa vía Tarifa, donde es la calor y la mar y la aspiración puede dar resultado en la post-aspiración)—mi español, latigazo caótico—es también derroche, abundancia y placer, una impresionante cadena de zafiros. ❧

My eldest son eats Takis, exclusively. Takis Fuego for
breakfast, lunch and dinner. And the youngest: mac 'n'
cheese, the cheesy cheesiest. That is all. Don't eat too early,
says one. Don't make us eat too late, says the other. I cook up
recipes from Istanbul and San Juan, from Paris and Ramallah,
and eat alone. A thin, brittle round of dough topped with
minced and seasoned beef, a squeeze of lemon and parsley
before I roll it up and gorge. My kids eat Takis, mac 'n'
cheese. I make crunchy tostones, though I prefer maduros,
because my youngest likes to squash unripe plantains, to
flatten them like mushy coins. I'm thinking gooey béchamel,
Gruyère, a crispy egg on my croquette. Instead, I surrender
to experiments with blue Gatorade, root beer and tajín and
keep the eggplants cured in olive oil to myself. No one will
miss them. My kids eat Takis, mac 'n' cheese. My youngest,
he likes to order what he won't eat: I changed my mind!
he protests. My eldest groans when I tell him I will not be
ordering a large anything for him, since he never eats or
drinks beyond a small size and the waste unhinges me. I
won't tell them there are people starving in Ethiopia, in
Yemen, in Chicago. I won't tell them how my cousin cried
over a plate of plump overcooked shrimp when I took her to
dinner in Havana. I never discuss how, as a kid, I spooned
government-provided cornmeal for breakfast, lunch and
dinner for weeks and months when we were refugees. I tell
them we—the three of us, now—are not kings, but we are
favored, and that, in this case, it means we usually eat what
we want, including the seventy-dollar Bag-o-Crab my eldest
constantly craves and which is strictly a twice-a-year event.
I cannot explain Ethiopia or Yemen, Honduras or Haiti.
My kids eat Takis, mac 'n' cheese. Sometimes, when we
seek to help unhoused people in our town, I see the fear

Mi hijo mayor come Takis, exclusivamente. Takis Fuego
para desayunar, almorzar y cenar. Y el menor: macarrones
con queso, con exceso de queso. Eso es todo. No comas muy
temprano, dice uno. No nos hagas comer muy tarde, dice
el otro. Preparo recetas de Estambul y San Juan, de París
y Ramallah y como sola. Una masa fina y frágil cubierta
de carne picada y sazonada, un chorrito de limón y perejil
antes de enrollarla y atiborrarme. Mis hijos comen Takis,
macarrones con queso. Hago tostones crujientes, aunque
prefiero los maduros, porque a mi hijo menor le gusta aplastar
plátanos verdes, aplastarlos como monedas blandas. Pienso
en una salsa bechamel pegajosa, queso gruyere, un huevo
frito encima de mi croqueta. En lugar de eso, me rindo a los
experimentos con Gatorade azul, cerveza de raíz y tajín, y
me guardo las berenjenas curadas en aceite de oliva. Nadie
las echará de menos. Mis hijos comen Takis, macarrones con
queso. A mi hijo menor le gusta pedir lo que no quiere comer:
¡cambié de opinión!, protesta. Mi hijo mayor gime cuando le
digo que no voy a pedir nada de tamaño grande para él, ya
que nunca come ni bebe más que un poco y el desperdicio me
desquicia. No les diré que hay gente muriéndose de hambre
en Etiopía, en Yemen, en Chicago. No les contaré cómo
mi prima lloró por un plato de gambas gordas demasiado
cocidas cuando la llevé a cenar en La Habana. Nunca hablo
de cómo, de niña, desayuné, comí y cené harina de maíz
suministrada por el gobierno durante semanas y meses en
nuestros días de refugiados. Les digo que nosotros—los
tres, ahora—no somos reyes, pero somos favorecidos, y que,
en este caso, eso significa que típicamente comemos lo que
queremos, incluido el Bag-o-Crab de setenta dólares que mi
hijo mayor anhela constantemente y que es estrictamente
un acontecimiento de dos veces al año. No puedo explicar

in my kids' eyes when those men and women loathe our efforts, threaten to throw back our modest sandwiches. Sometimes I see embarrassment when moms with kids their age take the little angel bags from their hands and mutter thanks. My eldest slumps when he gets back in the car, my youngest begs to go home. They're not strong enough for so much pain. I can't talk to them yet about Memphis, San Antonio. But then when? My kids eat Takis, mac 'n' cheese. When the boys are hungry, they can be a little rude, a little mean. They smile at their burgers (we all know from where, though no one admits they eat there). They fence with limp French fries, make endless scuba noises with their straws deep in whatever sugared swill is in their cups. My kids eat Takis, mac 'n' cheese. I know this will end. Someday my youngest might prepare a steak: heat high for a perfect brownish crust, rare pink inside and seasoned with fresh cracked pepper, kosher salt. They'll volunteer at a people's kitchen, stack cans of beans, ladle hot soup into bowls. My eldest will snack on Spanish macadamias while piling beets, arugula and sheep's cheese. My youngest will lean over to me then: I can help you eat healthier, more delicious. And I'll swirl my rosé and bite my tongue. ☙

Etiopía o Yemen, Honduras o Haití. Mis hijos comen Takis, y macarrones con queso. A veces, cuando intentamos ayudar a la gente desalojada de sus hogares en nuestro pueblo, veo el miedo en los ojos de mis hijos cuando esos hombres y mujeres detestan nuestros esfuerzos, amenazan con tirar nuestros modestos bocadillos. A veces veo vergüenza cuando las madres con hijos de su edad les aceptan las bolsitas de caridad de las manos y murmuran gracias. Mi hijo mayor se desploma cuando regresa al carro, mi hijo menor suplica volver a casa. No son lo suficientemente fuertes para tanto dolor. Aún no puedo hablarles de Memphis, de San Antonio. ¿Pero entonces cuándo? Mis hijos comen Takis, mac 'n' cheese. Cuando los chamas tienen hambre, pueden ser un poco pesados, un tin malos. Sonríen ante sus hamburguesas (todos sabemos de dónde, aunque nadie admite que coman allí). Esgrimen con blandas papas fritas, hacen un sin fin de ruidos de submarinismo con los pitillos hundidos en cualquier bazofia azucarada que haya en sus vasos. Sé que esto acabará. Algún día, el más chiquito preparará un filete: a fuego fuerte para conseguir una corteza dorada perfecta, casi crudo por dentro y sazonado con pimienta recién molida y sal kashrut. Serán voluntarios en un comedor comunitario, apilarán latas de frijoles y servirán sopa caliente en pozuelos. Mi hijo mayor comerá macadamias españolas mientras apila remolachas, rúcula y queso de oveja. Entonces mi hijo menor se inclinará hacia mí: puedo ayudarte a comer más sano, más delicioso. Y yo revolveré mi vino rosé y me morderé la lengua. ✍

Women—and some men, and a few people hailed by a
big sign that says *All Genders Welcome Here*—come in the
afternoons, wearing sneakers, lots of hand sanitizer in their
bags along with wet wipes, a bottle of water. There's no
snow, no ice, and so, even those who are in a genuine hurry,
stroll and skip as they approach the building where our
children gather. No one says this aloud but we all telegraph
it: Another day and still alive! I skip the coffee klatch. I sign
my name, check my watch and take my youngest home. He
gives me a big hug: I love you like a rock, I say. I love you like
a freight train, he replies. How was school today? Good, he
says. He cracks every code into my phone while I belt him
to the car. He's chasing zombies, racing mice. He's already
forgotten who I am. At home I make a pot of rice, season the
picadillo, slice tangy red tongues from olives in a jar. He's
on the couch or in his room, but when he comes for water,
he's instantly opposed. I want chicken, or fish sticks, he says.
Nope, it's picadillo tonight. But Mami! And this is where
everything goes awry. Maybe it's all mathematical, the result
of a stochastic process; there have to be better methods—I've
read so much about this already, I feel I'm going blind—but
how, how to measure, to begin to understand the gradient
changes that occur in such a brief moment of time? He's
crying in the back yard, and I'm standing in the doorway,
posed just like my mother with a chancla in my hand . . .
blood sizzling, nerves pulsing . . . the chancla now out of
my hand . . . now aimed like a harpoon at his . . . But no—
wait—this is the scene fear paints. Yes, he's crying in the
backyard, serenading the neighbors with throaty chants of
Chicken! Fish sticks! I'm pouring all the hand sanitizer on
my head to cleanse myself of my mother, father, uncles,

Las mujeres—y algunos hombres, y unas pocas personas reunidas alrededor de un gran cartel que dice *Aquí todos los géneros son bienvenidos*—vienen por las tardes, con zapatillas de deporte, un montón de desinfectante de manos en sus bolsas junto con toallitas húmedas y botellas de agua. No hay nieve, ni hielo, y así, incluso los que tienen auténtica prisa, pasean y saltan al acercarse al edificio donde se reúnen nuestros hijos. Nadie lo dice en voz alta, pero todos lo telegrafiamos: un día más y ¡aún con vida! Evito el café con los otros padres. Firmo, miro el reloj y llevo a mi hijo menor a casa. Me da un fuerte abrazo: te quiero como a las piedras, le digo. Te quiero como a un tren de carga, responde. ¿Qué tal la escuela hoy? Bien, dice. Descifra todos los códigos de mi teléfono mientras lo llevo al carro y le pongo el cinturón. Está persiguiendo zombis, corriendo atrás de una pila de ratones. Ya se ha olvidado de mí. En casa preparo arroz, aliño el picadillo, le corto las lenguas rojas a las aceitunas. Está en el sofá o en su cuarto, pero cuando viene por un vaso de agua, se opone al instante. Quiero pollo, o palitos de pescado, dice. No, esta noche hay picadillo. ¡Pero Mami! Y aquí es donde todo se tuerce. Tal vez todo sea matemático, el resultado de un proceso estocástico; tiene que haber mejores métodos—ya he leído tanto sobre el tema que siento que me estoy quedando ciega—, pero ¿cómo? ¿cómo medir? ¿cómo empezar a entender los cambios graduales que ocurren en un momento tan breve? Él está llorando en el patio trasero y yo estoy de pie en la puerta, posando igual que mi mamá con una chancla en la mano . . . mi sangre chisporroteando, los nervios palpitando . . . la chancla ahora fuera de mi mano . . . ahora apuntando como un arpón . . . Pero no—un momento—esta es la escena que pinta el miedo. Sí, está llorando en el patio trasero, dando

aunts, my old neighborhood in Indiana, whatever DNA from the father who scarred my father and then passed that sickness down to me. I sit down with my boy, place a gentle hand on his shoulder, rub his neck. Why are you crying? he asks. I have soap bubbles in my mouth—fucking hand sanitizer—my hair, my nose. We work hard to close the door to the back yard. In bed, I roll over a plastic racetrack, a ferine dinosaur. My son is curled away from me, hoarding something under the duvet. What's that? I ask. He grins. Your heart, he says, and holds up this blue and bloody thing. ❧

serenatas a los vecinos con guturales cánticos de ¡Pollo!
¡Palitos de pescado! Me estoy echando todo el desinfectante
de manos en la cabeza para limpiarme, quitarme de encima
a mi mamá, mi papá, mis tíos, mis tías, mi antiguo barrio en
Indiana, cualquier ADN del padre que dejó cicatrices en mi
papá y luego me transmitió la enfermedad a mí. Me siento con
mi hijo, le pongo una mano suave en el hombro, le acaricio
el cuello. ¿Por qué lloras?, me pregunta. Tengo burbujas de
jabón en la boca—puñetero desinfectante de manos—en el
pelo, en la nariz. Nos esforzamos por cerrar la puerta del patio
trasero. En la cama, ruedo sobre un hipódromo de plástico,
un dinosaurio ferino. Mi hijo está acurrucado lejos de mí,
acaparando algo bajo el edredón. ¿Qué es?, le pregunto.
Sonríe. Tu corazón, dice, y levanta algo azul, sangriento. ❧

My youngest son broke all the windows and cracked the walls before he packed his little bag to go to his other mom's for a few days. I'm going to see my dad this weekend, he said. His dad—his bio dad—is a charming bruiser of a guy, with a puckish sense of humor. We met for a moment, he turned to us and said, Yeah, you're all right, I'm okay if you raise my son. Last we heard, he'd just gotten out of jail. I'm going to see my mom and dad this weekend, my son says again, but mostly my dad. He can fix anything, my dad. With my dad, each side of the house is light, so light, he can pick each up with one hand, my dad is so strong, Mami. He could fix this window, all the cracks in the wall. Then, as he searched the playroom for his stuffies, my youngest son said: The river is deep where we're going; we've been there before, I remember the wind blowing. My dad's arm broke, then mine. The pain may never end. That's when he stopped talking. He is waiting for his other mom, glued to the broken window, his gaze far, far away. ✒

Mi hijo menor rompió todas las ventanas y agrietó las paredes antes de hacer la maletica para irse unos días a casa de su otra mamá. Voy a ver a mi papá este fin de semana, dijo. Su papá—su padre biológico—es el guapo del barrio, con un sentido del humor muy pícaro. Nos encontramos por solo un momento, se volvió hacia nosotros y dijo: "Sí, está bien, me parece bien que críen a mi hijo". Lo último que supimos es que acababa de salir de la cárcel. Voy a ver a mi mamá y a mi papá este fin de semana, vuelve a decir mi hijo, pero sobre todo a mi papá. Él puede arreglar cualquier cosa, mi papá. Para mi papá, cada lado de la casa es liviano, tan liviano, que puede levantar cada uno con una mano, mi papá es tan fuerte, Mami. Él podría arreglarte esta ventana, todas las grietas de la pared. Luego, mientras buscaba sus peluches en la sala de juegos, mi hijo menor dijo: el río donde vamos es profundo; hemos estado allí antes, recuerdo que el viento soplaba. Mi papá se rompió el brazo, luego yo el mío. Puede que el dolor no termine nunca. Fue entonces cuando dejó de hablar. Está esperando a su otra mamá, pegado a la ventana rota, con la mirada lejos, muy lejos. 🦢

There is a place under his bed where my youngest son sleeps. It's an empty mountain and sometimes the wind blows cold. When he hears the bluster, he shouts over the bridge, a bridge he builds and tends with thoughts of his lost parents, with dreams of family that can never be. Sometimes, at the supermarket, at the train station, his beauty draws attention and he performs excitedly, performs mischief and performs perfection but sometimes that beauty saddens the eyes of strangers, and they walk away not knowing why. My son may yet find a simple, humble life beyond his mountain under the bed, his bridge of longings. Perhaps fatherhood, perhaps not, there's no example to gift him, no prescription. Beauty gives meaning only to beauty. He loves and talks about love. No one will convince either one of us our hearts are cursed. ✐

Hay un lugar bajo su cama donde duerme mi hijo menor. Es una montaña vacía y a veces el viento sopla frío. Cuando lo oye, grita en el puente, un puente que construye y cuida con pensamientos de sus progenitores perdidos, con sueños de una familia que nunca podrá ser. A veces, en el supermercado o en la estación del tren, su belleza llama la atención y él actúa con entusiasmo, actúa travieso y con perfección, pero a veces esa belleza entristece la mirada de los extraños, y se alejan sin saber por qué. Puede que mi hijo aún encuentre una vida sencilla y humilde más allá de su montaña bajo la cama, de su puente de anhelos. Tal vez la paternidad, tal vez jamás sea padre, no hay ejemplo que regalarle, no hay receta. La belleza sólo da sentido a la belleza. Ama y habla de amor. Nadie nos convencerá que nuestros corazones padecen de alguna maldición. ✍

Holding hands, me and my eldest (then my only) son, a
beautiful green balloon between us in his tiny fist, the first
gust of air steals it. I jump, he stares after it, a leaf in autumn
floating into the filmy fog. Then he lowers and covers his
equally green eyes for a moment, streaming tears. The balloon
crosses the oceans, elegant and colorful, past El Paso and
Orlando, past Moura, Mo So, Mariupol and Kramatorsk,
past Kobo and Chenna, past Karachi, Haditha, Glogova and
Al-Wehda, Makran and Sagay. My son will never know. The
wind is too strong, then not strong enough. My son keeps
his eye on an invisible dot in the sky for a year. Remember
the green balloon, Mami? My son doesn't forget. It's on an
adventure, I say. On the plane, my son looks for the green
balloon cloaked in the clouds. He wonders if the green
balloon can survive the sun, dodge jets. When we disembark,
my son reaches into the air, his palm sticky and open. No
worse for the wear, the green balloon alights in his hand.
This is one of a million tiny lies I will gratefully tell. &

Tomados de la mano, mi hijo mayor (en ese entonces, el único) y yo, en su diminuto puño un hermoso globo verde entre nosotros. Cuando la primera ráfaga de aire se lo roba, yo salto y él se queda mirándolo, como una hoja otoñal flotando en la niebla. Luego se agacha y se tapa por un momento los ojos, igualmente verdes, derramando lágrimas. El globo cruza los océanos, elegante y colorido, más allá de El Paso y Orlando, más allá de Moura, más allá de Mo So, de Mariupol y Kramatorsk, más allá de Kobo y Chenna, de Karachi, Haditha, Glogova y Al-Wehda, Makran y Sagay. Mi hijo nunca lo sabrá. El viento es demasiado fuerte, luego no lo suficiente. Durante un año, mi hijo no pierde de vista un punto invisible en el cielo. ¿Te acuerdas del globo verde, Mami? Mi hijo no lo olvida. Está de aventura, le digo. En el avión, mi hijo busca el globo verde oculto entre las nubes. Se pregunta si el globo verde puede sobrevivir al sol, esquivar los jets. Cuando desembarcamos, mi hijo extiende la mano hacia el aire, con la palma pegajosa y abierta. El globo verde se posa en su mano. Esta es una de los millones de mentiritas que le contaré con gratitud. 🐦

My kid said he was so sick, he was going to die. I might
get angry about it later, he added. He wanted a drink so
we got a huge water bottle and filled it with ice. He had no
temperature but his body kept threatening to expel things: not
just food but photos and cats, friends and homework. He took
two hot showers, later a hot bath. He spent the night holding
an empty bucket. We tested for known viruses, I scratched his
back with a telescopic little rake made for that purpose. He
said it felt good. My other kid insisted on having lunch but
the very idea made my sick kid gag. We hid lunch from him,
squatted in the kitchen out of sight, ate hard-boiled eggs and
mac 'n' cheese. It felt like war in Europe. My sick kid was so
sick he couldn't bear to look at screens. My other kid dove
into a murder mystery where he turned out to be the killer,
which was upsetting to everyone. Are you going to stay with
me while I die? asked my sick kid. I said of course and patted
his naked thigh (he was too sick to wear clothes, this had been
established earlier). Winter gardens and cold weather make
me ill, he said. I feel incredible pain, he added. I thought I
wanted it but I don't want it anymore. This happens, I tell
him, it can be confusing, the thing you want and don't want
might be the same thing. It's a question of timing maybe, he
said sniffling. Yeah, like being on the verge of happiness and
suicide at the same time, I said. You're never supposed to talk
to us about stuff like suicide, he said. Oh, sorry, I said, you're
absolutely right. I tried to explain. Stop talking, said the other
kid, the one on the 55-inch screen. I'm sorry! I'm sorry! I said.
Stop talking! they shouted in unison, one live, one on the giant

Mi hijo dijo que se sentía tan enfermo que estaba a punto de morir. Puede que luego me encabrone por esto, añadió. Quería beber algo, así que agarramos una botella enorme y la llenamos de hielo. No tenía fiebre, pero su cuerpo seguía amenazando con expulsiones: no sólo comida, sino fotos y gatos, amigos y deberes. Se duchó dos veces con agua caliente y después se dio un baño abrasador también. Pasó la noche con un cubo vacío en las manos. Le hicimos pruebas de virus conocidos, le rasqué la espalda con un rastrillo telescópico hecho para ese fin. Dijo que le sentaba bien. Mi otro hijo insistió en almorzar, pero solo la idea le provocó arcadas a mi hijo enfermo. Le escondimos el almuerzo, nos acuclillamos en la cocina y comimos huevos duros y macarrones con queso. Parecía una guerra en Europa. Mi hijo estaba tan enfermo que no soportaba mirar las pantallas. Mi otro hijo se sumergió en un show de misterio con un asesinato en el que él mismo resultó ser el asesino, lo que nos disgustó a todos. ¿Te vas a quedar conmigo mientras me muero?, preguntó mi hijo enfermo. Le dije que por supuesto y le di unas palmaditas en el muslo desnudo (estaba demasiado enfermo para llevar ropa, ya se había comprobado antes). Los jardines de invierno y el frío me hacen mal, dijo. Siento un dolor increíble, añadió, creía que lo quería, pero ya no lo quiero. Esto pasa, respondo, puede ser confuso, lo que quieres y lo que no quieres puede ser lo mismo. Tal vez sea una cuestión de sincronización, dijo, sorbiéndose los mocos. Sí, como estar al borde de la felicidad y del suicidio al mismo tiempo, afirmé. Se supone que nunca debes hablarnos de

monitor. Then they coughed, taking turns, and laughed.
In fact, they couldn't stop laughing, couldn't stop
rolling around on the bed together, punching, pinching,
calling each other names. I sat back on the pillows to
watch. No one's dead yet. Everyone's alive. ❧

temas como el suicidio, dijo. Oh, lo siento, respondí, tienes toda la razón. Intenté explicar. Ya, deja de hablar, dijo el otro chama, el que aparecía en la pantalla de 55 pulgadas. Lo siento, lo siento, respondí. ¡Cállate ya!, gritaron al unísono, uno en directo, otro en el monitor gigante. Luego tosieron, por turnos, y se rieron. De hecho, no paraban de reír, no paraban de revolcarse juntos en la cama, de darse puñetazos, de pellizcarse, de insultarse. Me recosté en las almohadas para observar. Aún no ha muerto nadie. Todos seguimos vivos. ❧

On one of his first days at his new school, my eldest son comes home quiet, as if he'd traveled all day. I want to dance, I want to sing, but he demurs. He's out of focus, eyes moist. He sits on a broken barrel in the backyard and when I ask what's wrong, he says he has a dead tongue. This goes on for days. I have a presentiment, tell him I used to get beaten to a pulp at school, each year at a new school. Why? he asks. Because I couldn't speak English, said things wrong, was constantly tricked into pronouncing profanities: Couldn't say *sheet*. The teacher would wash my mouth out with soap. Soap! He thinks this is hilarious. Then he spills it: A couple of boys yelled at him: Your moms are queer! Yes, he tells me, I said yes, but they were still so angry, Mami. Someday I'll have to tell him about Sarah White Norman and Mary Vincent Hammon, convicted of lewd behavior in Plymouth almost six hundred years ago; about *Loving v. Virginia*; about how the Grand Ayatollah Ali al-Sistani issued a fatwa calling for the murder of gays and lesbians in the "worst, most severe way"; about the killing of Magne Andreassen in Lillehammer; the assassination of Kevin Fret, shot eight times on a savage night in San Juan; about Matthew Shepard and the grieving wastelands of Wyoming; about FannyAnn Eddy, Anele Bhengu, about Reinaldo Arenas, whom I loved. But right now all I want to do is sit here, on the barrel, holding hands, marveling at the miracle of his heart and how it just doesn't understand. ❧

Es uno de sus primeros días en su nueva escuela. Mi hijo mayor llega a casa en silencio, como si hubiera estado de viaje todo el día. Quiero bailar, quiero cantar, pero él se niega. Está desenfocado, los ojos húmedos. Se sienta en un barril roto en el patio trasero y, cuando le pregunto qué le pasa, dice que tiene la lengua muerta. Esto dura días. Tengo un presentimiento, le digo que en la escuela me molían a palos, cada año en un colegio nuevo. ¿Por qué? Porque no sabía hablar inglés, decía las cosas mal, me engañaban constantemente para que pronunciara palabrotas: no podía decir *sheet*. La maestra me lavaba la boca con jabón. ¡Jabón! Él piensa que esto es hilarante. Luego confiesa: Un par de chamas le gritaron: ¡tus mamás son maricas! Sí, me dice, les dije que sí, pero se encabronaron igual, Mami. Algún día yo tendré que hablarles de Sarah White Norman y Mary Vincent Hammon, condenadas por comportamiento lascivo en Plymouth hace casi seiscientos años; de Loving contra Virginia; de cómo el Gran Ayatolá Ali al-Sistani emitió una fatwa en la que pedía el asesinato de gays y lesbianas de la "peor y más severa manera"; le hablaré sobre el asesinato de Magne Andreassen en Lillehammer; del asesinato de Kevin Fret, muerto por ocho tiros en una noche salvaje en San Juan; de Matthew Shepard y los páramos en duelo de Wyoming; sobre FannyAnn Eddy, Anele Bhengu, de Reinaldo Arenas, a quien yo quería tanto. Pero ahora mismo todo lo que quiero es sentarme aquí, sobre el barril, cogidos de la mano, maravillándome ante el milagro de su corazón y de cómo simplemente no entiende. ✍

Some folks won't forgive my sons their moms, as if they had a choice. Why them, they ask . . . The world moves on and their necks rotate to see if there will be a nuzzle, a touch, something extraordinary and awful or beautiful that makes the boys special by virtue of us, just breathing, just moving along, each in our own lane, each checking our steps and heart rate. What do they do? Meaning us, in our separate homes, one of us going south for the winter, the other going north. The boys are comfortable taking turns, putting on layers, putting on sunscreen. When the air is full, my tongue goes tired. We were young once—I was young once— and lovesick and long limbed, open to kisses everywhere. And then a mouth on my breast came to mean something unexpected: the memory of a species at peace, of goddesses who could raise the dead, who could crack the earth open like an egg, who will be forever heralded by the cygnets to whom they taught their dazzling, righteous wingbeat. ❧

Hay gente que no les perdona a mis hijos sus mamás, como si ellos pudieran haber elegido. Por qué ellos, preguntan . . . El mundo sigue adelante y la gente gira para ver si habrá un morreo, un roce, algo extraordinario y horrible o hermoso que haga especiales a los chamas en virtud de nosotras, simplemente respirando, simplemente avanzando, cada una en su carril, cada una controlando nuestros pasos y ritmos cardíacos. ¿Qué hacen? Hablan de nosotras, en nuestras casas individuales, una rumbo al sur durante el invierno, la otra al norte. Los chamas se sienten cómodos turnándose, poniéndose capas, poniéndose crema solar. Cuando el aire está cargado, se me cansa la lengua. Fuimos jóvenes alguna vez—yo fui joven alguna vez—y enferma de amor, mis largas extremidades abiertas a besos por todas partes. Y entonces una boca en mi pecho pasó a significar algo inesperado: el recuerdo de una especie en paz, de diosas que podían resucitar a los muertos, que podían romper la tierra como un huevo, que serán eternamente anunciadas por los cisnes a los que les enseñaron su deslumbrante y justiciero batir de alas. ✑

I want to think that on the Thursday Rosa Parks sat down
on the Cleveland Avenue bus in Montgomery, Alabama,
my boys were on their way home from school, holding
on to the back of a seat, that maybe when she got on, my
oldest moved his brother from his lap, got up and said,
Here, ma'am, have a rest. I want to imagine that if they'd
run into a fourteen year-old black boy with a stutter and a
limp on a train from Chicago going south, they'd greet him
with that all-knowing nod boys use to say, It's cool, it's all
right, and maybe they could talk about the White Sox or
exchange baseball cards; that at the park they'd get Tamir
Rice to play soccer instead, that they'd walk Adam Toledo
home before dark. I don't want them in danger (though
they're always in danger), nor for them to be heroes, but I
want to leave this earth knowing they recognize the right
side of history, that they deliberately walk to where justice
is needed, that they know when to stand strong and when
to gather rocks and weigh them in their palms. ✒

Quiero pensar que el jueves que Rosa Parks se sentó en el bus de Cleveland Avenue en Montgomery, Alabama, mis hijos volvían a casa de la escuela, agarrados al respaldo de un asiento, que quizá cuando ella subió, mi hijo mayor apartó a su hermano de su regazo, se levantó y le dijo: "Aquí tiene, señora, descanse". Quiero imaginarme que, si se cruzaran con un muchacho negro de catorce años, tartamudo y cojo en un tren de Chicago yendo hacia el sur, lo saludarían con ese gesto omnisciente que los varones usan para decir: "No pasa nada, no pasa nada", y que tal vez podrían hablar de los White Sox o intercambiar cromos de béisbol; que en el parque harían que Tamir Rice jugara al fútbol y no a pistolero, que acompañarían a Adam Toledo a la casa antes de que oscureciera. No quiero que corran peligro (aunque siempre corren peligro), ni que sean héroes, pero quiero dejar esta tierra sabiendo que reconocen el lado justo de la historia, que caminen deliberadamente hacia donde se necesita justicia, que sepan cuándo mantenerse firmes y cuándo recoger piedras y pesarlas en las palmas. ❧

As we scan a list of the dead from a weekend shooting outside Chicago, my eldest son remembers another massacre in which a girl his age survived by swirling the blood of a murdered classmate on her face and arms. I'm not sure I could do that, Mami, he says. I could, intones my youngest son, pulling down on his eyelids to make a frightful face. The news reports, like the accounts from the carnage that girl survived by smudging blood, by filling her spongy pores and nostrils with the acerbic trails of her friend's death, describe the indescribable: the bodies blasted away, the faces flayed by sudden cruelty, left to strangers to recompose, to hold together, whether in pixels or the coroner's berth. My sons know how to hide under a desk, how to keep silent, both boys waiting their turns to be forever fallen. ✍

Mientras ojeamos una lista de los muertos en un tiroteo
ocurrido el fin de semana en las afueras de Chicago, mi hijo
mayor recuerda otra masacre en la que una niña de su edad
sobrevivió, manchándose la cara y los brazos con la sangre
de un compañero de clase asesinado. No estoy seguro si
podría hacer eso, Mami, dice. Yo sí, entona mi hijo menor,
bajando los párpados para poner cara de espanto. Las noticias,
como los relatos de la carnicería a la que sobrevivió aquella
niña manchada de sangre, llenando sus esponjosos poros
y fosas nasales con los rastros acerbos de la muerte de su
amiga, describen lo indescriptible: los cuerpos arrasados, los
rostros desollados por la crueldad repentina, abandonados
a extraños para recomponerse, para mantenerse unidos,
ya sea en píxeles o en la litera del forense. Mis hijos saben
cómo esconderse bajo un escritorio, cómo guardar silencio,
ambos esperando su turno para caer para siempre. ✍

There are fools who blame women for being women, and never see their own reflection. Sometimes I see them surrounding my sons, straining to overcome gravity, to lift them into their misanthropy. Of course my sons want to be brave before these mirrors of madness, but right now they're planting a garden. White lilies, cornflowers, red carnations. Take what you want, they say to the fools (I hope), take what you need and leave. But the fools persist: What a great joke, that taking, that needing. Simply and easily, I worry my sons have the same disease under the skin, that I won't ever do enough to root it out. In the foolish world, nobody wins. The fools will say whatever they receive is not a favor. The fools will turn with cruelty, will stake my boys. I've put everything they could possibly use in their pockets, all the loves, all the love. This is how my boys will confront their ghosts, their flesh, the world. ✒

Hay tontos que culpan a las mujeres por ser mujeres, y nunca ven su propio reflejo. A veces los veo rodeando a mis hijos, esforzándose por vencer la gravedad, por elevarlos en su misantropía. Claro que mis hijos quieren ser valientes ante estos locos reflejos, pero ahora mismo están plantando un jardín: lirios blancos, acianos, claveles rojos. Llévense lo que quieran, les dicen a los tontos (espero), llévense lo que necesitan y márchense. Pero los tontos persisten: tremenda broma, ese tomar, ese necesitar. Simple y llanamente, me preocupa que mis hijos tengan la misma enfermedad bajo la piel, que nunca hago lo suficiente para erradicarla. En el mundo de los tontos, nadie gana. Los necios dirán que cualquier cosa que reciban no es un favor. Los tontos se volverán con crueldad, pondrán mis hijos en riesgo. He puesto todo lo que podrían usar en sus bolsillos, todos los amores, todo el amor. Así es como mis chamas se enfrentarán a sus fantasmas, a su carne, al mundo.

The boys huddle together, they're made out of the substance squeezed from their own ribs. Their dicks in their hands. They compare all the time. Together these two giggle and snort and look out over my dead lands, the places they've forgotten I ever existed, the sites they conquered from me. It's not courage they have, it's force, it's muscle. The sun barely kisses the pillars toppled in their wake. Trees don't move. I worry about my last word, about everything I've ever said to them and what traces might remain: a whistle through the dry grass, a caution daubed in clay. They are made of a history I want them to recant. Foam collects on the riverbanks and naked bodies stop in their tracks when my sons come galloping. They freeze and stare as the boys slow to a trot. I want to—I desperately want to reassure them—to reassure myself—that they are safe from my sons. ❧

Los chamas se acurrucan, están hechos de la sustancia exprimida de sus propias costillas. Los penes en sus manos. Se comparan todo el tiempo. Juntos los dos ríen y resoplan y miran mis tierras muertas, los lugares que han olvidado, en los que alguna vez existí, los sitios que me conquistaron. No es coraje lo que tienen, es fuerza, es músculo. El sol apenas besa los pilares derribados a su paso. Los árboles no se mueven. Me preocupa mi última palabra, todo lo que les he dicho y las huellas que puedan quedar: un silbido entre la hierba seca, una advertencia embadurnada en arcilla. Están hechos de una historia de la que quiero que se retracten. La espuma se acumula en las orillas del río y los cuerpos desnudos se detienen en seco cuando mis hijos llegan al galope. Se quedan inmóviles y miran fijamente cuando los chamas reducen la velocidad al trote. Quiero, quiero desesperadamente asegurarles, asegurarme a mí misma, que están a salvo de mis hijos. ◆

The boys are still overflowing with joy, thinking every day is a thousand years for everyone. How long? Who knows? I'm the oldest mother, Sarah shuffling on her fallow path. Promises spring forth when the moon alights above the horizon, predictable and powerful. The boys don't have to move or look into my eyes. They know I'll catch my breath, climb, fall, keep up, all the gods in all the holy books be damned. I want my boys to know more than happiness, to know the pain that makes happiness a cool spring. I want them to know more than contentment, to feel the impulse of violence and the lure of danger so they recognize them, so they tame them. I want them to know love, with all its attendant shattering, with its redemption and transformation. I want them to love and be loved better than me, to be luckier than me. ❧

Los chamas siguen rebosantes de alegría, pensando que cada día son mil años para todos. ¿Cuánto tiempo? ¿Quién sabe? Soy la mamá mayor, Sarah arrastrando los pies en su camino de barbecho. Las promesas brotan cuando la luna se posa sobre el horizonte, previsibles y poderosas. Los chamas no tienen que moverse ni mirarme a los ojos. Saben que recuperaré el aliento, que subiré, que caeré, que me mantendré en pie, que se jodan todos los dioses de todos los libros sagrados. Quiero que mis hijos conozcan algo más que la felicidad, que conozcan el dolor que hace de la felicidad un fresco manantial. Quiero que conozcan algo más que la satisfacción, que sientan el impulso de la violencia y la atracción del peligro para que los reconozcan, para que los domestiquen. Quiero que conozcan el amor, con todos los destrozos que conlleva, con su redención y transformación. Quiero que amen y sean amados mejor que yo, que tengan más suerte que yo. ❧

There are many ways to translate fathers to boys. Son of
his father, son of the open sky. The river of laughter flows,
the surface trembling like war songs. One father can teach
the boys to be kings, or unknowns, the highest in human
consciousness. The other father takes them fishing, whipping
the line like skywriting, taglines about love and loyalty. Who
is happier? The boys and each of their fathers sit very close on
the shore's dull brown mud. The boys stare out at the water,
watching the baits dip and dunk. The fathers don't speak as
the boys reel in their catch, split the bellies, then tie fish guts
together to fashion two crowns. They use scales to make them
shimmer and shine. This is my father's all right, says one
son, as he admires his handiwork. The other son laughs. I
spawned, he says, I sprang from an egg, maybe two, or from a
rock struck by lightning. I'm here, he says as he calmly whirls
his crown over his shoulder and rubs his hands clean. ❧

Hay muchas formas en que los hijos descifran a sus padres. Hijo de su padre, hijo del cielo abierto. El río de risas fluye, la superficie temblorosa como cantos de guerra. Un padre puede enseñar a los chamas a ser reyes, o desconocidos, lo más alto de la conciencia humana. El otro padre los lleva a pescar, azotando el sedal como si escribiera en el cielo consignas sobre el amor y la lealtad. ¿Quién es más feliz? Los chamas y cada uno de sus padres se sientan muy juntos en el barro marrón opaco de la orilla. Los chamas miran fijamente el agua, observando cómo se sumergen los cebos. Los padres no hablan mientras los chamas recogen su pesca, parten los vientres y atan las vísceras de los peces para formar dos coronas. Utilizan escamas para hacerlas brillar. Esto sí que es de mi papá, dice un hijo mientras admira su obra. El otro hijo se ríe. Desové, dice, broté de un huevo, quizá dos, o de una roca partida por un rayo. Estoy aquí, dice mientras tira su corona tranquilamente sobre el hombro y se frota las manos. ❧

I bend under tropical weeds, unknown and mysterious, that keep repeating. These trees, they look loose, each branch a braid chock-full of misshapen fruit. The consequences of translation include prayer: hours; hours and minutes; seconds, seconds, seconds. Sometimes I find myself between two walls of water, the desert before me. The promised land. Everything in place before we're born. We feel the moment like devotions, translated many times over, finally landing on clicks and whistling, their own Silbo Gamero. I entreat my sons to look for rocks in the dilapidated buildings, to build altars, mark graves. We are here day and night, amidst the embers and the smoke, standing at a crossroads. One son might cleanse himself with the blood of a headless bird still fluttering about, the other might cover his face before the light. ෴

Me agacho bajo malezas tropicales, desconocidas y misteriosas, que se repiten. Estos árboles sueltos, cada rama una trenza repleta de frutos deformes. Las consecuencias de la traducción incluyen la oración: horas, horas y minutos; segundos, segundos, segundos. A veces me encuentro entre dos muros de agua, el desierto ante mí. La tierra prometida. Todo en su sitio antes de nacer. Sentimos el momento como devociones, traducidas muchas veces, aterrizando: finalmente en chasquidos y silbidos, su propio Silbo Gamero. Ruego a mis hijos que busquen piedras en los edificios derruidos, que construyan altares, que marquen tumbas. Estamos aquí día y noche, entre las brasas y el humo, en una encrucijada. Un hijo podría limpiarse con la sangre de un pájaro decapitado que aún revolotea, el otro podría cubrirse el rostro ante la luz. ◆

I knew something was up when everything was left in shambles. A sponge disappeared, the wi-fi connection, the glasses of water under the bed. I have the finest lines on my skin. And I think this much beauty . . . My oldest son peeks in and asks: Who's here? Love is Pavlovian, says my youngest, a conditioned response. The bell, salivation, that thing we need. I can't help myself and confess: What they never tell you is the end of the experiment: Bell, salivation, bell, salivation, bell bell bell. A Sunday's worth of bells in an undeveloped countryside marked by war, hurricanes, the false gods of colonialism, a call to prayer over fields of drought and famine. And then nothing, as if no bell had ever rung, no prayer had ever been held. I'm here for one to ten million years. ༄

Supe que algo pasaba cuando todo quedó hecho un desastre. Desapareció una esponja, la conexión wi-fi, los vasos de agua debajo de la cama. Tengo las arrugas más finas en la piel. Y pienso que tanta belleza . . . Mi hijo mayor se asoma y pregunta: ¿Quién está aquí? El amor es como Pavlov, dice mi hijo menor, una respuesta condicionada. La campanilla, la salivación, eso que necesitamos. No puedo contenerme y confieso. Lo que nunca te cuentan es el fin del experimento: campana, salivación, campana, salivación, campana, campana. Un domingo de campanadas en un campo sin desarrollar marcado por la guerra, los huracanes, los falsos dioses del colonialismo, una llamada a las plegarias sobre campos de sequía y hambruna. Y luego nada, como si nunca hubiera sonado ninguna campana, ni se hubiera rezado ninguna oración. Estoy aquí de uno a diez millones de años. &

PART 2

PARTE 2

There was no light, that last night all pitch. Wild humans
on the water, struggling onto the boat with muted horror.
I didn't agree or disagree, just tucked my head, scaled the
sides, did what I was told. What these people wanted was
to touch, relax, be safe. A black-eyed dog sniffed weeds on
an abandoned tarmac in an underdeveloped country where
everyone could read but, really, what good was that? We
weren't there, we were in the water, wading beyond territorial
lines, shoving each other. No one could speak, no one dared
recite poems of liberation or love. As such, there was no path
between pain and joy that I could see. Flying fish played in
a streak of moonlight as if there was no suffering, as if Babel
had been merely paused. We submerged, again, held hands
with our mothers and fathers and trusted they would not
drown us. I imagine my parents' debates, how they lined
up alphabets, threw a coin in the air but didn't stick around
to see its revelation. Could I ever do that? They herded
us to the beach in long black cars, taped our mouths shut.
You were saved, says a voice. You were stolen, says another.
Meanwhile, I listen to my eldest son insist on the force of his
breaststroke while my youngest floats leisurely on his back.
Neither of them can ever remember when I was a child. ❧

No había luz, todo negro la última noche. Humanos, salvajes
en el agua, luchando por subir al barco con horror mudo. No
estuve de acuerdo ni en desacuerdo, sólo agaché la cabeza,
escalé los costados, hice lo que me decían. Lo que esta gente
quería era sentir, relajarse, estar a salvo. Un perro de ojos
negros olfateaba las malas hierbas de un asfalto abandonado
en un país subdesarrollado donde todo el mundo sabía leer,
pero en realidad, ¿de qué servía? No estábamos allí, estábamos
en el agua, vadeando más allá de las líneas territoriales,
empujándonos unos a otros. Nadie podía hablar, nadie se
atrevía a recitar poemas de liberación o de amor. Como tal,
no había camino entre el dolor y la alegría que yo pudiera
ver. Los peces voladores jugaban a la luz de la luna como si
no hubiera sufrimiento, como si Babel se hubiera pausado.
Nos sumergimos, de nuevo, cogidos de las manos de nuestras
madres y padres y confiamos en que no nos ahogarían.
Imagino los debates de mis padres, cómo alineaban alfabetos,
lanzaban monedas al aire sin quedarse para ver su revelación.
¿Podría yo hacer eso alguna vez? Nos llevaron en manada a la
playa en extensos carros negros, nos taparon la boca con cinta
adhesiva. Te salvaron, dice una voz. Te secuestraron, dice otra.
Mientras tanto, escucho a mi hijo mayor insistir en la fuerza
de su brazada, mientras el pequeño flota tranquilo boca arriba.
Ninguno de los dos se acuerda de cuando yo era niña. ☙

The bus on the island, packed bodies, the road a glaring garish
white, ravishing sky, the purplish woman in front of us on
the bus cradling her head in her lap, my mother doubting for
a nanosecond, then leaning her arm hard on my back, her
hand on my head, everyone around us like ghosts praising,
doubling down, under the seat for me where it's sticky and
my mother is holding my head down. There was a shooting
or there may have been or we dreamt it together but maybe it
was just me. How fast is this world? I remember hearing that,
in winter, the macheteros leave their blades in the countryside
and pick up guns to bring to the cities, rice weevils writhe
in the pantries and everything has to be burned. I could see
flames on the bus, my mother's hand on my head keeping me
down down. Is the bus on fire? Is my mother on fire? Is her
hand on my head burning through to the back of my skull?
When I look past the sticky floor on the bus, I can see people
eating out in the streets, sugar cube upon sugar cube, and a
handful of snow to make it go down except there's never any
snow in Havana. There was a shooting, there may have been,
my mother and I leaned forward, ducked behind the seat in
front of us, her hand on the back of my head while we heard
someone was shot and someone else died and something
happened to a total of six people but we were doubled up
and I was down on the sticky floor and saw nothing nothing
at all but bursts of gunfire lighting up the bus windows and
the already blazing tropical sun and its torment of light.
Why? Why did my parents have children? I brought out
my Chinese checkers there on the sticky floor of the bus as
my mother held my head down. I watched the marbles roll
away as a sign of spring, roll down the bus steps and heard

El bus en la isla, los cuerpos abarrotados, la carretera de un blanco brillante y chillón, el cielo deslumbrante, la mujer morada delante de nosotros en el bus curvando la espalda sobre su regazo, mi mamá dudando durante un nanosegundo, y después su brazo apoyándose con fuerza en mi espalda, su mano en mi cabeza, todos a nuestro alrededor como fantasmas alabando, insistiendo, y mi mamá sujetándome agachada debajo del asiento donde está pegajoso. Hubo un tiroteo o puede que lo haya habido o que lo hayamos soñado juntas, pero puede que sólo fui yo. ¿Cuán rápido es este mundo? Recuerdo haber oído que en invierno los macheteros dejan las cuchillas en el campo y cogen armas para llevarlas a las ciudades, los gorgojos del arroz se retuercen en las despensas y hay que quemarlo todo. Veía llamas en el bus, la mano de mi mamá sobre mi cabeza me mantenía agachada. ¿Está ardiendo el bus? ¿Está ardiendo mi mamá? ¿Está su mano en mi cabeza quemándome hasta la pared posterior del cráneo? Cuando miro más allá del suelo pegajoso del bus, puedo ver a la gente comiendo en la calle, terrón de azúcar sobre terrón de azúcar, y un puñado de nieve para tragar, excepto que nunca hay nieve en La Habana. Hubo un tiroteo, puede que lo haya habido, mi mamá y yo nos inclinamos hacia delante, nos agachamos detrás del asiento de adelante, su mano en mi nuca mientras oíamos que habían disparado a alguien y que alguien más había muerto y que algo les había pasado a un total de seis personas, pero estábamos agachadas y yo estaba en el suelo pegajoso y no veía absolutamente nada salvo ráfagas de disparos que iluminaban las ventanas del bus y el tormento de luz del abrasador sol tropical. ¿Por qué? ¿Por qué fue que mis padres tuvieron hijos? Saqué mis damas chinas allí, en

them crunch under the feet of the macheteros without their machetes, the former passengers ordered outside. My mother didn't know what to do with me, except on the bus, when she pushed my head down down down. She didn't know what to do, that was clear, as clear as the rearview mirror on the bus where we could, for a nanosecond, see my father in his white suit being pushed around. How can this be acceptable? The bus radio is on and there's a sweet little charanga and I can feel my mother's hand on the back on my head pulsing to the beat. Someone said everyone survived, everyone survived with their own story. We laughed, my mother and I, her hand on the back of my head, not a caress exactly. We laughed and then she admonished me for losing the Chinese checkers, for the sticky stuff on my dress. There was a shooting or there may have been or we dreamt it together. A mystery on that bus, a mystery on the day of my oldest son's birth when I held up his head, on the day my youngest came home and rested his whole being against me. ✍

el suelo pegajoso del bus, mientras mi mamá me sujetaba la cabeza. Vi rodar las canicas como un signo de la primavera, las vi rodar por los escalones del bus y las oí crujir bajo los pies de los macheteros sin sus machetes, los antiguos pasajeros anteriores bajados del bus. Mi mamá no sabía qué hacer conmigo, salvo en el bus, cuando me empujaba la cabeza hacia abajo cada vez más. No sabía qué hacer, eso estaba claro, tan claro como el espejo retrovisor del bus en el que pudimos, durante un nanosegundo, ver cómo empujaban a mi papá en su traje blanco. ¿Cómo es que esto sea posible? La radio del bus está prendida, suena una dulce charanga y puedo sentir la mano de mi mamá en la nuca palpitando al compás. Alguien dijo que todo el mundo sobrevivió, que todo el mundo sobrevivió con su propia historia. Nos reímos, mi mamá y yo, su mano en mi nuca, no era una caricia exactamente. Nos reímos y luego me amonestó por haber perdido las damas chinas y por lo pegajoso de mi vestido. Hubo un tiroteo o pudo haberlo o lo soñamos juntas. Un misterio en aquel bus, un misterio el día del nacimiento de mi hijo mayor cuando sostuve su cabeza y un misterio el día en que mi hijo menor llegó a casa y apoyó todo su ser contra mí. ✍

Dead leaves and bricks on the edge of the brown slush. Cracks in the sidewalks. A collection of cigarette butts. Nothing separates me from the cemetery where my grandfather was buried for years and years. He had no idea he'd end up here, in a northern Indiana town where laid-off steel workers steal flowers for the living. He had no idea he'd have to wait years and years and years for my grandmother to die so he could be transported and they could be buried side by side, finally, in hurricane weather. I never understood why it mattered, I don't need to gaze on a tombstone to remember. My sons never knew my grandparents, which is not unusual. I barely knew them myself, growing up here, in Indiana, while they faced countless indignities in Cuba and Spain. Many years after they'd left the island, I visited Sagua la Grande, where the bridge was perilous and bloated fish swam in tanks of drinking water. I wandered through the ruins of my grandparents' old house with the permission of its not-so-new and deferential tenants. There was no sign of my family, or so I thought at the time. The people in the brownish framed photographs looked familiar enough. But photographs, I think, are not enough. In front of a window clouded by factory dust, I try to find my reflection, but I can't fit my sons' faces to my ancestors'. I walk to the northern edge of town and follow the boats on the lake's horizon. These are pleasure seekers, not in it for work, nor exodus. I overhear conversations about a wolf in a deserted shopping mall, a hot shower on a frigid morning, about burning the rotting alewives piled on the shores of Lake Michigan. ◈

Hojas muertas y ladrillos al borde del agua nieve marrón. Grietas en las aceras. Una colección de colillas. Nada me separa del cementerio donde mi abuelo estuvo enterrado durante años y años. No tenía ni idea de que acabaría aquí, en un pueblo del norte de Indiana donde los trabajadores despedidos de las plantas de acero roban flores para los vivos. No tenía ni idea de que tendría que esperar años y años y años a que mi abuela muriera para que pudiera ser trasladado y ellos pudieran ser enterrados uno al lado del otro, por fin, en tierras de huracán. Nunca entendí por qué importaba, no necesito leer una lápida para recordar. Mis hijos nunca conocieron a mis abuelos, lo cual no es raro. Yo misma apenas los conocí, pues crecí aquí, en Indiana, mientras ellos se enfrentaban a innumerables indignidades en Cuba y España. Muchos años después de que abandonaran la isla, visité Sagua la Grande, donde el puente era un peligro y los peces hinchados nadaban en tanques de agua potable. Deambulé por las ruinas de la vieja casa de mis abuelos con el permiso de sus no tan nuevos y deferentes inquilinos. No había ni rastro de mi familia, o eso creía yo entonces. Las personas en las fotografías enmarcadas en marrón me resultaban bastante familiares. Pero las fotografías, creo, no bastan. Frente a una ventana empañada por el polvo de una fábrica, intento encontrar mi reflejo, pero no consigo encajar los rostros de mis hijos con mis ancestros. Camino hacia el extremo norte del pueblo y sigo las barcas en el horizonte del lago. Buscan placer, no trabajo ni éxodo. Escucho conversaciones acerca de un lobo en un centro comercial abandonado, de una ducha caliente en una mañana gélida y sobre la quema de las alevines podridas amontonadas en las orillas del Lago Michigan. ✐

The lives of my mother fit in one name, typed on envelopes cut open like fish bellies. She makes them dance, like she does. On her night table she keeps a few photographs, black and white, of someone she knew: a familiar woman with simmering coal eyes on the arm of a gent in white linen; their long-ago poses exotic, ordinary. Today, my father falls asleep, his muscles soft before the hum of the TV screen. She complains (complains), hiding the trace of comfort trailing her words. Decades tumble into a thimble on the sewing table where she keeps her embroidery, store-bought patterns. In the garage, he keeps every nail, every screw, every pin, according to size, length and weight; little jars catalogued like a library, never used. They wear pajamas, cotton synthetic blends of extraordinary softness, the kind that sprout tight little beads of fuzz around the elbows, belly worn. They hold each other all night. Forty-odd years and, in the morning, he silences a cough, unknots the blankets and sheets, brings her coffee. With an impulse she might spill it, but it's too long in the same cup.

Sometimes I swallow glass, but no one names me against my will. It's never planned, but I make my own calling. These are familiar lives in foreign languages, intimate tongues. (My mother refuses to read the subtitles; she acknowledges nothing.) These are sharp, salty loves. Death on the first kiss. My father shakes his head; he wants no descendants from me. He complains (complains). She has a question: How long can you keep your head under water? (My mother is amphibian, a lizard whose tail will grow a new head.) She says she'd rather not know. My chest is tight, bursting. Death on every first kiss. (My mother is immortal, posthumous nails grow on the cadaver.)

Las vidas de mi mamá caben en un solo nombre, escritas a máquina en sobres abiertos como vientres de pescado. Los hace bailar, como ella. En su mesa de noche guarda unas cuantas fotografías en blanco y negro, de alguien conocida: una mujer familiar con ojos de carbón hirviendo en el brazo de un caballero vestido de lino blanco; sus poses de antaño, exóticas, ordinarias. Hoy, mi papá se duerme con sus músculos blandos ante el zumbido de la pantalla del televisor. Ella se queja (se queja), ocultando las huellas de consuelo que arrastran sus palabras. Las décadas caen en un dedal sobre la mesa de costura donde mi mamá guarda sus bordados, patrones comprados en tiendas. En el garaje, mi papá guarda cada clavo, cada tornillo, cada alfiler, según tamaño, longitud y peso; tarritos catalogados como una biblioteca, nunca usados. Ellos llevan pijamas, mezclas de algodón y sintético de una suavidad extraordinaria, de esos de los que brotan bolitas de pelusa alrededor de los codos, de los vientres gastados. Se abrazan toda la noche. Cuarenta años impares y, por la mañana, él acalla una tos, deshace los nudos de las mantas y las sábanas, le trae café. Con un impulso ella podría derramarlo, pero lleva demasiado tiempo en la misma taza.

A veces trago vidrio, pero nadie me nombra contra mi voluntad. Nunca está planeado, pero yo hago mi propio camino. Son vidas familiares en lenguas extranjeras, lenguas íntimas. (Mi madre se niega a leer los subtítulos; no reconoce nada.) Son amores agudos y salados. La muerte en el primer beso. Mi padre sacude la cabeza; no quiere descendencia mía. Se queja (se queja). Tiene una pregunta: ¿Cuánto tiempo puedes mantener la cabeza bajo el agua? (Mi madre es anfibia, una lagartija de cuya cola le crecerá una nueva cabeza.) Dice que prefiere no saberlo. Tengo el pecho apretado,

These photographs are different. She avoids them. I tell
her in my glove compartment there's another brand-
name envelope swollen with nearly instant photos; they
were processed overnight. But my mother wants to hire
a professional, a photographer who will shoot me in
black and white at family occasions. She'll wait for days
and sometimes weeks for memory's return, enlarged and
pinned like dried flowers to the page. This is her calling.

My mother wants to be annihilated with happiness.
She wants to take me with her to a happy hell where
there's never the individuality of pain.   ❧

a punto de estallar. La muerte en cada primer beso. (Mi madre es inmortal, le crecen uñas póstumas al cadáver).

Estas fotografías son diferentes. Ella las evita. Le digo que en mi guantera hay otro sobre hinchado de fotos casi instantáneas; se procesaron de la noche a la mañana. Pero mi mamá quiere contratar a un profesional, un fotógrafo que me tire en blanco y negro en ocasiones familiares. Esperará días, a veces semanas, al regreso de los recuerdos, ampliados y pegados como flores secas a la página. Es su vocación.

Mi mamá quiere ser aniquilada por la felicidad.
Quiere llevarme con ella a un infierno feliz donde nunca exista la individualidad del dolor. ✍

My father closes his eyes and picks me up after he smacks me. I let go of the knife in my hand. He still holds his belt, tells me how he'll use it to bind me. Red stripes fresh on my arm, my leg, my neck. The belt swinging from his fist, an upside-down lasso. He presses his eyes tight, he wants to be someplace else, to be someone else. When his eyes open, he sees his father and a heaven without angels, without dawn. ✌

Mi papá cierra los ojos y me carga después de pegarme. Suelto el cuchillo que llevo en la mano. Sigue sujetando su cinturón, me explica cómo lo usará para atarme. Rayas rojas frescas en mi brazo, mi pierna, mi cuello. El cinturón pendiendo de su puño, un lazo al revés. Aprieta los ojos con fuerza, quiere estar en otro lugar, ser otra persona. Cuando sus ojos se abren, ve a su padre y un cielo sin ángeles, sin amanecer. ❧

It's almost impossible for me to imagine my father traveling
alone. He was a man of dependence, and not just on the road,
who imagined himself sovereign. What he said was that, at
seventeen, he stowed away on an American freighter docked
in the Bay of Gibara. He sailed north, then hitchhiked from
Key West to San Francisco. I don't know if he stopped in
Savannah and strolled the waterfront, if he saw the St. Louis
arch—he talked with great emotion about the vastness of the
U.S. (never America, *we are all America*, a lesson I learned
from him) and the expert engineering of the highways: He
could trace hot-mix asphalt all the way back to the Romans.
I don't know if he suffered altitude sickness in the Rockies,
this boy who grew up below sea level, or if he lost his grip
the moment he saw bliss in the colors of New Mexico. I don't
know if he touched or was touched by anyone in a car at the
side of the road, or in a truck-stop motel, or if he saw the
world's largest ball of twine in Kansas. His story was always
about grandeur, about magnitude; it was about a kind of
religion without a god. I try to imagine him as a gaunt, gawky
teenager leaping in and out of truck beds, handling money
he might have earned washing dishes in Oklahoma (where
they might have thought him Cherokee or Kaw, but never
Jewish, never Spanish, never Cuban, until he talked). Maybe
he picked persimmons and plums with migrants, fruits as
strange and delicious as what tempted Eve. Maybe this is
when he developed his taste for apples, such an untropical
fruit. I see him circling those ticky-tacky city hall plazas in
the Midwest, the locals staring at the bounty of frizzled hair
on his head, the faint skin of his quivering lip which gave
him away more than any accent, more than any wrong turn.
Did he gingerly avoid the white boys loitering at the local

Me resulta casi imposible imaginar a mi papá viajando solo. Era un hombre que dependía de otros y no sólo en la carretera, aunque se imaginaba soberano. Lo que contaba era que, a los diecisiete años, se embarcó de polizón en un carguero americano anclado en la bahía de Gibara. Navegó hacia el norte y luego viajó de Cayo Hueso a San Francisco como mochilero. No sé si paró en Savannah y paseó por los muelles, si vio el arco de San Luis . . . hablaba con gran emoción de la inmensidad de Estados Unidos (nunca América, *todos somos América*, una lección que aprendí de él) y de la experta ingeniería de las autopistas: podía contar la historia del asfalto mezclado en caliente desde los romanos. No sé si sufrió el mal de altura en las Rocosas, este joven que se crió por debajo del nivel del mar, o si perdió el control en cuanto vio la santidad de los colores de Nuevo México. No sé si acarició o fue acariciado por alguien en un carro al borde de la carretera, o en un motel en alguna parada de camiones, o si vio el ovillo de hilo más grande del mundo en Kansas. Su historia siempre era acerca de grandeza, de magnitud; era como una especie de religión sin dios. Intento imaginármelo como un adolescente enjuto y desgarbado que saltaba dentro y fuera de las camas de los camiones, manejando el dinero que podría haber ganado lavando platos en Oklahoma (donde lo podrían haber confundido por cherokee o kaw, pero nunca judío, nunca español, jamás cubano, hasta que hablaba). Quizá recogía caquis y ciruelas con los emigrantes, frutas tan extrañas y deliciosas como las que tentaron a Eva. Quizá fue entonces cuando desarrolló su gusto por las manzanas, una fruta tan poco tropical. Lo veo dando vueltas por las plazas de los pequeños ayuntamientos del medio oeste, con los lugareños mirando en fijo a los bucles

gas station? I know nothing of his return to Gibara, if there was glee, a welcome, or if he was reproached or ignored. That never figured in any tale. When my sons ask about him, I'm careful to honor his silences but always find myself later, sitting with that decision, and wondering why. ❧

encrespados de su cabeza, la tenue piel de su labio tembloroso
que le delataba más que cualquier acento, más que cualquier
giro equivocado. ¿Evitaba con cautela a los blanquitos
que merodeaban por la gasolinera local? No sé nada de su
regreso a Gibara, si hubo júbilo, una bienvenida, o si fue
reprochado o ignorado. Eso nunca figuró en ningún relato.
Cuando mis hijos preguntan por él, me cuido de respetar
sus silencios, pero siempre me encuentro más tarde
contemplando esa decisión, y preguntándome por qué. ✎

My father saw himself a raconteur, the protagonist in stories of heroism and confrontation—a stark contrast to the man we often saw struggling to conform, diminished in interactions with the cashier at the 7-Eleven. There was a tale of defiance before a court judge, a tale of defiance before the doctor who delivered my brother on New Year's Day in 1959 and wanted my parents to name him Fidel. (*My son has a mother*, my father allegedly replied.) But one story came to me whispered like a confession. It happened our first year in Florida, in what were then long, lush green fields of tomatoes where my parents picked the fruit bare-handed, working calluses and rashes. (Years later, after they retired, they bought a house right on those fields, now a whole other municipality.) They'd been brought in along with a group of other newly arrived immigrants, all Cubans, everyone still shaking off seaweed and salt. When the lunchtime food trucks rolled out, marked "whites only" and "colored," the Cubans ambled up to the "whites only" truck (Was it shinier? A cleaner truck? Did its menu provide more choices?). There they were told some, like my dad, could stay, but the others would have to go to the "colored" truck. That's when my father said they were all brothers and sisters of all colors, that they would all eat together, and promptly led the entire group over to the "colored" truck. Many things are curious to me about this story. One is that while my father is identified as white enough to stay at the "whites only" truck, no one is fingered as too dark. I've often wondered if his actions were less a matter of unity, or, much less, racial sensitivity, than perhaps a question of saving face. Did he fear my mother would be singled out as not white enough? (She always walked in the shade, in the shade, afraid of the sun and what its heat might

Mi papá se veía a sí mismo como un cuentista, el protagonista de historias de heroísmo y confrontación, un marcado contraste con el hombre al que a menudo veíamos luchando por conformarse, disminuido en las interacciones con la cajera de la bodega. Hubo una historia de desafío ante un juez, una historia de desafío ante el médico que trajo al mundo a mi hermano el día de Año Nuevo de 1959 y que quería que mis padres lo llamaran Fidel (*Mi hijo tiene madre*, contestó mi papá, supuestamente.) Pero una historia me llegó susurrada como una confesión. Ocurrió nuestro primer año en la Florida, en lo que entonces eran largos y frondosos campos verdes de tomates donde mis padres recogían la fruta a mano desnuda, trabajándose callos y sarpullidos. (Años después, cuando se jubilaron, compraron una casa justo en esos campos, que ahora son un municipio). Los habían traído junto con un grupo de otros inmigrantes recién llegados, todos cubanos, todos todavía sacudiéndose las algas y la sal. Cuando salieron los camiones de comida para el almuerzo, que decían "sólo blancos" y "de color", los cubanos se acercaron al camión de "sólo blancos" (¿brillaba más?, ¿estaba más limpio? o ¿su menú ofrecía más opciones?). Allí les dijeron que algunos, como mi papá, podían quedarse, pero que los demás tendrían que ir al camión "de color". Fue entonces cuando mi papá dijo que todos eran hermanos y hermanas de todos los colores, que comerían todos juntos, y enseguida condujo al grupo entero al camión "de color". Hay muchas cosas que me resultan curiosas de esta historia. Una de ellas es que, mientras que a mi papá se le identifica como lo suficientemente blanco como para quedarse en el camión "sólo para blancos", a nadie se le señala como demasiado prieto. A menudo me he preguntado si sus acciones fueron menos una cuestión de unidad, o, mucho menos, de

reveal.) This would have prompted my father; it would have called on his chivalry, or perhaps his fears. Another curiosity is that, though in this narrative my father acts heroically—precisely in the ways he tried to paint himself in his other tales—he never told this story. I first heard it from my mother as an adult, in my late forties, after my father had passed away and she was feeling her own mortality. I remember one afternoon a decade later, after the birth of my eldest son, when she and I were lying in bed together in that very house built on those fields, and she repeated it. It is the only story about my father I ever want to tell my sons. ✍

sensibilidad racial, que quizá era una cuestión de salvar las apariencias. ¿Temía que mi mamá fuera señalada como no suficientemente blanca? (Siempre caminaba en la sombra, en la sombra, temerosa del sol y de lo que su calor pudiera revelar). Esto habría incitado a mi papá; habría apelado a su caballerosidad, o quizá a sus temores. Otra curiosidad es que, aunque en esta narración mi papá actúa heroicamente—precisamente de la forma en que trataba de pintarse a sí mismo en sus otros cuentos—nunca contó esta historia. Se la oí a mi madre por primera vez de adulta, cuando yo tenía cuarenta y algo, después de la muerte de mi papá, cuando ella sentía su propia mortalidad. Recuerdo una tarde, una década después, cuando nació mi hijo mayor, cuando ella y yo estábamos acostadas en la cama juntas en esa misma casa en esos campos, y ella me lo repitió. Es la única historia sobre mi papá que quiero contarle a mis hijos. ✍

My mother injected my son into her veins and cured herself. She coughed it out: all that fear, all that public shame. My son, a ball of dough and hope, slid off her lap in TV light into a puddle on the floor and warmed her feet instead. Before—before my son, the eldest, the one with gossamer skin—before he'd swallowed a scoop of air in this world, my mother hated me. Hated the way I cocked my hip. Hated the way I said here and guided my lover's fist inside me. Hated the way I stirred my coffee and my dreams. Before— before my son—my mother loved me like a pot of boiling water, like solar flares skipping over the Atlantic, seething with their own predacious wrath. That was before. Before her light found a rest, and a place for its reflection. ✑

Mi mamá se inyectó a mi hijo en las venas y se curó a sí misma. Tosió: todo ese miedo, toda esa vergüenza pública. Mi hijo, una bola de masa y esperanza, se deslizó de su regazo en la luz del televisor a un charco en el suelo y le calentó los pies. Antes—antes de mi hijo, el mayor, el de la piel de gasa—antes de que hubiera tragado una cucharada de aire en este mundo, mi mamá me odiaba. Odiaba cómo ladeaba la cadera. Odiaba la forma en que decía aquí y guiaba el puño de mi amante dentro de mí. Odiaba cómo removía mi café y mis sueños. Antes—antes de mi hijo—mi mamá me amaba como una olla de agua hirviendo, como llamaradas solares saltando sobre el Atlántico, hirviendo con su propia ira depredadora. Eso era antes. Antes de que su luz encontrara un descanso, y un lugar para su reflejo. ✌︎

PART 3

PARTE 3

If I didn't believe in the foolishness of the mountains and a
thousand ways to fall, in their dangerous and covert violence,
if I didn't believe in karma, in defying logic, if I didn't believe
in what I do and don't, if I didn't use my silence and my
voice, if I didn't trust my tongue, my bones, I'd be threading
ropes, spilling poison in the broth, if I thought it was an act
of love, then the cheating wouldn't count, the stones would
move all on their own, if I didn't believe in that desire, in the
sacred, in the inevitability of liars, if I didn't believe the fall
will take our minds into the void, that someone will guide
my fist into the hole, if I didn't take my life each time I cried,
if I didn't boil my children in their mother's blood, then
I'd be threading ropes and ropes and ropes, I'd be pouring
water in a new cup, if I believed it was an act of love. ❧

Si no creyera en la insensatez de las montañas y en las mil
formas de caer, en su violencia peligrosa y encubierta, si no
creyera en el karma, en desafiar la lógica, si no creyera en lo
que hago y no hago, si no usara mi silencio y mi voz, si no
confiara en mi lengua, en mis huesos, estaría enhebrando
cuerdas, derramando veneno en el caldo, si pensara que
es un acto de amor, entonces las trampas no contarían,
las piedras se moverían solas, si no creyera en ese deseo,
en lo sagrado, en la inevitabilidad de los mentirosos, si
no creyera que la caída llevará nuestras mentes al vacío,
que alguien guiará mi puño al agujero, si no me quitara
la vida cada vez que lloro, si no hirviera a mis hijos en
la sangre de su madre, entonces estaría enhebrando
cuerdas y cuerdas y cuerdas, estaría vertiendo agua en
una taza nueva, si creyera que es un acto de amor. ✍

There's chaos in my house, an unpleasant stench. I'm going from room to room, touching the leather couch, the pile of masks on the tiny table in the vestibule, the weird little machine that can turn almost anything to compost. That's the kind of homeowner I am: I compost. Someone's been here though, stealing my rotting food at night, staring at my kids, checking my home value. I remember when I first came to this house—it's not a big deal, it's nothing but a seventies ranch in a California town with no distinguishing features except good schools—the realtor was wearing a green and brown Hawaiian shirt and shook my hand. The bedrooms were too small, the kitchen cramped and weird. My eldest son and I (there was no other son then) ran through the big front room, stood on the tip of the deck out back and, though the yard was dry, Saharan dry, we saw rolling hills of green, saw a pool, soccer games and bbqs. I knew there'd be sunflowers and banana trees where neighborhood cats would sniff about. My ex-wife didn't come with us, didn't approve, nodded reluctantly though she was quick to sign the deed. I will probably lose my house this year. Goodbye avocado harvest, pomegranates, cherries, peach tree. Goodbye little shed where I wrote a few good poems, where my eldest vanquished enemies on screen with kids in Wales and Warsaw. There are no potential customers, no one will see my house at all, it'll transform into fine particles my ex-wife will shape into something novel, all the rage. ✐

Hay caos en mi casa, un hedor desagradable. Voy de habitación en habitación, tocando el sofá de cuero, el montón de mascarillas en la mesita del vestíbulo, la extraña maquinita que puede convertir casi cualquier cosa en compost. Así soy como dueña de casa: Hago abono. Sin embargo, alguien ha estado aquí, robando mi comida podrida por la noche, mirando a mis hijos, comprobando el valor de mi casa. Recuerdo cuando llegué por primera vez a esta casa—no es gran cosa, no es más que una casa estilo rancho de los años setenta en un pueblo de California sin más rasgos distintivos que buenas escuelas. El agente inmobiliario llevaba una camisa hawaiana verde y marrón y me estrechó la mano. Las habitaciones eran demasiado pequeñas, la cocina estrecha y extraña. Mi hijo mayor y yo (entonces no había otro) corrimos por la gran sala, nos paramos en la punta de la terraza de atrás y, aunque el patio estaba seco, seco como el Sahara, vimos colinas verdes, vimos una piscina, partidos de fútbol y barbacoas. Sabía que habría girasoles y plataneros por donde husmearían los gatos del barrio. Mi ex pareja no vino con nosotros, no aprobó, asintió de mala gana aunque se apresuró a firmar el título de propiedad. Probablemente pierda mi casa este año. Adiós cosecha de aguacates, granadas, cerezas, melocotones. Adiós al pequeño estudio donde escribí algunos buenos poemas, donde mi hijo mayor venció enemigos en la pantalla con amiguitos en Gales y Varsovia. No hay clientes potenciales, nadie verá mi casa, se transformará en finas partículas que mi ex pareja moldeará en algo novedoso, la moda del momento. ❧

We tell the kids in two parts: First, we say we're going to
have two houses, not one. And our eldest cries and cries
and asks us to move back in together in three years (we
demur, we skim the surface with our shame) while the
youngest looks around bewildered. In no time at all, he'll
have no memory of our ever sharing anything but tension,
anything at all but strained expressions when together. Then
the second part, a few weeks later, like an afterthought:
that you're moving in with someone else, and our eldest,
without missing a beat, understands it all too well. Will
she be our new stepmom? he asks. I was scared, I was
embarrassed he felt her solar shadow on your skin so clearly,
that he understood she'd hold the fruit you peeled. And
though we had a speech prepared about how she was your
partner and not their mom, he sensed those future holiday
cards, the way he and his brother would pose among our
ruins so you could build your new foundation. ❧

Se lo comunicamos a los chamas en dos partes: Primero, les decimos que vamos a tener dos casas, no una. Y nuestro hijo mayor llora y llora y nos pide que volvamos a vivir juntas dentro de tres años (nosotras evitamos el tema, rozamos la superficie con nuestra deshonra) mientras el pequeño mira a su alrededor desconcertado. Dentro de poco, no recordará que hayamos compartido nada más que tensión, nada más que expresiones tiesas cuando estamos juntas. Luego, la segunda parte, unas semanas más tarde, como una ocurrencia tardía: que van a vivir con otra persona y nuestro hijo mayor, sin perder un segundo, lo entiende perfectamente. ¿Será nuestra nueva madrastra? pregunta. Me asusté, me dio vergüenza que él sintiera tan claramente la sombra solar sobre tu piel, que entendiera que ella sostendría la fruta que tú pelarías. Y aunque teníamos un discurso preparado sobre cómo ella era tu compañera y no su mamá, él intuyó esas futuras tarjetas navideñas, la forma en que él y su hermano posarían entre nuestras ruinas para que tú pudieras construir tus nuevos cimientos. ❧

When it came to raising children, sometimes it felt like jelly, sometimes like ice. We could go from zero to sixty in a billionth of a second—not about the kids, but about us. The kids? We compromised. And us? You said, We'll be all right. Scientists have measured the shortest interval of time, clocking how long it takes a mote of light to cross a maiden molecule of hydrogen. The instrument to gauge what it took us to cut the cords, to tell the kids, to delete every single speck of what we once were is yet to be invented, the rate still to be named, the story of how love turned to disdain ongoing. ❧

Cuando se trata de criar a los hijos, a veces es como la gelatina o hielo. Podíamos pasar de cero a sesenta en una milmillonésima de segundo, no por los chamas, sino por nosotras. ¿Los niños? Acuerdos mutuos. ¿Y nosotras? Dijiste: "Estaremos bien". Los científicos han medido el intervalo de tiempo más corto, cronometrando cuánto tarda un átomo de luz en atravesar una molécula de hidrógeno. El instrumento para medir lo que tardamos en cortar las cuerdas, en decírselo a los chamas, lo que se necesita para borrar cada partícula de lo que una vez fuimos aún está por inventarse, la tasa por nombrarse, la historia de cómo el amor se convirtió en desdén sigue en curso. ✍

Love was over when the marriage fell apart. The bright star had fizzled out. Every morning for years she slept in my bed. After we each went our own way, I thought about her on nights it rained, when I could hear stars crashing, each string of black smoke quickly smothered by the downpour. Sometimes, I listened to her. Sometimes I couldn't hear a word she said. Sometimes I marveled at how far things had gone, as if we were just happily walking along and tripped suddenly into one of those water-park slides with giant S-curves, tunnels and air drops and we were just holding on, and holding each other as we flew and laughed, still in a haze and terrified. When we splashed down, we scrambled out of the pool. I was sure it was she who'd made us fall, she was sure it was me. Then we switched sides and sympathized and then got bored and frustrated. We walked past the charred stars, not an ember left, just dry ash, barely any evidence of its once radiant promise. ✍

El amor terminó cuando el matrimonio se vino abajo. La estrella brillante se había apagado. Durante años, todas las mañanas durmió en mi cama. Después de que cada una siguiera su camino, pensaba en ella las noches que llovía, cuando oía las estrellas chocar, cada ristra de humo negro rápidamente sofocada por el aguacero. A veces, la escuchaba. A veces no oía ni una palabra de lo que decía. A veces me maravillaba de lo lejos que habían llegado las cosas, como si estuviéramos paseando alegremente y de repente nos hubiéramos tropezado con uno de esos toboganes de los parques acuáticos con gigantes curvas en forma de S, túneles y caídas en el aire, y nos hubiéramos agarrado y abrazado mientras volábamos y reíamos, todavía en una nebulosa y aterrorizadas. Cuando caímos, salimos corriendo de la piscina. Yo estaba segura de que había sido ella la que nos había hecho caer, ella segura de que había sido yo. Luego cambiamos de bando y nos compadecimos y luego nos aburrimos y frustramos. Pasamos por delante de las estrellas carbonizadas, no quedaba ni una brasa, sólo ceniza seca, apenas alguna prueba de su promesa antaño radiante. ❧

My boys scamper through a field of grass after their soccer games. They kick a ball between them, ahead of them, lose it in the tall grass and have to go back. It's a maze. One boy is dotted with sweat, the other's slick as a hiss. They lie on their bunk beds, one with a weighted baby blanket over his always-cold feet, the other with a black and white cat on his head. They're flesh, they're red marble and maize, they're rum because I insist and coffee every blackish morning because I can't live without them. They're a curse, have no doubt about it, an improvised detour after detour after detour after a malicious earthquake, a road carved through ever shifting and impossible lava. I'm free to want, and I'll do what I want, I'll fall head over heels over this ball and chain. There's no point in worrying about the past. ❧

Mis hijos corretean por un campo de hierba después de sus partidos de fútbol. Patean un balón entre ellos, delante de ellos, lo pierden en la hierba alta y tienen que volver. Es un laberinto. Un hijo está salpicado de sudor, el otro resbaloso como un siseo. Están tumbados en sus literas, uno con una manta de bebé tirada sobre sus pies siempre fríos, el otro con un gato blanco y negro en la cabeza. Ellos son carne, son mármol rojo y maíz, son ron porque insisto y café cada mañana negruzca porque no puedo vivir sin ellos. Son una maldición, no debe haber duda, un desvío improvisado tras otro desvío, tras otro desvío, tras un terremoto malicioso, un camino labrado en lava siempre movediza e imposible. Soy libre de querer y haré lo que quiera, caeré de cabeza sobre este peso y esta cadena. No tiene sentido preocuparse por el pasado. ✍

She grips my naked wrist, this woman with hooded morning eyes and says, sincerely: My own kid is almost out of the house, out in the world, and I can see the light at the end of the tunnel—but, you, oh you, you have a two-year-old son and . . . I can't. She can only see what's straight in front of her, and all my attributes become blurry asides. This repeats itself over and over, when my youngest is three, then four, now five. You're so fantastic, the women say, pushing their feet into their shoes, but . . . then they pause to disentangle my son's yo-yo from their laces. In another life, maybe . . . But even when my adrenaline's pumping, the circle of this life of mine, the only one I own, keeps getting smaller and thinner. Women visit, pull on my branded arm, sleep with a scar-free hand on my shoulder, then arise in the morning and make their way through a maze of Hot Wheels, avoid the spilled pink slime, the full drum set like a throne in the playroom. By the time my youngest takes his place with the sticks to show off his alarming talent—his limb independence defies the laws of nature—they're gone and I'm on a train, blasting through zone after zone of slightly rarified air. ✒

Me agarra de la muñeca desnuda, esta mujer de ojos matutinos encapuchados y dice, sinceramente: mi propio hijo está casi fuera de casa, ya en el mundo, y puedo ver la luz al final del túnel . . . pero, tú, oh tú, tienes un hijo de dos años y . . . no puedo. Ella sólo ve lo que tiene delante, y todos mis atributos se convierten en apartes borrosos. Esto se repite una y otra vez, cuando mi hijo menor tiene tres años, luego cuatro, ahora cinco. Eres fantástica, dicen las mujeres, metiendo los pies en sus zapatos, pero . . . luego hacen una pausa para desenredarse de los cordones del yoyó de mi hijo. En otra vida, tal vez . . . Pero incluso cuando me sube la adrenalina, el círculo de esta vida mía, la única que tengo, sigue haciéndose más pequeño y más delicado. Las mujeres me visitan, tiran de mi brazo marcado, duermen con una mano libre de cicatrices sobre mi hombro, luego se levantan por la mañana y se abren paso a través de un laberinto de Hot Wheels, evitan el limo rosa derramado, la batería completa, como un trono en la sala de juegos. Para cuando mi hijo menor toma su sitio con las baquetas para demostrar su alarmante talento—la independencia de sus miembros desafía las leyes de la naturaleza—ellas ya se han ido y yo estoy en un tren, atravesando, una tras otra, zonas de aire ligeramente enrarecido. ❧

There's a woman who loves me but things are getting tense. We walk around my sons, each in a different direction, pass each other and look away. After a while, I step away, I leave the boys with her for a moment and go look for a light. They stare up at her as if she were the loveliest star, the beacon they've been waiting for, but she's shaking her head. And then she puts her hands to her face and says, Okay, for you, because I love you. We walk around the boys again, pass each other on the right, against the flow. We look at houses in up-and-coming towns and imagine our distribution, our flowering garden, where we'll put the trampoline. She wants to take her life, she wants to take my life, our lives, far and away. You still love me? She nods, I nod, nobody knows who asked the question. Is there any question? Take our lives to North Carolina, to Philly, Belize, Paris. We can speak French in bed, she can learn Spanish, I'll memorize the shabbat prayer for once instead of unfolding that savage little piece of paper each and every time. Take our lives before winter comes, take our lives before the rains, before we can promise any more. Leave everything and everyone behind, plunge into the dark of April, into the cold of May. We'll leave, someday. &

Hay una mujer que me quiere pero las cosas se están poniendo tensas. Caminamos alrededor de mis hijos, cada una en una dirección diferente, nos cruzamos y miramos a otro lado. Al cabo de un rato, me alejo, dejo a los chamas con ella un momento y voy en busca de luz. La miran como si fuera la estrella más hermosa, el faro que han estado esperando, pero ella niega con la cabeza. Y entonces se lleva las manos a la cara y dice: "Vale, por ti, porque te quiero". Volvemos a caminar alrededor de los chamas, nos cruzamos por la derecha, a contracorriente. Valoramos casas en ciudades emergentes e imaginamos cómo nos podríamos acomodar, nuestro jardín florido, nos preguntamos dónde pondríamos el trampolín. Quiere llevarse su vida, quiere llevarse mi vida, nuestras vidas, lejos, muy lejos. ¿Todavía me quieres? Ella asiente, yo asiento, nadie sabe quién hizo la pregunta. ¿Hay alguna pregunta? Llevar nuestras vidas a Carolina del Norte, a Filadelfia, Belice, París. Podemos hablar francés en la cama, ella puede aprender español, yo memorizaré, por fin, la oración del shabat en lugar de desplegar cada vez ese salvaje pedacito de papel. Seguir nuestras vidas antes de que llegue el invierno, llevar nuestras vidas antes de que llueva, antes de que no podamos prometer nada más. Dejarlo todo y a todos atrás, sumergirnos en la oscuridad de abril, el frío de mayo. Nos iremos, algún día. ꙮ

After I break up with her, there's a new girl in my ex-lover's life. She busted my watch, picked it up or stole it. Not sure, but she gets to wear it now, because my ex-lover wants it that way. I say, well fine, then tell me about her. I know my toothbrush will fly out of the cup in my ex-lover's bathroom, be snapped in two and buried before she's finished answering. She'll galvanize her key to my house to spear it in my side. I want to lie down and make her lie down too but no—she's at a table with a fountain of flowers and I'm over here in a chair, strapped in by god knows what, waiting to bleed out. My ex-lover says the two of them hit all their milestones at the same time, check them off in unison and it's so much fun. My ex-lover says the new girl lives nearby and she doesn't have to drive forever to spend the night, like she did with me. She says the new girl's house is cozy, a real hearth, a delight, no bouncy balls to trip on, no junk food or dairy in the house. My ex-lover's so relieved she never has to worry about keeping cream for coffee again.

My ex-lover licks her lips: No kids, she says, there are no kids, no *fucking* kids, no custody arrangements, no kid bday parties, no kindergarten or middle-school graduations, no kid colds, no Legos to step on, no feverish bodies to interrupt the night, no sex toys to hide, no profanities to swallow, no need to be dressed all the time, no bedtime, no worries about what they might get into, no need to get them to school on time.

Después de romper con ella, hay una nueva chica en la vida de mi ex amante. La nueva desbarató mi reloj, lo recogió o lo robó. No estoy segura, pero ahora lo lleva ella, porque mi ex amante lo quiere así. Digo, bien, entonces cuéntame de ella. Sé que mi cepillo de dientes saldrá volando de la taza del baño de mi ex amante, se partirá en dos y quedará enterrado antes de que ella conteste. Ella galvanizará su llave de mi casa para clavármela en el costado. Quiero desplomarme y hacer que ella se desplome también, pero no, está sentada en una mesa con una fuente de flores y yo estoy aquí en una silla, atada por dios sabe qué, esperando desangrarme. Mi ex amante dice que ellas dos alcanzan todos los hitos al mismo tiempo, los marcan al unísono y es muy divertido. Mi ex amante dice que la chica nueva vive cerca y que no tiene que conducir eternamente para pasar la noche, como hacía conmigo. Dice que la casa de la nueva chica es acogedora, un verdadero hogar, una delicia, sin pelotas con las que tropezar, sin junk food ni lácteos. Mi ex amante está tan aliviada que nunca más tendrá que preocuparse de guardar nata para el café.

Mi ex amante se lame los labios: No hay niños, dice, no hay niños, no hay ni un *puñetero* chiquillo, no hay acuerdos de custodia, no hay fiestas de cumpleaños, no hay graduaciones, no hay resfriados, no hay Legos que pisar, ni cuerpos febriles que interrumpan la noche, ni juguetes sexuales que esconder, ni blasfemias que tragar, ni necesidad de vestirse todo el tiempo, ni hora de acostarse, ni preocupaciones por en lo que puedan meterse, ni necesidad de llevarlos a la escuela a tiempo.

My ex-lover's new girl checks my broken watch on
her wrist, takes my car and drives herself to the same
yawning job she's had since the day she was born.
When I protest, my ex-lover looks the other way.

What's the purpose of this story?

It's for me to ask: How could you lie to me like that? ✍

La nueva chica de mi ex amante comprueba mi reloj roto en su muñeca, coge mi carro y corre al mismo trabajo aburrido que tiene desde el día en que nació. Cuando protesto, mi ex amante desvía la mirada.

¿Cuál es el objetivo de esta historia?

Es para que pregunte: ¿Cómo pudiste mentirme así?

Friends choose my hotel room, spacious, one bed, giant
windows that will let the light in at morning's first break. I'd
been crying in airport cafés, shrinking in size, drawing too
much attention. Come home soon, they said. They meant
Chicago, Havana, imagined cities between the American
Midwest and, maybe, Patagonia. My body resists the cold
but every cell resurrects with each step on the harsh frozen
ground. My friends meant Oakland, or a small beach
town on the coast of North Carolina—not Oakland, let's
be frank, they meant Miami and deep soul meditations
in a slightly lemony mikveh with an attendant, a Russian
refugee from Soviet days who wants to compare our exiles.
She shakes her head and strokes my hair with her left
hand. She'll do the tally as she brings her palms to my chest
and neck, moves her hand to my waist. (None of this is
kosher.) Your life doesn't threaten the American dream,
she said with a heavy accent. She spun me around, handed
me a room service menu. I ordered accordingly. ❧

Mis amigos eligen mi habitación de hotel, espaciosa, con una cama, ventanas gigantes que dejen entrar la luz al amanecer. Había estado llorando en los cafés del aeropuerto, encogiéndome, llamando demasiada atención. Decían: vuelve pronto. Se referían a Chicago, La Habana, ciudades imaginarias entre el medio oeste americano y, tal vez, la Patagonia. Mi cuerpo resiste el frío, pero cada célula resucita con cada paso sobre el duro suelo helado. Mis amigos se referían a Oakland, o a una pequeña ciudad playera en la costa de Carolina del Norte; Oakland no, seamos francos, se referían a Miami, y a las profundas meditaciones del alma en una mikve ligeramente alimonada, con una encargada rusa, una refugiada de la época soviética, que quiere comparar nuestros exilios. Menea la cabeza y me acaricia el pelo con la mano izquierda. Hace el recuento mientras lleva sus palmas a mi pecho y cuello, mueve su mano a mi cintura (nada de esto es permitido). Tu vida no amenaza el sueño americano, dice con un fuerte acento. Me hizo girar y me entregó el menú del servicio de habitaciones. Ordené enseguida. ✍

Everything is written with clay and oil.

They used to be of good quality. But now the road is long and difficult and my feet get stuck. I've been married too long, but it's just on paper; it's been that way for years. If I had my way, there would be no fire, no wind, no trees decomposing on the forest floor, initials abstracting on the disintegrating bark. I'd take my sons to meet my lovers. We could do the blessings, we could learn what words to say as we made our way through the bush. What is that, a seed? A tooth? A shard of amber entombing a forever love? ❧

Todo se escribe con arcilla y aceite. Antes eran de buena calidad, pero ahora el camino es largo y difícil y mis pies se atascan. Llevo demasiado tiempo casada, pero es sólo una cuestión oficial; ha sido así por años. Si por mí fuera, no habría fuego, ni viento, ni árboles descomponiéndose en el suelo del bosque, ni iniciales abstrayéndose en la corteza que se desintegra. Llevaría a mis hijos a conocer a mis amantes. Podríamos hacer las bendiciones, podríamos aprender qué palabras decir mientras nos abrimos paso entre la maleza. ¿Qué es eso, una semilla? ¿Un diente? ¿Un fragmento de ámbar enterrando un amor eterno? ❧

At the end of June, I replace the lightbulbs and plants near the windows. Today, we are blanketed by fog and ashes, so I finish pruning the spring-flowering shrubs, the corydalis, the bleeding hearts. Pick up the balls the boys have left scattered in the yard. Spray the hardwood trees. Prune the boxwoods and yews. Check for slugs, aerate the compost. Tie the perennial vines to their supports. I'll cage the peppers, tomatoes and eggplants. Water the melons until they almost drown. When his body rises from the bed we've ravished together, his mouth is lopsided and game. Tonight, when he falls asleep inside my body, I worry we'll perish like that. ❧

A finales de junio, cambio las capullos y las plantas de las ventanas. Hoy nos cubre la niebla y la ceniza, así que termino de podar los arbustos de floración primaveral, los corydalis, las flores de lira. Recojo las pelotas que los chamas han dejado esparcidas por el jardín. Rocío los árboles de madera dura. Podo los bojes y los tejos. Compruebo si hay babosas, aireo el compost. Ato las parras perennes a sus soportes. Luego enjaularé los pimientos, tomates y berenjenas. Regaré los melones hasta que casi se ahoguen. Cuando su cuerpo se levanta de la cama que hemos arrasado juntos, su boca está ladeada y juguetona. Esta noche, cuando él se duerma dentro de mi cuerpo, me preocupa que perezcamos así. ❧

This is the love you find when you're not looking, when you're not trying to fool yourself into thinking you're not looking, but when you really aren't, because you've gotten used to going without it, or it got used to being without you. It broke your neck, crushed your hands. You can stop asking yourself how old you are now. You see, all love is hard, no matter when it comes, and most of all, when it doesn't. Your mouth is always the most beautiful part of your body because of kissing, but also—and most importantly—because this is where truth emerges, or should. It connects in a bloody spiral to your broken neck, the pulp of your hands, your heart. This is the most dangerous part of your body because when someone loves you now, at this age, they're loving your mortality, they can see it blinking off and on down your throat, they can almost make out the when and where. When someone loves you now, they're loving your wisdom and your helplessness, your children and your irascibility. When someone loves you now, they're loving all your past loves, your past mistakes, all the ways that brought you here, to them, covered in your shame. You might ask: How does this work? I love you, you are my love. How does this work? How does this work? ❧

Este es el amor que encuentras cuando no buscas, cuando no intentas engañarte pensando que no buscas, sino cuando realmente no lo haces, porque te has acostumbrado a no tenerlo, o el amor se acostumbró a pasar sin ti. Te rompió el cuello, te aplastó las manos. Ya puedes dejar de preguntarte cuántos años tienes. Ya ves, todo amor es difícil, no importa cuando llegue y, sobre todo, cuando no llega. Tu boca es siempre la parte más bella de tu cuerpo a causa de los besos, pero también—y sobre todo—porque es aquí donde surge, o debería surgir, la verdad. Se conecta en una espiral sangrienta a tu cuello roto, a la pulpa de tus manos, a tu corazón. Esta es la parte más peligrosa de tu cuerpo porque cuando alguien te ama ahora, a esta edad, está amando tu mortalidad, puede verla parpadear intermitentemente por tu garganta, casi puede distinguir el cuándo y el dónde. Cuando alguien te ama ahora, ama tu sabiduría y tu impotencia, tus hijos y tu irascibilidad. Cuando alguien te ama ahora, está amando todos tus amores pasados, tus errores pasados, todos los caminos que te trajeron aquí, a ellos, cubierta de vergüenza. Te preguntarás: ¿Cómo funciona esto? Te quiero, eres mi amor. ¿Cómo funciona esto? ¿Cómo funciona esto? ✍

She'll love the dark, not just the night sky and the long shadows of a tropical afternoon, but impure intentions too, the secrets that leak from our souls. Nothing I say will frighten her. She won't care about my flawed living room furniture, the music I play, or the circular architecture of my house which sets the boys (and her too sometimes) racing round and round. She'll stock good coffee—the best coffee, with notes of cocoa-toned guava and a very full, satiny mouthfeel—and there will be sex that tastes like coffee. Coffee and cream, the real thing, frothy top milk. And she'll be a fighter and fight me, bare-fisted, bared breasts, unafraid of the way the ground might quake. In winter, when it's gusty and cold and we are both beautiful, she'll lift my scarf and kiss my neck and say, We have fallen and we will not fall in vain. ✌

Amará la oscuridad, no sólo el cielo nocturno y las largas sombras de una tarde tropical, sino también las intenciones impuras, los secretos que se filtran de nuestras almas. Nada de lo que le diga la asustará. No le importarán los desperfectos de mis muebles de salón, ni la música que pongo, ni la arquitectura circular de mi casa que pone a los chamas (y a veces a ella también) a dar vueltas y más vueltas. Se abastecerá de buen café—el mejor café, con notas de guayaba entonadas con cacao y una sensación en boca muy plena y satinada—y habrá sexo que sepa a café. Café y nata, de verdad, espumosa. Y será una luchadora y peleará conmigo, con los puños desnudos, los pechos descubiertos, sin miedo a que tiemble el suelo. En invierno, cuando haga viento y frío y las dos seamos hermosas, me levantará la bufanda, me besará el cuello y dirá: Hemos caído la una en la otra y esto no será en vano. ❧

On the longest night of the year, we light candles and squeeze
and mold the dripping wax between our fingers into tiny
animals, a plane, a three-petal flower. We will give these
away to those we love, we will kiss them, each one, as if they
were who we love. We will unbind the god's ankles, we will
unknot any knot that needs to be unknotted; we will set free
any divinity who promises to refract to our will. We will
wear white gowns with red sashes and twirl on one foot.
We used to send heads to Hades, phota to Saturn—lights,
we are very careful with the lights. On the longest night of
the year, we surrender to unrestrained glee, to the delight of
many banquets, the feasts, the lavish streams of wine. There's
hooting and clapping and singing and playing games, and
false kings in every home telling someone to dance naked
or eat a peach or clean up after themselves. On the longest
night of the year, the world is still cursed with loneliness
even in our unrestrained glee, with hunger even amidst the
delight of our many banquets. We can't feed everyone, we
can't turn every life around. We pray for blessings, we wait,
we hold each other that we might be again and always in our
beloved broken world, that we might find a moment's balm,
a fragile peace, an appetite for forgiveness. On the longest
night of the year, we wait for daybreak to catch the first
sparks, the light pillars holding up the nascent sun. ❧

Durante la noche más larga del año, encendemos velas y apretamos y moldeamos la cera que gotea entre nuestros dedos para formar animalitos, un avión, una flor de tres pétalos. Los regalaremos a nuestros seres queridos, los besaremos, a cada uno de ellos, como si fueran los que amamos. Desataremos los tobillos del dios, desataremos cualquier nudo que necesite ser desatado; liberaremos a cualquier divinidad que prometa desviarse hacia nuestra voluntad. Llevaremos vestidos blancos con fajas rojas y giraremos sobre un pie. Enviaremos cabezas al Hades, claridad a Saturno—luces, tendremos mucho cuidado con las luces. Durante la noche más larga del año, nos entregamos al júbilo desenfrenado, al deleite de los muchos banquetes, los festines, los derroches de vino. Hay gritos y palmas y cantos y juegos, y falsos reyes en todas las casas diciéndole a la gente que baile desnuda o se coma un melocotón o que limpie lo que ensucia. Durante la noche más larga del año, el mundo sigue sufriendo de soledad, incluso en nuestra alegría desenfrenada, por el hambre, incluso en medio del deleite de nuestros numerosos banquetes. No podemos alimentar a todo el mundo, no podemos cambiar todas las vidas. Rezamos por bendiciones, esperamos, nos abrazamos para poder estar de nuevo y siempre en nuestro querido mundo quebrado, para poder encontrar un momento de bálsamo, una paz frágil, un impulso hacia el perdón. Durante la noche más larga del año, esperamos que amanezca para captar las primeras chispas, los pilares de luz que sostienen el sol naciente. ✍

PART 4

PARTE 4

I want you strong, like elephants, crushing rocks under their feet. I want you sweet, like elephants, but with skin as thick to repel fears and hate. I want you to have forty-pound hearts, to smell a storm coming from more than one hundred miles away, to walk stealthily. I want you to click, purr, bark, squeal, trumpet and roll in the mud in utter glee. I want you to stomp and send your joyful tremors through the earth's core to the other side of the world. I want you buoyant, like elephants, and careful, like elephants, pushing little ones to shore, working together, walking together. I want you to learn from your mothers (all your mothers), to know you'll be there for the sick, the injured, the young, the old, the tender-hearted, like you. I want you always near, like elephants, to hold my bones close, like elephants, to remember, remember like elephants. ✑

Los quiero fuertes, como los elefantes, aplastando rocas bajo sus pies. Los quiero dulces, como elefantes, pero con la piel tan gruesa como para repeler los miedos y el odio. Quiero que tengan corazones que pesen cuarenta libras, que puedan oler una tormenta a más de cien millas de distancia, que caminen sigilosamente. Quiero que chasqueen, ronroneen, ladren, chillen, trompeteen y se revuelquen en el barro con total regocijo. Quiero que pisen fuerte y envíen sus alegres temblores a través del núcleo de la tierra hasta el otro lado del mundo. Los quiero boyantes, como elefantes, y cuidadosos, como elefantes, ayudando a los pequeños a llegar a la orilla, trabajando juntos, caminando juntos. Quiero que aprendan de sus mamás (de todas sus mamás), quiero saber que estarán presentes siempre para los enfermos, los heridos, los jóvenes, los viejos, los de corazón tierno, como ustedes. Los quiero siempre cerca, como los elefantes, con mis huesos cerca, como los elefantes, para recordar, recordar como los elefantes.

How to explain that life is worth living only when it has meaning, and that meaning comes only from knowing what you know, being open to what you don't, and being glad to give it up, to lay it down, not just for self or even love. How to let you know life is worth living only if you see the gifts in yourselves and others, if abundance is a whisper and an outcry, an outpouring of justice from your hands and throats. Life is worth living only if you don't ignore the sorrows or the silence, only if you grapple with grief and shame and pin them to your chests, each one an unseen badge with ribbons wafting, each one a promise to decode and keep. ❧

Cómo explicar que la vida sólo merece la pena cuando tiene sentido y que ese sentido sólo viene de saber lo que se sabe, de estar abierto a lo que no se sabe y de estar dispuesto a renunciar a ello, a dejarlo, no sólo por uno mismo, sino incluso, por amor. Cómo hacerles saber que la vida sólo vale la pena vivirla si ven los dones en ustedes mismos y en los otros, si la abundancia es un susurro y un grito, una efusión de justicia en las manos y gargantas. La vida sólo merece la pena si no se ignoran las penas o el silencio, sólo si se enfrentan el dolor y la vergüenza y los prenden en sus pechos, como una insignia invisible con cintas ondeando, una promesa que descifrar y cumplir. 🖎

I had a dream last night, a holy snow of memories, writing on ice. I wrote in blue looking at the sky. Tonight I climbed a steeper hill to tell you I'll never forget. I'll wave a flag, I'll take you in each and every time. There is no moon tonight but I can see, and you can see all those moments of our lives in which the uncertainty is finally gone. Last night I had a dream of purity and typed it in the text box where the moon should have been. I drew a line so high I almost toppled, almost dove into the moonlight. I drew a line so thin only a black-eyed dog could find its frequency. ❧

Anoche tuve un sueño, una santa nieve de recuerdos, escritos en el hielo. Escribí en azul mirando al cielo. Esta noche subí una colina empinada para decirles que nunca olvidaré. Alzaré una bandera, siempre les daré amparo. No hay luna esta noche, pero puedo ver y ustedes pueden ver todos esos momentos de nuestras vidas en los que la incertidumbre por fin se desvanece. Anoche soñé con la pureza y la describí en el cuadro de texto donde debería haber estado la luna. Dibujé una línea tan alta que casi me caigo, casi me zambullo en la luz de la luna. Dibujé una línea tan fina que sólo un perro de ojos negros podría encontrar su frecuencia. ❧

The grass is bright again, the first orange poppies dot the
side of the freeway up the coast, the bright red throats of
hummingbirds flicker as they rise and dive. In the temples, no
one's praying today. The lines along the road are still flaky and
dry. Geese trumpet and trombone, march on green-sprinkled
dirt. And all the wounded creatures test the edges of the cliffs,
the rocks, the elfin branches. Tonight, city lights will compete
with the Black Moon. We'll park in a field of ashes, lay out
a labyrinth with whatever's in the back seat and the trunk:
a tire jack, a bag of dirt, four packets of arugula seeds, an
empty soda bottle, bandages and salves from our emergency
medical kit, a Rubik's cube, bike helmets, McDonald's toys,
an empty sock, broken headphones, two YA mysteries with
dog-eared pages, a bag of M&Ms. We'll fall asleep wrapped in
blankets smeared with grease. Towers may fall while we're
in our dreams, waters may bloat, fires might seethe just out
of sight. Your heads are on my arm, sweet boys, your hands
below my ribs. Stars radiate, but not from the sky. ✎

La hierba brilla de nuevo, las primeras amapolas naranjas salpican la orilla de la carretera que sube por la costa, las gargantas rojas y brillantes de los colibríes parpadean al elevarse y zambullirse. En los templos, hoy nadie reza. Las líneas a lo largo de la carretera siguen, secas y resquebrajadas. Trompeta y trombón de gansos marchan sobre la tierra salpicada de verde. Y todas las criaturas heridas prueban los bordes de los acantilados, las rocas, las ramas de los elfos. Esta noche, las luces de la ciudad competirán con la Luna Negra. Nos estacionaremos en un campo de cenizas, construiremos un laberinto con lo que haya en el asiento trasero y en el maletero: un gato neumático, una bolsa de tierra, cuatro paquetes de semillas de rúcula, una botella de refresco vacía, vendas y pomadas de nuestro botiquín de urgencias, un cubo de Rubik, cascos de bicicleta, juguetes de McDonald's, un calcetín suelto, auriculares rotos, dos novelas juveniles con las páginas dobladas, una bolsa de M&Ms. Nos dormiremos envueltos en mantas manchadas de grasa. Puede que caigan torres mientras soñamos, puede que las aguas se eleven, puede que los fuegos bullan justo fuera de nuestra vista. Sus cabezas reposan en mi brazo, dulces niños, sus manos bajo mis costillas. Las estrellas irradian, pero no del cielo. &

You were called, both of you. You were called to learn a language, to learn two, or many. You were called to cultivate a new world, to adorn your bodies with charcoal and hematite. To know the frailty of the skin on your belly, how it will tear like an onion peel. To cover your heads in the presence of women, especially crones and hags. To bend your knees before your lovers, especially if they are women. To learn to unfold the folds. To savor the brine. To learn to read the cave drawings in the darkest dark, through twisting red passages and chambers. You were called to be patient, to learn the use of a thousand tools, to leave your handprints on the wall for future men to evidence, to emulate. ❧

Ustedes, ambos, recibieron el llamado. Recibieron el llamado a aprender una lengua o dos, o muchas. Fueron llamados a cultivar un mundo nuevo, a adornar sus cuerpos con carbón y hematites. A conocer la piel frágil de sus vientres y verla desgarrarse como capas de cebolla. A cubrirse la cabeza en presencia de las mujeres, sobre todo de las arpías y las brujas. A doblar las rodillas ante sus amantes, especialmente si son mujeres. A desplegar los pliegues. A saborear la salmuera. A leer los dibujos de las cuevas en la más oscura oscuridad, a través de retorcidos pasadizos y rojas cámaras. Fueron llamados a ser pacientes, a aprender el uso de mil herramientas, a dejar las huellas de sus manos en la pared para que los hombres futuros vean la evidencia y los emulen. ✍

Maybe the end of the world is coming and love may not be ideal, but it's worth the hazards. I'm here to tell you: Hearts break but you can learn to embrace the flawed, the imperfect, highlighting the cracks and repairs as simply one more thing that happened on your journey. The end of the world may yet come but time is with you always, like kintsugi, in thick belts of gold. They bind and fortify you, they hold you and suspend you until the next time, and your next life.

Puede que se acerque el fin del mundo y que el amor no sea lo ideal, pero merece la pena arriesgarse. Aquí estoy para decírselo: los corazones se rompen pero pueden aprender a abrazar lo defectuoso, lo imperfecto y destacar las grietas y las reparaciones simplemente como algo más que ocurre en el viaje. El fin del mundo puede estar aún por llegar, pero el tiempo está siempre con ustedes, como kintsugi y sus gruesos cinturones de oro. Estos los atan y los fortifican, los sostienen y los suspenden hasta la próxima vez, y la próxima vida. ✌

When the world falls apart, you need to build it back up.
Have something with you, a postcard or a pocketful of
change. Make coffee, peach pudding, varnish the table,
mop the floors. Take a deep breath, reach out, go deep.
You are not responsible for this disaster. It's been coming.
There will be rejoicing, there will be opportunities, there
will be a phoenix star that breaks through the dark and gets
pinned to the night sky. It may flare, may set the world on
fire, may disintegrate before your very eyes like a string of
fluttery ash, but it will be replaced by another and another
until there's a sublime display of lights and you can step
out of your huddle with your children and your children's
children and live knowing you have me and everyone who
ever came before us inside each and every one of you. ⤳

Cuando el mundo se desmorona, hay que reconstruirlo.
Lleven algo con ustedes, una postal o un bolsillo lleno de
monedas. Preparen café, pudín de melocotón, barnicen
la mesa, frieguen el suelo. Respiren hondo, extiendan la
mano, profundicen. No son responsables de este desastre.
Se veía venir. Habrá regocijo, habrá oportunidades, habrá
una estrella fénix que irrumpa en la oscuridad y quede
clavada en el cielo nocturno. Puede que se prenda, puede
que incendie el mundo, puede que se desintegre ante sus
propios ojos como un hilo de ceniza aleteando, pero será
reemplazada por otra y otra hasta que haya un sublime
despliegue de luces y puedan salir de sus apiñamientos con
sus hijos y los hijos de sus hijos y vivir sabiendo que me
tienen a mí y a todos los que alguna vez vinieron antes que
nosotros, dentro de todos y de cada uno de ustedes. ✍

May you breathe, live, have fun. May you read in bed, at home, on the go. May you make a sign with your hand and post it on the door, the windows. May you collect fresh flour, wine and oil. Don't eat the crops before their time. Remember these words: Mark them on your wrist and on your forehead; teach your children to recognize them when they come in and out of the house, and when you wake up from a dream. You and your children are at your door in the land you and your children promised your ancestors to reach at the end of the sky. This should last forever. Indeed, you are the eternal shield. True for all generations, from first to last. Remember everything and your lovers will sing beautiful songs to you, praise you. Is there anyone in such a pure and precious light as you? Your lovers sing a new song for you, a chorus to your love. ☙

Que respiren, que vivan, que se diviertan. Que lean en la cama, en casa, en la calle. Que hagan una señal con las manos y que la pongan en la puerta, en las ventanas. Que recojan harina fresca, vino y aceite. Que no se coman las cosechas antes de tiempo. Recuerden estas palabras: márquenlas en las muñecas y en las frentes; enseñen a sus hijos a reconocerlas cuando entren y salgan de casa y cuando se despierten de algún sueño. Ustedes y sus hijos están a las puertas de la tierra que ustedes y sus hijos les prometieron a nuestros ancestros que iban a alcanzar al fin del cielo. Esto debería ser para siempre. En efecto, ustedes son el escudo eterno. Seguro para todas las generaciones, de la primera a la última. Recuérdenlo todo y sus amantes les cantarán bellas canciones, los alabarán. ¿Hay alguien con una luz tan pura y preciosa como ustedes? Sus amantes les cantan una nueva canción, un coro a su amor. ✒

The love given to you is yours, and when you wake up, my loves, you'll see the world in all its blissful, brutal truths. Choose beauty, align yourselves with goodness, learn wisdom. Love will keep you, even when happiness eludes you. Give flight to the black birds, let the wild dogs free, loosen your tongues, release the roar and pain in your throats, be kings of kindness and know I will come and I will love you, I will love you love you love you all my days and all the days beyond the days. ❧

El amor que se les ha dado es suyo, y cuando despierten, mis amores, verán el mundo en todas sus dichosas y brutales verdades. Elijan la belleza, alinéense con la bondad, aprendan la sabiduría. El amor los mantendrá, incluso cuando la felicidad los eluda. Den vuelo a los pájaros negros, dejen libres a los perros salvajes, suelten las lenguas, liberen el rugido y el dolor de sus gargantas, sean reyes de la bondad y sepan que vendré y los amaré, los amaré los amaré todos mis días y todos los días más allá de los días. ❧

ACKNOWLEDGMENTS

So grateful to Gayatri Patnaik, Catherine Tung, and everyone at Beacon. I'm especially in debt to Helene Atwan, who continues the conversation.

Thank you to Rachel Beser, Mabel Cuesta, Anne-Christine D'Adesky, Carolina de Robertis, Desireé Díaz, Cristina García, Haley Totherow, Kris Kleindienst, Iris Moore, Phyllis Oscar, Lola Proaño Gómez, Patrick Reichard, and Elizabeth Tanner.

For the time, for the spiritual peace they afford me, I'm in debt to MacDowell and Ragdale, both artist colonies that have meant so much to me. I first went to Ragdale before I'd ever published a book and Alice Ryerson Hayes assured me there would be many, many books.

I can't say enough about Jonah Straus, the world's most patient man.

And, of course, and forever, Ilan and Pablo.

AGRADECIMIENTOS

Muchas gracias a Gayatri Patnaik, Catherine Tung y a todos en Beacon. Tengo deuda especial con Helene Atwan, que continúa la conversación.

Gracias a Rachel Beser, Mabel Cuesta, Anne-Christine D'Adesky, Carolina de Robertis, Desireé Díaz, Cristina García, Haley Totherow, Kris Kleindienst, Iris Moore, Phyllis Oscar, Lola Proaño Gómez, Patrick Reichard y Elizabeth Tanner.

Por el tiempo, por la paz espiritual que me proporcionan, estoy en deuda con MacDowell y Ragdale, dos colonias de artistas que han significado tanto para mí. Fui por primera vez a Ragdale antes de haber publicado un libro y Alice Ryerson Hayes me aseguró que habría muchos, muchos libros.

No tengo palabras para describir a Jonah Straus, el hombre más paciente del mundo.

Y, por supuesto, y para siempre, a Ilan y Pablo.

HOUSE

OF

SMOKE

A Southerner Goes Searching for Home

JOHN T. EDGE

CROWN
NEW YORK

CROWN
An imprint of the Crown Publishing Group
A division of Penguin Random House LLC
1745 Broadway
New York, NY 10019
crownpublishing.com
penguinrandomhouse.com

Library of Congress Cataloging-in-Publication Data
Names: Edge, John T., author.
Title: House of Smoke : A Southerner Goes Searching for Home / by John T. Edge.
Description: New York : Crown, 2025. | Includes bibliographical references.
Identifiers: LCCN 2024049197 (print) | LCCN 2024049198 (ebook) |
ISBN 9780593241028 (hardcover) | ISBN 9780593241035 (ebook)
Subjects: LCSH: Edge, John T. | Food writers—United States—
Biography. | Southern States—Civilization.
Classification: LCC TX649.E35 A3 2025 (print) | LCC TX649.E35 (ebook) |
DDC 614.5092 [B] —dc23/eng/20250210
LC record available at https://lccn.loc.gov/2024049197
LC ebook record available at https://lccn.loc.gov/2024049198

Hardcover ISBN 978-0-593-24102-8
Ebook ISBN 978-0-593-24103-5

Editor: Francis Lam
Editorial assistant: Darian Keels
Production editor: Patricia Shaw
Text designer: Amani Shakrah
Production: Heather Williamson
Copy editor: Dianna Stirpe
Proofreaders: Sasha Tropp, Lisa Lawley, Andrea C. Peabbles
Publicist: Tammy Blake
Marketer: Kimberly Lew

All interior images courtesy of the Edge family except page 66: Gretchen Barron, reproduced with permission; page 112: Pableaux Johnson, reproduced with permission; page 146: The Southern Foodways Alliance, logo by Keisha Okafor, design by Richie Swann; page 202: courtesy Bluefoot Entertainment; page 224: Erin Austen Abbott, reproduced with permission; page 236: Pableaux Johnson, reproduced with permission.

Azalea illustrations by Shutterstock.com/Muhammad Mijil Pamungkas
Author photo: Erin Austen Abbott, reproduced with permission. Courtesy of the Hambidge Center, with the permission of photographer Amanda Greene.

Jacket image: Noah Saterstrom, a Nashville-based painter with Mississippi roots, made the painting that graces the jacket.

Manufactured in the United States of America

1 3 5 7 9 10 8 6 4 2

First Edition

The authorized representative in the EU for product safety and compliance is Penguin Random House Ireland, Morrison Chambers, 32 Nassau Street, Dublin D02 YH68, Ireland, https://eu-contact.penguin.ie.

For VBH and VJB,
who showed me the way home

"Where you come from is gone, where you thought you were going to never was there, and where you are is no good unless you can get away from it. Where is there a place for you to be? No place . . . Nothing outside you can give you any place . . . In yourself right now is all the place you've got."

—FLANNERY O'CONNOR, *WISE BLOOD*

HOUSE

OF

SMOKE

A Note About Sources

Nothing here is fabricated. If quote marks appear, I heard the words and wrote them down or read the words and copied them down. If italics appear, they mark my recollection of the words spoken. An independent researcher fact-checked this book. That said, any errors are my responsibility. To understand the sources I consulted for inspiration and information, please turn to the Bookshelf section at the rear. Finally, a name change: To cut down on potential confusion between characters, I made one slight edit. Here, the young man I knew as Charles Stanley is referred to as Chester Stanley.

—JTE

Contents

My mother and me

Prologue

RUNNING

I burst out the screen door, bare feet on gravel. Twenty feet ahead, my mother runs toward the dark woods, her red housedress trailing like a cape. She couldn't take another minute inside our house. She couldn't take another minute inside her head.

The light from our porch doesn't reach where she's going. At first, I can see the pistol in her hand. But as my mother crosses into the clearing, the red of her dress fades and everything turns black.

The crack of that pistol splits open the night. I stumble, catch myself, and plunge forward, past the sand pile where, just a few years before, I plowed toy dump trucks along pretend roads lined with mud skyscrapers.

I find her in the rock garden, among the pink azaleas, beneath a cedar arbor. Momma sits on a bench beside the old jail kitchen that she never quite turned into an antique shop. She cries into her dress.

Tears fall down her face. The pistol lies on the ground. Smoke trails from her cigarette.

Was that a warning shot? Did my mother push the door open and run toward the woods to fire her pistol into the blue-black sky? Or did she plan to shoot herself? Did she aim above her earrings, change her mind, and crumple to that bench?

Five decades later, I stand at the edge of that memory and peer back in, like I'm watching a scratched print of a black-and-white film about my childhood. She wanted to make a break. She wanted to make a change. And there was no better way to mark before and after than a run toward the woods and a shot in the night.

I ran for a long time, too. Away from that house. Away from my family. Away from what my past taught. Away from what the South demanded. Until, finally, I turned to face the dark woods.

Home for my first seventeen years

Chapter One

KUDZU AND LIES

Grade school friends on sleepovers were my first audience. I stood before them in our dining room, my mouth full of battlefield stats, to tell a story that began long before I was born, with people I claimed as family because their lives gave luster to mine. I received strangers, too. Drawn to our home by the historical marker out front, they turned up our gravel drive, expecting to find costumed interpreters from Colonial Williamsburg. An only child who wanted an audience, I met them on the patio, climbed atop an overturned washpot, and leaned into their expectations.

The words on that marker, embossed in gold on a dull green field, told a story of Confederate valor that shaped my Georgia childhood. I recited the pedigree of Brigadier General Alfred Iverson as if he were a great-uncle from a splintered branch of our family tree. He was reserved and dignified, I told audiences. Beard trimmed, eyes piercing, he looked dashing in gray and quoted Shakespeare from memory. A man of character, Iverson knew victory and suffered loss.

Some of his biography I borrowed from the marker by the road. The rest came from the genealogy room at the public library in nearby Macon. Born in our home in 1829, Iverson accepted an 1855 lieutenant commission in the U.S. Cavalry. The next day, his father took the oath of office as a U.S. senator from Georgia. As father ascended, so did son. In March of 1861, young Alfred Iverson resigned from the U.S. Army to join the Confederates, I said, my tone going low to reflect the seriousness of the moment.

He went down in defeat at Gettysburg, I told them, when the war could have gone either way. But he went down in honor, like the great Robert E. Lee. I didn't know then how spectacularly Iverson failed that day. I knew precisely what a white boy growing up in Georgia in the 1960s and 1970s was supposed to know.

My best friend, Clinton Roberson, never heard me tell Iverson stories. From the time we were out of diapers, Clinton and I raced Hot Wheels through his swept dirt yard and floated toy boats in a brook on the far side of our drive. His mother, Elizabeth, worked for my mother, mopping our floors and washing our bedsheets. She cooked for me and Clinton in their house, near the center of our little town. But on lonely summer days it seemed like her real job was to deliver Clinton to my doorstep and then track our movements around the community for which he was named.

We imagined a lifelong friendship, like generations of white and Black boys before us. But then came integration. After my parents transferred me, age eight, to a white academy in nearby Macon, stories of Iverson became a kind of passkey to belong. And my friendship with Clinton became collateral damage.

Once I had the attention of an audience, I talked about the

waning days of the Confederacy, when men marched home from battle without shoes and widows boiled dirt from smokehouse floors in search of the salt that dripped from hams. To offer a glimmer of hope for that hopeless cause, I told of a battle fought the year after Gettysburg at Sunshine Church, a chinked-log sanctuary ten miles from my house on a ridge near the village of Round Oak.

The Union outmanned Iverson that July day in 1864. But superior forces don't win all battles. Men who fight on the land where they were born summon strength they don't suspect. Iverson was said to know where creeks ran, where boulders blocked trails and gullies swallowed men and horses whole. Knowledge bred in his bones, I said, helped Iverson trick Union general George Stoneman into believing he was surrounded by Confederates.

Stoneman surrendered by waving the white tail cut from his dress shirt. Or maybe he held aloft his hat. Iverson captured the officer and five hundred of his men. When Stoneman learned that Iverson's force was actually much smaller than his own, he sat on a log and cried. Or he cried on the back porch of our house. No one in Jones County seemed to agree on the details. But all knew Iverson was the hero of the Battle of Sunshine Church.

In the years that followed the Civil War, white Southerners made Iverson into an idol. Historical markers and monuments told of Iverson's exploits. They went up in Athens near the arched entrance to the University of Georgia, and near Atlanta at the gate to a U.S. Army supply depot. They seemed to go up everywhere white Southerners needed reminders of the gallantry of the men who fought to defend a civilization built on the backs of Black people. They remained to remind Black Southerners of their so-called rightful place.

I didn't know then to connect my family story to this bigger story. I didn't yet understand that because our family adopted the

Iverson family, I would have to answer for both. As a boy, all I knew was the good guys wore gray.

MARY BEVERLY EVANS EDGE and John Thomas Edge moved to Jones County in 1959. "We were in love with the idea of that house," my father told me decades later. Cedars lined our property, marking the borders of our seven acres, blocking the roar of the busy two-lane that ran below the bluff where our house sat. Thatches of privet obscured our view of the single-wide across the road, where kudzu climbed out of a rain-washed gully to wrap the land in accidental topiary.

Gnarled oaks anchored our front yard, where my father napped on Sunday afternoons in a rope hammock. Opposite a bank of azaleas stood the old jail kitchen he had moved to our land after my mother talked him into buying the building to open an antique shop. He stripped chifforobes and I polished silver to stock the store she imagined.

Daddy and I spent Saturdays pulling up stretches of rotted flooring, eating sandwiches and stew from the barbecue joint up the road, listening to college football games on a box radio with a universe of silver dials. By the time the new boards were down, my mother lost interest in the shop. *It's too much trouble,* she said. When my mother was in a sangria phase, everything was too much trouble.

You had to overlook a lot to think our house was grand. A foursquare elaborated with wainscoting, it was built as a dogtrot in 1821. A different windowsill rotted out each year. Tucked in a side window in the den, our sole air conditioner never really worked in my seventeen years under that roof.

A medusa of wires snaked from the fuse box. My father predicted electrical fires and feared lightning strikes. *Our house is heart pine,* my mother said. *That means it's kindling,* my father said. Our house is historically significant, my mother wanted him to know. My father reminded her that the roof leaked around each of the four chimneys and pooled beneath the coal grates.

My bedroom connected to my parents' bedroom through our only bathroom. When I was eight, my father convinced an architect friend to draw up plans for a second bathroom and a laundry room. Daddy bid out construction projects that came back with estimates we couldn't stomach. Our house was a ruin, said the contractors. My mother told them it was a relic. She loved that turn of phrase. I can see her smiling, a goblet of sangria in hand.

MY MOTHER HELD COURT IN THE DEN, where Caroline Goode Holt Iverson gave birth to Alfred. Tucked in a bentwood rocker, she wrapped an orange-and-brown shawl around her bird-bone shoulders. Cigarette smoke haloed her bobbed hair. Lilliput, our Yorkipoo, sat at her feet. Smiling through rouge, she would reach for a silver goblet and talk of what the Yankees took from her Southland.

My mother spoke playfully, a lilt in her voice. She didn't talk about saving Confederate money or restaging Pickett's Charge. That was gauche. My mother's attitudes about Southern honor and Yankee thievery lived in the gaps between her life and her dreams. The losses she compiled were societal. In the wake of the Civil War, they were inevitable, and they were conveniently out of her control.

The South was a proud and powerful force on the world stage, she said. Then came Reconstruction. In the aftermath of Federal occupation, the story of the South played like a tragedy. A pursed smile on her lips, my mother mourned that tragedy and delighted in the chance to recount the fall.

After the Creek Indians signed over the land between the Oconee and Ocmulgee rivers in 1805, she told me, the plantation belt that stretched across Middle Georgia became one of the leading cotton-producing regions in the nation. Newspapers from that era promised high yields to whites willing to fight Native tribes and haul Black men and women to places like Jones County to crop cotton in the virgin soil.

Clinton was the fourth largest town in the state by 1820. Jones was the second most populous county. The Clinton Academy soon incorporated to serve the sons and daughters of the white gentry. In 1830, Samuel Griswold of Jones County manufactured as many cotton gins as any firm in the nation.

Three hotels operated in Clinton back then, my mother reminded me. And a thespian society staged costumed productions of *Hamlet*.

The decline came as swiftly as the rise. River towns like Macon and Columbus grew in the years before the war. During the war, Federals burned houses and gins and other factory works. When the gentry of Clinton talked about that era, they talked about property. A century and a half later, that strikes me as logical, for the war was a fight over human property.

In a 1975 newspaper article my mother saved, Valentine Barron Blair of Clinton remembered Union general George Stoneman as the man who ransacked her 1810 home. She spoke of the hand-painted wallpaper decorated with horsewomen in red jackets, which his troops tore from the living room walls, and of the harm done when those men hatcheted open barrels of molasses. Blair told the reporter, "I didn't know damn Yankee was two words until I was thirteen years old."

The railroad bypassed Clinton after the war. My mother said the gentry repelled the intrusion of those infernal machines. Locomotives would scare horses; smoke from their stacks would foul the air. Truth was, Clinton solicited the railroad, but the development company chose Gray, less than two miles east, because the land was easier to navigate.

By 1888, only one store operated in Clinton. The county moved government to Gray in 1905. When the courthouse closed, the county sold off the wrought-iron fence that bordered the property and hauled off the granite steps. Decades passed before the roof on the old courthouse collapsed under the weight of neglect, but the town was already gone.

My mother leaned in and reached for the jug of wine at her feet. *That loss connected our hometown to other failed and beautiful places,* she said, gesturing toward a volume from *The Decline and Fall of the Roman Empire.* Stacked on a shelf above the television, alongside a plaster bust of a regal woman in a green headdress rescued from an estate sale, that book connected my mother to the ancients. *Rome is gone now,* she said. *But lessons from Rome still shape our lives.*

CLINTON WAS A PROP FOR WRITERS who walked the small street grid, surveyed the early nineteenth-century architecture, and indulged in nostalgia. In 1922, a writer for *House & Garden* invited readers to "turn down the narrow elm lined road where wisteria hangs purple festoons from tree to tree."

Writers came to rediscover a world preserved in amber, a remnant of the day when the village of Clinton thrived and Macon, thirteen miles away, was a "block house and a few Indian huts." Reporters described Clinton as a frontier town, inspired by villages in Connecticut and Massachusetts, with homes that showed "fineness, restrained beauty, and charming severity." The "beauties which remain are worth a trip for anyone who cares to recall the glories of the past."

That narrative changed after the movie *Gone with the Wind* debuted in 1939. Instead of identifying the New England street plan, writers searched Jones County for the columned facades of Twelve Oaks and Tara. Those glories got amplified, when I was a boy, as the centennial of the Civil War approached and a federal commission celebrated the men who fought for the blue and gray.

Spectators in Charleston, South Carolina, gathered on the Battery to watch a reenactment of the Confederate shelling of Fort Sumter, cheered as flames geysered toward the sky. Faced with the change that the civil rights movement promised, stories of resistance entertained and seduced white families like mine and white children like me.

By the 1970s, in the national run-up to the bicentennial, my town took on a new role. The rest of the nation plunged forward. Downtowns emptied and developers built malls on the grounds of old plantations. Mothballed towns like Clinton were recast as tourism prospects. Clinton will become to Georgia what Colonial Williamsburg was to Virginia, an *Atlanta Constitution* columnist wrote. "It's there, waiting for tender handling. The authenticity is there. The history is known."

My family bought into these Williamsburg stories on a summer road trip. My mother purchased pewter serving platters and beer mugs from the gift shop. Wandering the streets, she reimagined our house in muted shades of green and red and cream, inspired by paint chips scraped from Williamsburg houses. Watching the tourists, intent on reliving our nation's past, my parents glimpsed a future.

AN OLD CLINTON HISTORICAL SOCIETY brochure from 1974, the year of its founding, described our village as an "aristocratic community in a typical 'Gone with the Wind' Georgia county." My parents were charter members. For culture they looked to Atlanta, an hour and a half up the road, but for gravitas they depended on Clinton. They believed our town was overdue for recognition. That brochure, with a blurb about our house on page 2, validated their belief.

My mother stacked those brochures on our granite-topped coffee table like a storefront preacher stacks Bibles on a plywood dais. The text on the historical marker out front was our gospel. In the beginning, the Old Clinton Historical Society was her church.

Supporters said my hometown could be a counterpoint to the "relentless urban forces of modern civilization." My mother grew up in the orbit of Charleston, South Carolina, the first Southern city to develop a historic district and declare its history endangered. In her mind, Clinton and Charleston were sister cities, backward-glancing places joined by loss.

Formed as the Sunbelt economy grew and subdivisions sprouted along the blacktop roads of Jones County, early Old Clinton Historical Society meetings revolved around preserving our town by getting it added to the National Register of Historic Places. They would use the power of the federal government to throttle developers. Then society members could rehabilitate the antebellum houses, stake out archaeological digs, and restore overgrown green spaces.

My father served as secretary. My mother, membership committee chair, recruited friends and family. On the 1975 roll, I showed as a twelve-year-old associate member. The effort drew attention. Writers for the Atlanta and Macon papers published call-to-arms editorials. Historic preservation classes from the University of Georgia toured our home. Led by professors in actual tweed coats, they studied the sharp pitch of our roof and marveled over the fingerprints left in fireplace bricks made by enslaved masons. I stood alongside the students, scribbling notes on one of my father's legal pads.

The fight that splintered the society and community began when the state planned to four-lane the highway that connected us to Macon. No longer a place of "Indian huts," Macon was the economic center of Middle Georgia. Commuter traffic and pulpwood trucks clogged the highway. On Saturday nights at Ollie's Dairy Bar, families counted up the weekly wreck totals over popcorn shrimp baskets.

My parents argued that four lanes would mean fewer sideswipes by pickups in the passing lane. William Cawthon, a law student at the University of Georgia, argued that two additional lanes would destroy the site of a historic women's school. He predicted that a commercial strip would form along the highway. With it would come noise pollution. Truck traffic would shake apart the foundations of the buildings.

The faction led by my father won a vote of support to four-lane. Just as it was with the Civil War, though, the losers would not give up. Round after round of accusations and petitions followed. Sometime between the day the society printed brochures for the 1975 tour of homes and the April weekend they staged that tour, my parents dropped out or got kicked off. Instead of reprinting the brochure, someone crossed out the entry for our house with a ballpoint pen.

That's just plain tacky, my mother said of the organization she began calling the Old Clinton Hysterical Society. In a public meeting, she called out our neighbor, society president Anne Hamilton. Standing before a courthouse crowd, my mother sing-songed, *Bury me shallow or bury me deep, just don't bury me at Annie's feet.*

My father showed comparative restraint when, as the highway department began to map its work, he wrote a valedictory letter, published in the Macon *Telegraph:* "When you quote preservationists, one naturally pictures stalwart, sincere, dedicated people working for things that are good and right. Many of the people associated with the Old Clinton Historical Society and the Clinton Foundation are good, well-intentioned people. A few of them, however, fall short of the description outlined above." It's clear, I hope, that any talent I have with words, I owe to my namesake.

ON A PATCH OF HIGH GROUND, on the far side of that highway, the Coulter family ran Old Clinton Bar-B-Q, my hometown joint. Rough-cut cedar poles framed the porch of a cinder-block building. Sawdust speckled the concrete floor inside. Smoke poured from a chimney that connected to a dogleg pit, fed by ricks of hardwood.

The sauce that ran my veins came from Mittie Coulter, wife of founder Roy Coulter. The Brunswick stew came from her family, too. The Coulters stocked bottles of Mountain Dew and Orange Crush in a slide-top cooler. Sweet tea arrived in a tall plastic tumbler. A bag of Colonial white bread sat at the center of each table.

Five weeks before I was born, Roy fell out on the floor of the kitchen and died. Their son Wayne would soon call himself the owner of Old Clinton Bar-B-Q, but his mother, Mittie, ran the place. Wayne walked the dining room with a knot of keys on his belt that jangled like warning bells. His brother, Little Roy, who lived with what appeared to be Down's syndrome, wore short-sleeved dress shirts and a pocket protector and sat in the alcove behind the bathrooms to watch westerns on television.

Mittie Coulter wore a white apron and, often, a plaid smock dress. She teased her hair into white curls and wore a pair of granny glasses on her nose. A slight smile creased her wrinkled face. By the time I reached the porch, I could hear the thwacks of cleaver on cutting board. Her favorite had a wooden handle and a rectangular blade that sparkled and shined in the afternoon light.

The sound was measured and deep, and it carried through the dining room, across the ladder-back chairs, past the collection of antique cash registers that lined the back wall and the mummified wasp's nest that hung above. To keep the meat warm, she draped cooked hams with kitchen towels. As Mittie hacked fat and skin into a smoky jumble, she poured on a sauce that tasted of cider vinegar and red pepper, ketchup and black pepper, family and time.

Working his federal court job, my father made a study of barbecue joints like Old Clinton. Driving Georgia to check in with probationers and parolees, attorneys and judges, he planned routes around his favorites. From a no-name hutch in the shadow of the Greensboro courthouse, he bought takeaway orders, chopped on an oversized block behind the counter. He ate ribs dripping with red-brown sauce and stew ladled over white rice at Mitchell's in Valdosta, buying extra sauce to bring home in whatever bottle Mrs. Mitchell could find.

On weekends, we retraced his steps. In court before a judge in a robe, Daddy wore tailored suits and wing-tip shoes. For our road trips, he dressed in yard-work clothes: khakis and old button-downs with ink-pen stains on the front pockets. Our favorite destination was a smokehouse outside Sandersville, where George Hooks cooked six or eight hogs a week. Tongs in hand, we ducked around back to pull meat from a carcass, broken open on a wire net like a book with a cracked spine, reaching for threads of belly or hunks of shoulder.

Behind the wheel of a Volkswagen or one of the used Mercedes diesels he bought on the cheap, we got time to talk, or just watch dirt roads fade into deep and numbing stretches of pine, brown and green tumbling into abstraction. Later, when my mother became too much to bear, we drove most any road, bound for the Kmart in Macon or Southlake Mall near Atlanta.

Daddy called it "running an errand." But we were really just running. Away from the tensions of Clinton. Away from the small-town gossips who feasted on stories about our family. As I grew older, I kept running.

THE SUMMER BEFORE I BEGAN FIRST GRADE, my mother tacked a poster to my bedroom wall, opposite color prints of Confederate generals Jeb Stuart and Stonewall Jackson, above the switch for the merry-go-round her father built in the backyard from a junked Gulf Oil sign and a lawn-mower engine. Other kids had to go to the county fair to ride such a thing. I could flip the switch and run the distance before the contraption finished its first revolution.

The poster text came from *Walden,* published by Henry David Thoreau in 1854 as the United States teetered toward war: "If a man does not keep pace with his companions, perhaps it is because he hears a different drummer. Let him step to the music which he hears, however measured or far away."

Thoreau gained new popularity in the 1960s as a generation of young people planned their escapes. Twenty-three editions published during my first-grade year, when *Walden* served back-to-the-land kids bent on quitting what the United States was becoming. Worried their sons would come home from Vietnam in body bags, lots of mothers wanted their children to listen for different music. Attuned to those fears, wary of the conformity that small towns coerced, my mother asked me to listen harder.

Small-town life stifled my mother. After her family left the village of Bowman, South Carolina, for the nearby town of Orangeburg, they lived in a bungalow opposite the railroad tracks. Her father, Jesse Clifton Evans, ran a filling station, a used car lot, and, eventually, a lawn-mower repair shop, source of the motor in my backyard plaything. Her mother, Azalie Smith Evans, grew roses to sell from a front-yard stand and took in laundry at the back door.

As her father grew older, he spent more time at his fish camp on the Edisto River, where he hunted raccoons and squirrels and caught bream and catfish. He raised chickens and hogs out there and kept a big garden. But each night, my grandfather returned to Orange-burg, where my grandmother put two meats on the supper table. Each sunrise, my grandfather woke to eggs and grits and often liver pudding. Watching her mother's life count down, my mother told herself that she would make a different life.

My mother believed, with all her heart, that she belonged on Broadway, like her idol Bette Davis. If not as a star, then as a chorus girl. She got as far as Winthrop College, a women's school in Rock Hill, South Carolina, where she wore a navy-blue skirt and a jacket to class and curled her blond hair atop her head.

At Winthrop she began to believe that drink could take her where dreams could not. Before she quit college, my mother marched in the band, twirling a wooden baton. Decades later, she still twirled at parties. I can see her now, prancing the brick patio outside my bedroom window, knees pumping high, head reared back, the life of every party she hosted.

My mother willed me to escape the small-town South, strapping her dreams to my back in a way she thought would give me lift and propulsion. Raising me to believe I belonged somewhere else, she protected me from the low horizons of her own childhood. That Thoreau poster broadcasted her aspirations. Over time, our aspirations joined.

. . .

ON WEEKEND MORNINGS, MY FRIENDS hunted deer from stands nailed to pines or shot squirrels out of white oaks. My family drove an hour and a half north, to the Buckhead neighborhood of Atlanta, where my mother shopped for scoop-necks at the Casual Corner and we ate club sandwiches at Twenty-Seven Birds and prime rib at Victoria Station.

Wandering an audiophile store where clerks wore black turtlenecks and the speakers blasted jazz, I pretended to be the city kid my mother raised. Or I dug an Ellery Queen mystery out of the back seat of our car and disappeared into a corner in a furniture store while my parents shopped for floor lamps. Getting to know the city, they ate egg foo young and egg drop soup at House of Eng at Peachtree and 10th, and Tex-Mex at the restaurant on Peachtree Industrial that advertised itself as Spanish.

My father fell hard for the biggest city in Georgia. Inspired by what he read in *The Atlanta Constitution,* he drove to Lenox Square mall and parked around back to eat braunschweiger on rye at a German restaurant. Born in small-town Florida, raised on Vienna sausages and white bread, he bought packs of dried squid from the Asian market in Lindbergh Plaza and black chickens from lowboy freezers at Buford Highway grocery stores. My father told himself, *I'm forever a small-town kid, but I live within reach of the world.*

Underground Atlanta was our family's Bourbon Street. My parents ducked in and out of clubs, with me in tow. A quick beer at Muhlenbrink's Saloon, where Piano Red played. A walking-around cocktail from Ruby Red's. At Dante's Down the Hatch, a crocodile swam in the moat and a jazz band played on a Huckleberry Finn raft. Sipping cocktails in souvenir glasses, eating fondue laced with kirsch, my parents became, for a couple of hours, the sophisticated people they wanted to be.

Like the catacombs of Paris I read about in school, Underground

Atlanta was a lost place. Walking those alleys reminded me of the tunnels that were said to cut across Coleman Hill in Macon, connecting storehouses of Confederate gold to the columned homes where the grandchildren of planter scions lived. As Atlanta grew into a rail hub in the late 1800s, the city abandoned the warehouses by the railroad tracks, building viaducts above, spanning the culverts beneath to make a new street level. What they left behind was a netherworld where Southerners came to witness the ruins they made.

In the 1970s Underground Atlanta felt dangerous, like the fringes of the French Quarter where streetlamps don't reach and wild shit goes down. I wandered brick passageways that leaked humidity and dumpster juice. Dodging the organ-grinder and his evil monkey with a taste for small fingers, I imagined that if I walked the right alley, I would step back into the past that everyone around me seemed to value so much. On the drive home, as the dark woods closed in and Clinton neared, the breach between my parents' dreams and our reality opened wide.

MY MOTHER COSTUMED OUR FAMILY like actors in a pageant. She wore pillbox hats and carried a black valise purse. Borrowing ideas from *Vogue* magazine, she designed her own clothes, using materials from the local fabric store. Josie Lee, who worked a machine in a ranch house down the road, did the sewing for me, too. My friends wore Wranglers. My mother dressed me in knickers. On big nights out, I wore blazers with coats of arms and ascots fixed in place with stickpins.

I became the out-of-step child my mother wanted, a dandy in the land of coveralls. I played Little League baseball and Midget League football like the other Jones County kids. Unlike the other kids, I saved my allowance to buy art. I hung a long-shadowed De Chirico print in my bedroom opposite those Confederate portraits. I bought a Picasso self-portrait, rendered as a lithograph, with his sweeping signature across the lower third.

My friends took piano lessons; I studied the banjo ukulele because my mother liked to watch Tiny Tim play the ukulele on *The Tonight Show.* I lived in the cleft between the Jones County I knew and the world my mother wanted me to know.

Sara Roberts brought a Native American bracelet for our first-grade show-and-tell. I came with the *Yellow Submarine* album and compared our homeroom to a submersible. Standing before my classmates, I recruited new members to Sgt. Pepper's Lonely Hearts Club Band so that we could join together and fight the Blue Meanies.

The barber in Gray clipper-cut my friend Keith Martin's hair into a tight buzz. I wore my hair so long that when I asked to go to the bathroom at department stores, clerks steered me toward the girls' room. To accentuate my curls, my mother took me to a beauty school and talked the young women-in-training through how to cut my hair in layers. When they balked, she brought in a picture of shaggy-haired George Harrison in his *Abbey Road* prime.

It was as though she lived somewhere else. Not in Clinton, and certainly not in Gray, our county seat. Everybody else seemed to conflate the two. My mother wanted me to claim Clinton. *Gray is a drab color,* she liked to say, looking directly at me, letting me in on the joke to come. *And Gray is a drab place,* she said as cigarette smoke drifted across the den. *But I'm trying to do something about that.*

THIRD GRADE IS THE YEAR SCHOOL BEGINS TO MATTER, my mother told me in the summer of 1970, after the Supreme Court made it clear that they were serious this time. That fall, my public school would enroll Black students like my friend Clinton for the first time. My mother believed in the concept of integration. Integrated public schools reflected her ideals. But they would not serve my needs. *You are gifted,* she told me. *If you are going to reach your potential, we have to act.*

My move to Stratford Academy, a private school in Macon, actually began eight years before I was born, after the Supreme Court handed down the 1954 *Brown v. Board of Education* decision. Judge William Augustus Bootle joined the federal bench in Macon that year. Two years later, the State of Georgia tried to void *Brown.* That same year, my father became an officer of the court, working as a federal probation and parole officer one floor above Bootle.

They worked together on federal cases, including the 1964 Klan-fueled murder of Lieutenant Colonel Lemuel Penn on a bridge outside Athens. Judge Bootle dictated the desegregation of Middle Georgia public schools and forced the desegregation of the University of Georgia. In response, students burned crosses and hung effigies.

Inspired to resist by politicians in search of votes, conservative whites pulled their children from public schools. So did moderates like my parents. Between the fall of 1969 and the fall of 1970, more than fifty private schools opened in Middle Georgia, including Jonesco Academy, three miles from our house, set in a gravel parking lot alongside a mobile home assembly plant. By February of 1970, more than one hundred fifty families with almost three hundred children committed to Jonesco.

In the run-up to the opening, a leader of the new school approached our family. Most of my white friends were making the move, he told my father. My third-grade class would include twenty-plus kids. *What kind of school will it be?* my father asked.

What are the admission requirements? The man looked at my father like he was daft and said, *The only test is the white reflection test.*

My father wanted me to stay in public schools. But my mother won the argument. "I wish I'd been stronger," he told me much later. By sending his son to a segregation academy, my father thought he compromised his beliefs and failed Judge Bootle. His work to overcome those perceived failings would, over the decades that followed, inspire my own work.

My mother never spoke of the real reasons I changed schools. She grew up lower-middle class. Instead of talking about her family struggles during the Depression, she told and retold a childhood story of how she once rode from Orangeburg to Bowman in the back seat of a white Cadillac.

After I enrolled in Stratford, where the carpool line clogged with Cadillacs, she told that story more often. Driven by the knowledge that she was not gentry, my mother aspired to the gentry. Stratford was a rung on that ladder.

LETTERS TO THE EDITOR OF *The Jones County News* stoked bigotry. A cartoon published the year our schools integrated shows a bus on fire: A Black student with exaggerated lips and an Afro runs to join a fight in front of a building labeled PUBLIC SCHOOL. A crowbar juts from his back pocket. He holds a switchblade knife. At the bottom, two white men in coats and ties, their disdain vivid, stare down the violence that integrationists have wrought.

Jonesco Academy got its name from combining the name of our county and an abbreviation of the word *county*. My new school took its name from Shakespeare, born in Stratford-upon-Avon in central Britain, and the Lee family of Stratford Hall in Virginia, where two signers of the Declaration of Independence lived and

Robert E. Lee was born. My mother said that Stratford was a better sort of academy.

The house at the core of our campus was part of the appeal. Built beginning in 1836 by enslaved men, the mansion I knew as Overlook gleamed like a block of divinity draped in fondant. Fronted by eighteen two-story columns, bisected by a spiral staircase, perched at one of the highest points in the city, the place came with a pedigree that connected both sides of the Civil War.

Before his men captured Confederate president Jefferson Davis downstate in Irwinville, Union brigadier general James H. Wilson headquartered at Overlook. Two decades later, Davis and his family, in town for an agricultural fair and Confederate reunion, gathered there for a ball that honored his daughter Winnie.

The Overlook front yard was our playground. We wrestled beneath the boughs of a sprawling magnolia and swung from its tangled limbs. We slid down a long wooden banister at the heart of the old house. A Black kitchen crew fed us in the cafeteria. A Black custodial crew cleaned up our messes. We played the parts of lords and ladies, testing the limits of our domain.

Stratford Academy opened a decade before Jonesco, but the intent was the same. White parents, fearful of what integrated public schools would become, made plans to cull their children. Jonesco separated students based on race. Stratford also sorted for class. Newspaper reports promised that Stratford students were "ladies and gentlemen." One teacher had studied ballet with Martha Graham in New York City. All students were said to be bound for college.

A 1960 Macon *Telegraph* article reported that the crest Stratford chose reflected the school motto: FREEDOM FOR EXCELLENCE. The design showed a young white man, arms raised in conquest. A wreath represents excellence achieved. A broken chain represents freedom won.

One hundred years before, the great-grandparents of some of those students started a war with the federal government over the right to hold workers in chains. Their descendants believed that the federal government held their children in chains. To fight off integration, they were ready to go to war again.

MY FATHER CAME UP HARD. His father, James Alexander Edge, moved the family often, following road construction projects. From Toccoa, Georgia, to Holly Hill, South Carolina, he carved grooves in old roadbeds so that his crew could lay down new pavement. Asphalt pebbles blackened his fingernails; smoke from tar buckets choked his lungs.

In the only picture I have of my father's father, he wears a leather football helmet. The tolls that drinking will take do not yet show, but the anger is already there. Head cocked, chin jutted, he looks ready to fight or run.

When my father was ten or so, the family settled in Columbia, South Carolina, south of the statehouse in a neighborhood called Black Bottom. Their house sat directly across the street from the state hospital for the insane. William Price Fox, author of the book *Southern Fried,* grew up nearby. Fox wrote Edge characters into his short stories and novels. One is a bully. Another gets into trouble and joins the service to escape jail. "I ran with a pretty rough crowd back then," my father told me.

My grandmother Hazel Pritchard Edge hunkered at the kitchen table, where she filled out newspaper contest entries in pursuit of transistor radios and windup clocks. Born in Ogdensburg, New

York, near the border with Canada, she met my grandfather in Jacksonville, Florida, where he worked in a shipyard and she worked as a domestic. My grandmother could clean houses anywhere. She thought, *Why not do that work where it's warm?*

Daddy was three when the Depression began. Home was a series of rentals, sometimes with backyard bathrooms. Dishes piled high in sinks and crabgrass splotched dirt yards. My father ran the streets. Come summer, he borrowed other kids' gloves to play baseball. Years later, my father described his mother as an agoraphobic. He also said she was loveless. Daddy worked hard to become the kind and loving man I knew.

In 1936, my father and a friend ran away to Atlanta, where they slept among a network of culverts downtown that would become Underground Atlanta. He was ten, about the same age I was when I began exploring that place. Before my grandfather returned them to Columbia a few days later, they sold newspapers, earning enough money to imagine they might make new lives in the big city.

At twelve he began to smoke. Daddy got a rap sheet at thirteen after he busted out the back window of a corner store and crawled through to take a carton of cigarettes. Drunk or just showing off, he never said why. He enlisted in the Navy at seventeen.

In the Pacific, he trained to serve as a coxswain on a landing craft. In San Francisco, he ate Chinese food and watched an all-male burlesque show. He served on the USS *Bronx* and the USS *Kershaw*. His crew docked in Manila and at Corregidor. When the United States dropped atomic bombs on Japan, they shifted from practicing an invasion to hauling troops off islands. Riding the waves, bound for home, my father swore to quit Columbia within a month.

A year after my father died at age ninety-six, I visited the graveyard where his parents were buried. His father died in 1969, his mother in 1978. I was there for both of their funerals but had not returned since. It seems that no one else had, either. Where grave-diggers laid his father, at about the spot where a headstone should have gone, weeds sprouted from the ground. Near his mother's feet, a tuft of bird feathers skittered across the loam until it tangled in a nest of twigs.

MY FATHER RARELY TOLD STORIES of the houses in which he grew up. My mother, on the other hand, lavished attention on our house, layering story on top of story, exaggeration on top of embellish-ment. The provenance she established included ghosts. *Any house as old as ours has to have some,* she said.

Standing at the stove in our kitchen, stirring a pot of vegetable soup with marrow bones, she talked of Caroline Goode Holt Iverson, first wife of the elder Alfred Iverson, who died in our house soon after she gave birth to their son Alfred. *We don't know where she was buried,* my mother would say. *Do you think they laid her down in the cellar? Is that her I hear on the front porch at night?*

Every few years, my mother lured a newspaper reporter to Clin-ton with tales of flickering lights in what we called the red room and rolling thuds in the attic. My mother preened for their cam-eras, spinning stories to land quotes in their notebooks, saving the newspapers where the stories appeared, writing corrections in the margins, underlining each Iverson reference and starring the best.

For a Macon *Telegraph* story that spanned the front page of the Living section, I posed with her on our brocaded chaise lounge in front of two hurricane lamps. I wore tube socks, pulled to my knees. My mother wore a halter top. We pretended to enjoy a conversation. We pretended a lot back then. My mother told stories of ghosts to win attention, but she never talked about the ghost that really walked our floors.

ON A FEBRUARY NIGHT IN 1971, my mother and I ate salmon croquettes and grits at the kitchen table. We sat at that table most nights to talk through homework. Daddy had gone down to Albany for a trial. Momma and I were conjugating verbs when I heard a small pop in another room. She heard it, too. We often heard odd sounds. *That was the house settling,* my father would say. *Probably a squirrel in the furnace,* my mother would guess. This sounded different.

I walked twenty feet, past the kitchen, through the hall, into my parents' bedroom, to find Charles Roberson, older brother of my best friend Clinton, lying face down on the far side of my parents' bed. Blood spilled from his head and pooled on the heart pine planks.

I ran for my mother. She called my father. My father called the sheriff to tell him that Charles, who sometimes did work for our family, had been shot. For an ugly minute, my mother stomped through the house, looking for a burglar. She peered out windows, thinking someone must be hiding in the woods beyond the clearing.

Sheriff Hawkins turned Charles over. The gun lay beneath his chest. For reasons I still do not understand, Charles shot himself with the pistol my father kept on the fireplace mantel behind a stack of books. Charles was twelve. I was eight, and so was Clinton.

Their mother, Elizabeth, arrived, trailed by two white ladies. I hugged her tight around the waist and cried until I soaked her blouse. The sheriff asked gentle questions. *Was your mother with you just before you heard the pop? Had anyone else been inside the house?*

And then the sheriff and the body were gone, bound for the hospital in Macon, where a doctor declared Charles dead that night.

I don't know when my parents returned to sleep in the room where Charles shot himself. I don't know what day his family buried him. My discovery of Charles still plays in my head on a loop, but my brain has pulled a cloak over what came next. Did my family attend the funeral? Did we pay for it? If so, did we act out of love or guilt or obligation? Did I go to school the next day? Did the news carry to Stratford? Did I tell my friends there? Did they already know?

It was an accident: That's what the sheriff told my father. That answer satisfied no one. We played back scenes from Charles's time in our house, patching window screens and dusting bookshelves. We wondered if Charles played with the gun before he shot himself. We remembered that he was vacuuming before the pop. We wondered if Charles thought the gun was a toy. We found a snapshot of Charles and me, side by side, and stared into his eyes in search of answers. He was a star student, a bright presence. Surely he didn't mean to kill himself.

The day after Charles died, the *Jones County News* published an account of a moonshine raid near the Baldwin County line that turned up a still capable of churning out three hundred gallons a week. An editorial by FBI director J. Edgar Hoover ran in that same issue. "Much of the turmoil in our country today," he wrote, "is caused by the unreasonable demands of irrational misfits." No record of the life or death of Charles Roberson appeared in my hometown newspaper that month. Or any month that followed.

INSTEAD OF GOING QUIET, which Jones County expected, my mother amped up the pageant. Like a performer in a bankrupt canteen, she danced faster and smiled bigger. When I played quarterback for the Saints in the Jones County Midget League, our team rode through Gray in the fall parade. I can see the goalpost mounted on the cab of the flatbed truck, and the black and gold crepe paper my mother used to wrap the uprights.

Wearing a white halter top and a black skirt, she marched behind us. In a picture shot as we crossed in front of the post office, a black El Camino with wire wheels and white-letter tires trails the procession. Sitting on the roof, feet planted on the driver's-side window, I wave to the crowd in my best imitation of her.

When our Little League all-star team mourned a loss at Shoney's over fried shrimp, my mother gave my teammates half-dollar coins embossed with John F. Kennedy's likeness. Blond-brown hair tucked beneath her team-mother cap, she stood alongside a U.S. flag, beneath the seal of a Macon Rotary Club. "Ask not what Little League Baseball can do for you," she declared. "Ask what you can do for Little League Baseball."

Momma was at her best that day. As she spoke, my mother smiled big, charmed by her own cleverness. I pretended to be embarrassed. But as I watched and listened, I wondered if I would ever be able to hold the attention of a crowd like she did.

Appearances mattered more than ever. Each December, my father and I tramped the woods to cut down a Christmas tree. After we guy-wired it to the red room walls, my mother took over. Instead of ruining the period aura of our home by draping our family tree with strings of electric lights, she decorated it with garlands of holly and white candles backed by tin reflectors.

My mother knew those candles were a fire hazard. She also knew they looked beautiful in the early light of a winter morning. When my father bought a washer and dryer to install on the back porch, she insisted that workers build a wooden box around those metal boxes. *We can't break the spell,* she liked to say. *The spell is all we have.*

To cast that spell, she sidestepped the present to call on the past. Somewhere along the way, my mother decided the state-installed Iverson marker out front was not enough. After she found a decommissioned marker, she had it hauled up our driveway and bolted to a black metal pole. The text on that one told the story of Stoneman's Raid, plotting Union efforts to burn Confederate supply trains. More important, the new sign referenced Iverson's "distinguished parentage." My mother loved that phrase.

WE DIDN'T ACTUALLY NEED ALFRED Iverson to burnish our family story. My mother's people claimed their own pedigrees. According to family lore, Rowland and Richard Evans left Wales around 1750, sailing for America. Their parents died of typhoid on the ship. Orphaned, the boys learned trades in Boston before they left for South Carolina, where Richard Evans slipped out of sight and Rowland Evans, through a grant from the British Crown, acquired land in what is now Orangeburg County.

He bought enslaved men and worked a farm near Bowman, the town where my grandmother gave birth to my mother one hundred fifty years later. During the Revolution, Rowland served with Francis Marion, the famous Swamp Fox, rising to the rank of captain. Home on furlough after the Battle of Eutaw Springs, Tories shot Rowland down in his yard. Retribution came a few years later, when John Evans, his son, killed one of the Tories at a church camp meeting.

These were my people. My mother knew their stories, or at least a version of the one I know now. But I cannot recall her telling it. Maybe she told herself the story the times demanded. Maybe she told me the story I wanted to hear.

My mother's family stories began with her father's generation.

As electric light spread from cities to small towns in the early 1900s, my grandfather Jesse Clifton Evans built a generator in his Bowman garage. He strung wires and sold power to neighbors, she said, charging by the lightbulb.

Later, he ran a state dispensary, making and selling taxed alcohol during South Carolina's long flirt with Prohibition. For much of my childhood, my mother searched antique stores for one of the blue-green bottles his dispensary filled. On a shelf in my bar in Oxford sits the one she bought, blazoned with a palmetto.

A black-and-white snapshot of a locomotive hung on the wall in my parents' bedroom, above the spot where Charles collapsed on the floor. In the photo, smoke pours from the stack. Hitched to the rear is a coal car, embossed with the logo of the B&B railroad company. Three men pose for the camera. Jesse Clifton Evans stands in the gap between the locomotive and the coal car. My mother told me that he ran a narrow-gauge railroad between the Orangeburg County towns of Bowman and Branchville, inland from Charleston. He owned the railroad, she suggested, or at least managed it.

Our branch of the Evans family was something close to wealthy, my mother told me, until a fire burned up a trainload of cotton on its way to market. With those flames went the family fortune, and with her story came the saga of a noble but faded Southern family who sacrificed money for honor. My grandfather paid for the cotton lost on his watch, she told me, and the Evans family began a long financial decline from which they never recovered.

I was in my fifties before I traveled to Branchville to chase that story. Thumbing records at the old rail station, I found no reference to an Evans, but I did learn why my mother might have wanted to associate our family with the railroad. The second commercial rail line in the nation ran from Charleston through Branchville to Hamburg, South Carolina. When the tracks were laid in 1833, that was the longest rail line in the world. Two decades later, as rail lines began to web the South, Branchville built the first depot café in the nation. A historical marker, much like the one that stands before our old house in Clinton, told those stories. But a day wandering the station and its museum told me little about my family.

Many white families depended on stories of ruined businesses and spent fortunes. They explained the rotting facades of once grand homes and the elbow patches sewn onto cashmere sweaters. Handed down across generations in lieu of cash or land, those stories served my people as cultural dowries. They explained away failures of enterprise and morality. They rationalized lives lost to drink and depression and gunshot.

Layer upon layer, generation after generation, those stories added up. Hundreds of thousands of Lost Cause narratives fed the grand cultural lie the white South told itself about what went wrong. The lie my family told me. The lie I learned to tell myself.

TO FILL A VOID IN OUR FAMILY that only she could see, my mother shopped for stories that belonged to other families. To acquire those stories, she bought their objects, collecting their cast-asides like a quilter gathers fabric swatches.

My mother's tastes were expansive and subversive. She saw beauty others missed. When the Krystal in Macon switched to plastic, my mother bought a set of their logo-embossed plates and bowls from the restaurant manager. After the city of Macon condemned a stretch of Greek Revival and Victorian homes, she negotiated with the wrecking crew to crowbar out the porcelain tile surrounds from their fireplaces. When the federal court installed metal bookcases in my father's office, my mother bought the old glass-fronted oak cases she called barrister bookshelves and got them hauled home.

She arrayed what she called conversation pieces on our coffee table, grouped like a Joseph Cornell assemblage: a tin box for Sheik brand condoms, decorated with a cartoon image of a man in a turban; a dull brass lock, salvaged from demolition work done on the University of Georgia library in Athens; a bamboo hash pipe with a curlicue bowl, purchased in a midtown Atlanta head shop. (On my mother's suggestion, I taped that pipe to a poster board and brought the display to a fourth-grade show-and-tell on drug abuse.) Instead of reading just the Macon *Telegraph,* like most of her friends, my mother stacked our coffee table with copies of *The Great Speckled Bird,* the underground newspaper hippies sold on the street near that head shop.

Called to explain her, I told friends that my mother was an antiques dealer. That was almost true. She never actually bought to resell. Despite the work my father and I did to get that old jail kitchen ready, no matter the checks she bounced at estate sales for what she called inventory, my mother collected to embellish and to project ideas about our home, our family, our life.

That's how I came to live in a house decorated with Belgian statuettes pulled from ruined drawing rooms and French gilt mirrors liberated from demolished townhomes. Each acquisition came with a backstory, which my mother often wrote on the rear of the object. "Bought from the Rossers of New Smyrna Beach" on an oil landscape. "Borrowed from Winthrop" on a calling card, mounted beneath a monogrammed linen from her college.

The estate sale at Bolingbroke was her big score. When the owners of Great Hill Place, a former cotton plantation in a community north of Macon, announced they would sell their furnishings, my mother arrived as the sun rose. I went with her, carrying two baseball gloves and a ball in case anyone wanted to play catch. She

stuffed the rear of our Volkswagen Squareback with souvenir plates
from the World War One armistice, a set of bone dinnerware that
included a gold-rimmed soup tureen, a Confederate flag she called
an heirloom, and the grandest prize of all, a French theater poster
from the aftermath of World War One.

Water-stained, rumpled by the weight of time, that poster shows
a troop of young French boys, circa 1918, wearing cast-aside Ger-
man helmets, playing in the ruins of a French village. In the fore-
ground, a young girl comforts a crying child. A portrait of rebirth
in the aftermath of the Great War, that image reflected her belief in
the possibilities of post–Civil War Clinton.

Buying that poster, my mother bought into the status of the
railroad financier who once owned Great Hill and the grandeur of
his manor home at the center of that plantation. When my mother
said "Bolingbroke," she taffied three syllables into four and con-
jured a faded civilization.

ONE SUNDAY AFTERNOON, MY MOTHER drove to a cross burning
out toward the settlement of James to see who in Jones County
belonged to the Klan. *I could tell who they were,* she said, *by the look
of their shoes and the sound of their voices.* Listening to her describe a
skinny man in jeans and cowboy boots, I wanted to believe. But as
she talked, I imagined a more likely story: My mother drove by a
group of men she suspected were Klansmen, who were nailing to-
gether what looked like a cross. In her rearview, exaggerations
blossomed and a story formed.

Did my mother tell that story to make a point about the evil
that lurks in any community? Or did she just want to broadcast
that she was better than those peckerwoods? I'm not sure. Much of

my childhood comes back to me in brief and gauzy moments. I didn't keep a journal. To reckon what happened, I coax scenes from photographs and memories that leave me with questions.

I know my father quit our Methodist Church in Gray over a new preacher's decision that God didn't want dancing in the fellowship hall. But when our church asked me to join at thirteen, did my mother take me on a tour of houses of worship, from a Catholic cathedral to a Jewish synagogue to a Muslim mosque? At the close of a month of visits, did she ask me what I believed? Did she smile when I said, "I don't know"? What I do remember is that after we quit going to our church, my mother and father began to talk smugly about how the local Methodists were as small-minded as the Baptists. Fact and fiction blurred in my head as my mother juggled who we were and who she wanted us to become.

As I grew older, I told that house of worship story to the parents of girls I dated. When they wanted to know where my family went to church, I said my mother was a free spirit, as if that were a denomination. Those stories nested inside the fictions my mother nurtured. They bundled inside the lies the South told about itself.

In a photograph from my youth, I sit in the kitchen, wearing a red-and-white Jones County All Stars uniform, waiting for my father to drive me to a baseball game. When my mother took the photograph, she chopped off my head, shifting the focus to a stack of wooden wine crates, piled with bottles of her favorite red. The photograph shows something I tried to overlook. When I was a young boy, I believed that my mother was naturally gregarious. I knew she drank. But I told myself that her presence and verve came naturally.

Slowly, I recognized that much of her boldness came from the jugs she stowed in the bathroom cabinet alongside bottles of mouthwash and the time she spent sitting on the edge of the tub, door locked, screw top off. As she grew older, my mother grew more reckless. On afternoon drives to the mall, she balanced what looked like a glass of orange juice between her legs. On the way home from the grocery store, she drove our car into a ditch and got fished out by the sheriff.

I WAS RIDING A BUS home from a Little League playoff game when a teammate called my mother a drunk. He said it in a tone he might have used to say she was a brunette. I flashed to the pitchers of sangria she poured for friends and the picture we pasted in our family scrapbook of the two of us, reclining in bed, playing cards on New Year's Eve, toasting with flutes of Champagne. I dialed up an image of my mother on a couch, laughing, as a friend bent toward her with a B_{12} hypodermic to fix her hangover.

Drink changed my mother. Once, on a trip to Tampa, Florida, to visit the godmother I called Caro, she slapped me hard across the face. I don't remember the moment or the reason. But my father did. Fifty years later, he spoke with awe about the clap of her hand, as if he had watched my mother transform into an animal that was unrecognizable to him.

More than once she ran into the night with a pistol, threatening suicide. At least twice she fired it. Each episode began in our back hall. My mother screamed, throwing herself at the feet of my father, like a spurned woman in a B movie. My father looked sheepish, almost embarrassed, as if he couldn't believe this was his life. Each episode ended beneath the arbor, among the azaleas, on the edge of the dark woods, as my mother cried into her housedress and begged forgiveness. She would promise a new beginning, but we kept acting out the same ending.

The violence and lies that alcoholism fuels will seep into the stories you tell about your people. The house you build will shift on its foundations. Smoke from unseen fires will soot the drapes and sneak up around the eaves. Fictions and gaps in memory will rot out the flooring. As my house shifted and the smoke tumbled, the stories on which I depended came unmoored. And so did my ideas about my place, my people, myself.

My father in our backyard

Chapter Two

THE SIEGE

The woods were my childhood playground. I built tree forts with fallen logs, imagining turrets in the gaps. I played Grand Canyon in the deep gulley behind the springhouse and sling-bladed wide paths through those woods, thinking of the four lanes we traveled in Atlanta. Come summer, my friends and I soared on a zip line tacked between two pines.

My parents talked of the woods like they were a frame. When the power company arrived to trim trees from the lines that ran to our house, my mother met the bucket crew out front. Hands on hips, a playful scowl on her face, she was there to make sure they didn't scalp the black walnuts and cedars that defined what was ours.

Old houses, she said, deserved old trees and thick foliage. If I proposed cutting back the privet by the road, she stood guard to make sure I didn't remove too much. *There should be some mystery,* she would say. *A beautiful home should slowly reveal itself on the approach.*

Those same woods connected us to a community of Black families, reached by a road that narrowed as it receded from the highway. Back there, where the trees closed in, the gravel gave out, and a concrete-block church stood, some families lived without running water. Driving to Gray, we passed young children carrying metal buckets and plastic jugs from a public well near the VFW hall.

Paul Stanley, who played on my Little League team, lived back there with his preacher father and his siblings. Tucked into a warren of dirt streets on land that Iverson likely owned and the women and men he enslaved may have worked, their house was a mile from us by car. Through the woods, the distance was just a few hundred yards.

More than woods separated us from our closest neighbors. Neither of my parents inherited much money after their parents died. We weren't wealthy, but maybe we were wealthy for Jones County. My father worked a government job and polished his wing tips on Sunday nights. My mother wore rings on every finger, a gold tiger beside a diamond stud on her pinkie.

As a boy, I did country things, like ride around in the bed of a pickup truck, cutoffs on, shirt off. Later, trying to signal I belonged, I turned the air intake on my straight-6 Camaro upside down to make the engine sound like a big block V-8. But my parents brought me up to think of myself as something other than country.

People talk about us because we are distinctive, my mother would say as she arranged conversation pieces on our coffee table. She knew the families at the end of that road. The Robersons had recently moved there. My mother canvassed those houses for the U.S. Census and made baseball carpool pickups and drop-offs back there in our VW Squareback. What she didn't say was that some of the families who carried those buckets of water back and forth probably resented our easy whiteness and seeming wealth.

Chester Stanley, older brother to Paul from my Little League team, was a teenager when he first cased our house. That's the way my father remembered it. One fall morning, he watched someone who looked a lot like Chester prowl the clearing, near where my grandfather planted a bank of azaleas. He dodged from pine to cedar until my father yelled Chester's name and fired a rifle into the air to warn him off. The sound bounced off the back of our house like a thunderclap. Until that moment, I had never seen my father even hold a rifle.

ON THANKSGIVING DAY IN 1977, thieves kicked in our back door and ransacked our home. Over the next year, they stole again and again, mostly taking stuff they could fence: a stereo receiver, a pair of speakers and a turntable, a shortwave radio. They usually struck after we went to Atlanta on shopping trips.

We would return home with a trunk full of new treasures to discover that our old treasures had been plundered. Knowing we had insurance meant the thieves could return to steal the replacements. Knowing they could escape through the woods made them brazen.

As Chester Stanley grew older, the break-ins grew more violent and frequent, and the hauls became more personal. That next spring thieves busted out a window, knocked over a dresser, and took off with my collection of Confederate banknotes and the silver pocket comb my mother gave my father on their twenty-fifth wedding anniversary. My father had cages installed on our windows, iron bars on our doors.

One summer morning, thieves broke in by bending the bar that spanned the double doors at the front of our house. Years later, I picked up one of those lengths of iron, turned it in my hand, and marveled at the violence that took.

Each time we walked across broken glass, my mother's ruined antiques crunching beneath our feet, I obsessed over who might remain in the house, hidden in the back closet of my bedroom. At least once, my father believed the crooks were still in the house when we rolled up the driveway.

A security company installed pressure-sensitive carpet pads, part of an alarm system that rang the sheriff. Before technicians from Macon could return to Clinton to finish the job, thieves busted out the bars in my bedroom. Work paused. Ten minutes after the crew finally completed the install the next week, burglars shot out the exterior alarm. With a fire poker from our den, they smashed an infrared motion detector and an interior alarm. Our yippy nine-year-old dog wouldn't stop yipping, so they gouged her with that same poker.

I found Lilliput in the courtyard, trembling against the boxwood hedge. Blood from her neck clotted her apricot curls and stained the soft orange bricks beneath. A few weeks later, the thieves returned to smash through the bars on our windows with an axe. Did Lilliput bark that time? I wondered. Or did she cower and try to lick at her neck sutures?

To document what he called the siege, my father wrote letters to insurance companies and law enforcement officials. He bought a better-than-average camera and took photos of what he thought they might steal next, including a rank of silver estate-sale goblets stacked on a sideboard in the back hall. And that Picasso lithograph I bought with my allowance.

A pair of binoculars in a leather case hangs from a doorknob in those pictures. My father bought them to watch birds. After the break-ins began, he used them to scan the trees for thieves. Decades later, I discovered a series of photos he took then. Bound in a small booklet, they look a little out of focus, as if my father's hands shook with anger or fear or both as he clicked the shutter. Growing up, I never saw my father scared. Knowing he probably was broke my heart again.

A badge and a pistol came with my father's job as a probation officer. But I can't recall him pinning that badge to his coat or stowing that gun in his glove compartment like cops did on television. My father built a career around redemption and rehabilitation. For a man who went to jail before he could drive, those beliefs sustained him.

He played Johnny Cash's "Folsom Prison Blues" on the turntable in our den and talked about how honorable men retire the debts of their past through service. He subscribed to *The Angolite*, the literary magazine published out of Angola Prison in Louisiana, to read the poetry and investigative journalism that won the inmates awards. In their plights, he saw a version of himself, if he had continued on the course he began in Columbia.

Daddy didn't hunt deer. When he heard a report from a rifle, he winced. He wanted nothing to do with guns, especially after Charles Roberson shot himself in our house. The siege changed that. My father worried that Chester Stanley would come for me. My father worried that Chester would come for him. His worries carried into the bedroom he shared with my mother, where blood stained the pine floor. Those worries lingered in the woods that ringed our house.

My gentle father faked family trips, sending me and my mother out of the house while he hid inside. Figuring he might face down a gang of thieves, he waited, back against our rear door, cut-down shotgun in hand. His worries carried all the way to his office in the federal building in Macon. In his mind's eye, my father would soon look up from his desk to see Chester Stanley standing on the other side, fire poker in hand.

THREE WEEKS BEFORE CHRISTMAS IN 1978, the Jones County sheriff responded to a car fire just down the road from our house. As the tires on a Chevrolet Caprice melted, the blacktop beneath did, too, and an oval scar emerged on the bleached gray pavement. The blaze burned so hot that the firemen couldn't see the charred body inside until they put out the flames.

A man's legs and arms had disintegrated. He no longer had a lower jaw, but his upper jaw showed two gold teeth. An autopsy revealed that he was already dead from a blow to the head when someone doused the rear of the Caprice with gasoline, placed him in the back seat, and torched the car and the man. When a newspaper deliveryman discovered the blaze, fire leapt from the four-door and smoke billowed toward the sky.

Reverend Stanley, father to Chester, preached funerals in concrete-block churches across Middle Georgia. He served Mount Gillard Baptist Church in Reynolds, Mount Zion Baptist Church in Butler, and Fellowship Baptist Church in Thomaston. Now a preacher from one of those churches would lay him in the ground.

According to a *Jones County News* reporter, the body of Reverend Stanley burned two hundred yards from his green cinder-block home, on the road that connected his home to ours. A year would pass before the county patched the road. I was sixteen, in love with my Camaro, convinced I could outrun anything. But each time I drove toward Gray, I felt a jolt through the steering wheel when I hit the scab on the pavement.

The sheriff questioned Reverend Stanley's children. They questioned their neighbor, Elizabeth Roberson, too, mother to Clinton and Charles. Those conversations connected Chester, then twenty, to the burglaries of our home. Officers fetched our stuff from his house and tagged it as evidence. In a front-page article that announced the indictment of Chester Stanley, readers learned that the reverend's wife died six weeks before. The reporter didn't mention her cause of death.

EARLIER THAT YEAR, REVEREND STANLEY made a complaint to police, saying his son was writing bad checks on his account. The preacher kicked him out. Georgia Bureau of Investigation officers learned that Chester Stanley still climbed through the back window of the family home late at night. They reported that Reverend Stanley threatened to kill his son if he kept it up.

The most recent argument may have begun when Chester tried to move back home. His father said no. To build a case that Chester murdered his father in retaliation, the district attorney displayed a blood-soaked mattress and blood-splattered shoes, recovered from the family home. He blew up photos of the burned-out Caprice.

Chester said it was an accident. He and his father fought that night. The preacher fell and hit his head on the floor. When Chester tried to clean his hands, he slung blood everywhere. Asked why there weren't bloodstains on the rug where Reverend Stanley supposedly fell, Chester told investigators that he cleaned that blood up with a mop. Asked why he set his father on fire, Chester said he panicked when he realized his father was dead. Thirty feet from the car, investigators found a plastic container that smelled of gasoline.

I knew how Iverson's war ended. That violence came at me in sepia. Creeping through the green-black woods that surrounded our house, dodging from pine to cedar, this violence played out in lurid color.

Murder charges didn't hold. The judge sentenced Chester to fifteen years for manslaughter. The day Chester went to prison, my father began counting the days until his release. *If Chester breaks into our house again,* my father told himself, *I'll have to shoot him.*

OUR FAMILY TRIED TO ADJUST. For eighth grade, I had moved from Stratford Academy in Macon back to public school in Gray. Now, for my sophomore year in high school, I transferred to Tattnall Square Academy in Macon. We told friends that I made the move because my headmaster at Stratford took a job there. I never fit in at Stratford, we said, but I always connected with Dr. Hill.

That story was somewhat true. What we didn't say was that my parents wanted me out of Jones County. Charles Roberson killed himself there and I found him. Chester Stanley broke into our house again and again. He or someone else gouged the throat of our dog with a fire poker and left her to bleed out. I found her, too, and the woods closed in around me.

My father believed that a change in scenery would lead to a change in family circumstance. Back in the summer of 1975, he applied for a Fulbright grant to study criminology at the University of Cambridge in England. When that didn't work out, he began pursuing a transfer away from the federal court in Macon. One day he would come home talking about Chicago. The next day the escape he planned would land us in Lexington, Kentucky. On a scouting trip to Tampa, our family toured white-painted brick ranches, flanked by spindly palms, set on man-made canals. Every time we walked through one of those houses, I counted the bathrooms. One time I counted four.

My father never made plans to leave my mother, because that would mean leaving me. *Try it, and I will win him in a custody battle*: That's what she threatened each time he plotted a new life for the two of us, free of her drinking, clear of her tantrums, removed from her wild threats of suicide. My father and I both wanted out, even as we recognized that her spectacles drew us in.

We spoke of the time she snuck us backstage at the Fox Theatre in Atlanta during Elton John's *Goodbye Yellow Brick Road* tour, and of how close we crept to his piano. We played back the afternoon by our hotel pool, down the street from the Fox, when she befriended Joel Grey from *Cabaret* and Rosey Grier, the football player turned actor. In family lore, stories of my mother's antics became a sort of repertory theater, reenacted for friends and relatives.

Bravado was her calling, in much the same way that other mothers were good at needlepoint. Back when I was in grammar school and we watched Stratford play high school baseball games at Luther Williams Field in Macon, she led me up and over the bleacher rails to lay quilts atop the home team dugout and claim our space. Her thin hair blew in the afternoon breeze. My classmates in the bleachers heckled, for we were nearly on the field and we were surely a spectacle. That was just the way my mother wanted it. *Keep your eyes on the field,* she'd say. *Don't look back; don't give your detractors an audience.*

A COUPLE OF MONTHS AFTER I graduated from high school, my father moved into a cheap apartment on the edge of Macon and filed for divorce. When our house sold, my mother hired a friend to pull the doorknobs as souvenirs. She couldn't imagine new people making their home in our old house. They couldn't possibly grasp the stories now entrusted to them. I returned for the estate sale to help her label and price her treasures.

The people who bought our house jacked it up during a failed renovation and broke it in half. Timbers splintered and plaster walls crumbled. The shift in weight tore apart the rock foundation. The new owners sued, claiming their work exposed foundation problems and termite damage my parents hid. They wanted those old doorknobs back, too.

My parents eventually won the suit but lost their long battle for pride of place. When the new owners walked away from the house, they draped the roof in tarps and left the toilet in the backyard. Though we no longer owned the Iverson birthplace, Daddy drove out there often to mark the losses.

Fire and smoke didn't take our house like he feared. Instead, the ivy that once blanketed the foundation and chimneys crept up the clapboard siding. Kudzu, which my father kept at bay with a sling blade and douses of motor oil, jumped the road and tentacled up the hill.

Social at the Sigma Nu house

Chapter Three

ANIMAL HOUSE

My cousin Meredith Barrett Berry parked her yellow Volvo in front of a movie theater at the back of a strip mall near her hometown of Columbia, South Carolina. It was late summer 1980. We were there to watch a second-run showing of *Animal House*. Twelve years older, a former college softball player, Meredith defined my idea of cool. In the light of a parking lot gooseneck, we passed a joint back and forth. The cabin fogged and Van Morrison played and Meredith asked what I believed Athens would be like. All I knew at seventeen was that college would get me out of Clinton.

Athens was already a part of my life. In the early 1970s, my father kept a second office in the white marble federal building downtown, where he wrote sentencing reports and counseled parolees. On summer trips, our family stayed at a motel on the back side of downtown with a pool in the middle and a basement bar my mother called the Boom Boom Room. At the newsstand across from campus, I bought pulp mysteries from spinner racks. Seated in a vinyl booth at a Chinese restaurant in the suburbs, my mother ordered pupu platters with Sterno-fed volcanoes, orbited by egg rolls and chicken wings.

When the houselights went down that night in Columbia and rush began at Faber College, after Bluto busted that guitar over the head of the singer on the stairs and the horse dropped dead in Dean Wormer's office, *Animal House* gave me an answer to Meredith's question: The University of Georgia would be the kind of place where the heels went to class and the suits conformed. For the next five-plus years, *Animal House* played across the screen in my head like a countercultural instruction reel, in which drinking was an engine of self-expression, double secret probation a badge of honor.

A week before classes began in September of 1980, I drove toward Athens in my father's Karmann Ghia, polo shirts and button-downs on the passenger seat, legal pads from his office on the floorboard. Listening to a boom box tucked into the polos, I imagined food fights and toga parties. Like my generation of white middle-class kids, caught between the radicalism of the 1960s and the materialism of the 1980s, I memorized the lyrics to "Louie Louie" as if those slurred words held existential truths.

My father wanted me to study political science and aim for law school. He graduated with honors from the University of Georgia night school while working at the federal penitentiary, managing an office full of inmates who were twice his age. "Fraternities are not for us," he told me before I left home. The first college graduate on his side of the family, Daddy wanted me to pick up where he left off. "Buckle down. It's time to get serious," he said.

"College will be mind-expanding," my mother told me. In Athens I would be free of small-town ideas. I could escape small-town judgments and follow Thoreau's drummer.

Only now do I realize that I made a choice on that drive to Athens: Instead of a scholar like my father wanted, I became a sort of provocateur like my mother. After she left the house that was her stage, I stepped in to play the role she taught me.

The day before school began, I celebrated the round snake badge on my polo with my new Sigma Nu brothers. Swaying arm in arm, we drank keg beer and sang about swimming with bow-legged women. Before I blacked out, I swallowed the worm at the bottom of a bottle of cheap tequila. During the night, I upchucked a clotted yellow ribbon of Krystal burgers. The next morning, I slept through the first and second classes of my college career.

WHEN THE PHONE RANG AT our fraternity house, I sprinted up and over the stair landing, down to the ice room, where a rotary box hung on the wall and brothers scribbled the sill with sorority house phone numbers. "Pledge Edge, how may I help you?" The want to belong strained my voice.

First-years were supposed to answer the phone in three rings. Most pledges moved lazily toward the stairs, if they moved at all. They knew it was a game. I believed what I read in the pledge manual about my responsibility to "walk in the light of truth," even though my call to the light seemed to translate as cleaning the toilets on Mondays before chapter meetings and suffering the hazing fantasies of brothers like Dan Hammack, who styled himself a minor-key Hitler, and Colton Sexton, a big-headed fellow we pledges called Hydro. I desperately wanted to believe that life in this house would go better than life had gone in our Clinton house.

Instead of a Southern mansion fronted by columns like most,

our frat house was a château built in the French style, a white brick three-story with a long and wide front gallery that faced Oconee Hill Cemetery and the big woods behind. Over the living room mantel hung a mirror etched with the snake that curled through our crest.

Brother Herman Talmadge, recently retired after six terms in the U.S. Senate, siphoned off the money to build our house: That's the story a senior told me during rush week. It wasn't true, I learned later, but to broadcast the power our people wielded, I told the story to each new pledge class.

On the way from the fraternity house to class on the second day, I hitched a ride to the main campus in the open trunk of a sedan. Legs hanging over the lip, feet nearly dragging on the pavement, two pledges and I banged on the back fender to signal the driver to take off. The brothers in the back seat got out in front of the history department, but we blew off our classes and stayed in the trunk. The driver knew a place down by the river where we could buy two-dollar gallons of draft. Waving to friends as we navigated class-change traffic, I was back on top of that dugout with my mother, posing for the crowd.

IN ATHENS, EVERYONE SEEMED TO try on new identities. Townie kids shopped at the Potter's House for wigs and paisley blazers. Frat pledges from New Jersey learned to swallow their consonants and quote Buford T. Justice lines from *Smokey and the Bandit.* I studied the unstudied gentry look from *The Official Preppy Handbook,* trying to project the wealth of my new brothers, angling for the status my mother coveted.

To aid the transition, my parents bought me Brooks Brothers shirts in soft pinks and baby blues. And my cousin Meredith and her family gifted me a rainbow of polo shirts with alligator insignias. Frat boys like I wanted to be wore white bucks and patchwork madras shorts. My kind starched our khakis and wore blue hopsack blazers fixed with brass buttons.

A decade before, Georgia students burned draft cards and tried to burn down the ROTC building. My rebellion was dancing at toga parties and ditching responsibilities. Without really knowing it, I was tapping a well of nostalgia that mirrored Ronald Reagan's promise to return our nation to a simpler past.

Like the brothers in *Animal House,* I went deep on rhythm and blues. My friends teased that a transmitter embedded in my car picked up a signal that originated in Myrtle Beach in 1945. Writing this book, I realized that I was listening to the same music my mother shagged to there after she came home from her failed college run.

Determined not to conform, I fumbled toward rebellion. For a California-themed social, I wore a flowered dress and tennis shoes. I told my brothers that I was dressing like gay boys did on the West Coast. I wasn't trying to make a statement about gender. I didn't connect with the drag that the B-52s, then the pride of Athens, were introducing to straight America. I didn't even know the term *drag.* I was acting outrageous at a time in my life when wearing a dress was the most provocative thing I could imagine. One of my new brothers ripped off my dress. Instead of fighting back, I threw the heap of cotton into the fireplace and ran upstairs in my boxers.

As I settled into fraternity life, I let rumors spread that I lacked resolve in college because I could fall back on a generous inheritance. I became a character from a gone-to-seed plantation who teetered on the brink of ruin. Like my boyhood home in the time my parents divorced, I became a shambled mess.

I batched kamikazes for band parties. At first, we set up shot glasses on folding tables at the top of the basement stairs, alongside the phone booth. One afternoon, my fraternity brother Brandt Furin and I came home from the hardware store with a better idea. We filled a bug sprayer with vodka, lime juice, and sugar syrup, and walked the party, pumping squirts from the long wand, modeling the technique for anyone who didn't grasp how to drink through what looked like an oversized dental hygienist's tool. By midnight, smeared lipstick and spritzed liquor covered my face.

At sorority dances, I made a show of drinking from one of my date's high heels, pulling her shoe off to pour from a bottle of André and sip the fizzy liquid that pooled in the toe box. When I didn't have a date, I drank from my own penny loafer. These were acts of bold decadence, I believed, the sort of things they did in West Egg, the kind of provocations we would have already known about had Fitzgerald pulled the curtain back a little more. Going wild, I told myself, meant I would never go quiet.

ATHENS IN THE 1980S WAS A PLACE of pageants and spectacles. Soul star James Brown from nearby Augusta pranced the sidelines at Sanford Stadium. Hair teased into a slick pompadour, his voice all gravel and ecstasy, he shouted "Dooley's Junkyard Dogs" as the bleacher faithful roared. Outside the student union, an itinerant preacher named Brother Jed wore a suit and tie and held a sign that read REPENT!

Rock and roll was *wicked, depraved, and diabolical,* Jed shouted. My friends and I shouted back, pleased that he seemed to speak directly to us. *I don't know how the whorehouses in this town stay open,* he screamed at women in sundresses. *All of you sorority girls are giving it away for free!* Pretending to suffer his wrath, we laughed off the small-town conservatism that we came to Athens to escape.

The spring before I arrived, R.E.M. played its first gig in a decrepit church less than a mile from my frat house. Their lyrics layered found images and eavesdropped conversations. Michael Stipe sounded inscrutable, like the South itself. "Gardening at Night" was maybe about taking a whiz. "Voice of Harold" definitely sampled the promotional text from a gospel record by a group called the Revelaires. The places and people R.E.M. sang about were easy to caricature but hard to understand. That seemed to be the point, or at least one of the points, along with dancing so hard at a show that the Old South would fade into the newer South our generation was trying to make.

R.E.M. subverted old ideas about the region while reminding us that the South was home. The band rejected the belief that home was a cultural backwater. Instead, they asked, *What if Athens is a headwater?* The magazine *Melody Maker* set the broader scene: "Buried deep in the land of rednecks, peanut farms, and wave-yer-hat-and-shout-yeehaw boogie bands, there's something stirring."

I first heard R.E.M. while riding around Athens in the back seat of my fraternity pledge brother Sam McNair's Galaxie 500, listening to "Radio Free Europe," liking what I heard, thinking that other stuff on WUOG was too weird for me. As the band grew in popularity, R.E.M. leaned harder into Southern images and ideas. For the *Fables of the Reconstruction* tour, they came onstage to a recorded tape loop of a train, a constant in the small-town South of my childhood, and left to the whistled theme of *The Andy Griffith Show*, the series about a bucolic North Carolina town that premiered on CBS the same decade the boys in the band and I were born.

Once I tried to get inside an Athens show R.E.M. played under the pseudonym Hornets Attack Victor Mature. By the time I heard the rumor, the line to get into the Uptown Lounge stretched down the block. I stood on the curb, catching snippets of lyrics each time the door opened. The rebellion I wanted forever waited on the other side, where R.E.M. played secret shows, and my crush, Laura Carter of the Bar-B-Q Killers, sometimes sang with tampons stuck in her ears and other times arrived onstage strapped to a cross, screaming "Fuck Jesus!" That's what it was like to be a frat boy in the time of R.E.M.

By my third year, I began to see my uniform of starched button-downs and boat shoes as a symbol of the conformity I came to college to reject. I didn't want to quit the fraternity; I wanted to remake it. I began by remaking myself.

Sitting in a salon chair in a button-down, I asked a moonlighting sorority girl to give me a rattail haircut. In the front row of a Sigma Nu band party, as the cuffs of my pants turned brown in the basement muck, my friend Pam Coleson pierced my ear with a stud attached to a dangling voodoo doll. I began to wear black T-shirts and skateboarding shoes and tune my car radio to the left end of the dial.

I ditched beach music and went hard for the Violent Femmes. When I looked in the mirror, I still saw myself at age twelve, a country boy from Clinton, shopping for records in Atlanta with kids who were older and cooler. They pooled money to buy the Beatles' *White Album.* I bought John Denver's *Back Home Again* and played "Thank God I'm a Country Boy" on repeat.

The veil that separated the country of my childhood and my college town ideas began to fall the night I saw Jason and the Nashville Scorchers play a campus double bill with R.E.M. To open, Jason Ringenberg shredded that musty old Hank Williams song "I Saw the Light," and the crowd screamed in recognition. From the front row, I watched him leap off the stage and into the audience. Guitar in hand, he sang as he fell.

I had never heard someone reinvent something in real time. I didn't know it was possible to sample your past to make a future. I didn't yet connect my wild stabs at reinvention to the music R.E.M. and the Scorchers made. But I was beginning to realize that change often requires someone or something to chafe against.

RALPH REED WON THE PRESIDENCY of our chapter of the College Republicans the year before I landed at the University of Georgia. He stood for everything I told myself I was going to oppose. Reed married religion to politics and promised to correct the social changes of the 1960s and 1970s. Charming and smart, he fed small-minded dislike of things that were odd or irregular.

In a column for our college newspaper, written in response to the 1982 film *Gandhi,* Reed told readers that the nonviolent Indian leader who inspired Martin Luther King Jr. was a "ninny" who "spent his mornings rolling around in bed with naked teen-age girls." That got Reed fired. Not for his claim; because he plagiarized some of his argument and much of his language.

My fraternity brothers from South Georgia were Reed's audience. Their mothers' people owned creosote plants; their fathers' people founded the seg academies where they played high school football. Heirs to convenience-store fortunes and turpentine dynasties, they wore oxford-cloth button-downs and spit dip into foam cups.

Most didn't care for me or the old Karmann Ghia my father eventually gave me. Red-dirt gentry, they could sense my deep want to belong. They could hear my grandfather's lawn-mower shop in my accent. They could read my father's government job on my face.

The kids from Atlanta were sons of airplane pilots and lawyers, daughters of doctors and accountants. Instead of falling back on inherited wealth, they wanted to make their own way while trying out new looks and attitudes. In my fourth year, I took my Atlanta friend Garlan Barron to the homecoming football game. She cut her hair into an asymmetrical bob and wore black combat boots laced tight. Garlan dressed the way I thought a radical dressed. Trying to figure out a way to match her anti-authoritarian cool, I bought her a mum and pinned it on upside down.

Being a townie came with its own risks. For a "40 Watt" party at Sigma Nu, Sam McNair and another pledge brother, Kelly Crow, booked Limbo District to play our basement. Michael Stipe of R.E.M. came to film the show. Tucked in the back corner, hair in his eyes, a camera trained on the stage, Stipe looked scruffy and cool. The band, which Kelly later joined, sounded like a hurdy-gurdy troupe on windowpane acid. I wanted to like them. Some of my brothers wanted something else. That night, two of them roughed up Stipe. Over breakfast the next morning, one explained himself, saying, "He looked weird."

MY FRATERNITY BROTHERS AND I teased a pledge we called Manchild. Lanky and muscled and seemingly country, John Cleaveland arrived from Jacksonville, Florida, in a Japanese pickup, jacked high on mudders. Manchild painted a moonshine still on the glove box, as if to say, *These are my people.* He was a work in progress. We all were.

When Manchild was a freshman and I was a sophomore, I adopted him as a running buddy. Late that fall, we traveled to his hometown for the Georgia–Florida football game. Other kids cruised Fernandina Beach, tall boys in hand, or booked tables at Bennie's Red Barn up on St. Simons Island to eat rib eyes and drink those ice cream and alcohol bombs they call Raccoons. Manchild planned a drive into the piney woods to an oversized barn lit by floodlights.

From a perch high in the wooden bleachers, we watched roosters and people lunge at one another. Money changed hands and fistfights exploded. Blood clotted the sawdust floor and cocks strutted. I would like to remember that what I saw that night disgusted me. But those cockfights were spectacles. On a search for all things outrageous, in an attempt to channel my mother's maximalism, spectacles were my currency of choice.

By his junior year, Manchild wore tight shorts and tube socks and raced his sixteen-speed around Athens. In that phase, we brothers called him Sportchild. In phase three, he invited us to his room in the fraternity house to drink Tanqueray. I began calling him Sophistichild. When John took to painting abstracts, inspired in part by Richard Olsen, a veteran of the Vietnam War who taught him to think about color in new ways, we called him Artchild.

After that persona took, a career as a landscape painter followed. Battle sites from the Civil War came first, then landscapes from World War One. By the time we caught back up with each other in the late 2010s, he was painting the wild places of Georgia, near his home in the little town of Farmington, down the road from Athens.

In college, we teased Manchild because his search was overt. Like generations of college kids before and after, we poked at what we couldn't understand. We were lost and trying hard to cover that up. Manchild lived the search, committing himself, again and again, to the change he wanted to make. In Manchild, we saw our weaknesses and aspirations amplified. We envied him, because we didn't yet know how to tap that drive in ourselves.

...

FRIENDS GRADUATED AND RUNNING BUDDIES grew younger. If you were a transfer student, I was your wingman. If you were a pledge, I was your shepherd. If you hadn't yet figured out where you fit in, I wandered with you. I drank to talk to girls I wanted to know. I drank to become someone I wanted to be. I drank to live up to expectations, and I drank to live down the fool I played.

I was the guy in the front row at the 40 Watt Club who danced so hard to the Flat Duo Jets that he sweated through his button-down. As "Kung Fu Fighting" played, I led soul trains. I pogo-danced through sorority formal crowds to "Rock Lobster" and pranced the stage at a shitkicker bar singing a Sinatra version of "New York, New York."

My body bears marks from that time. A crescent scar runs along the underside of my right forearm, a marker of the Easter Egg Beer Hunt I hosted in my fifth year. In a photograph from that day, I have one arm looped around one of our fraternity little sisters, the other around a white plastic bucket full of Jell-O shots. My tongue lolls. Red Jell-O leavings stain the rim of the bucket, same as they stain my cheeks. Two hours later, I punched a hole in my bedroom window. A flap opened on the underside of my forearm.

In the emergency room, my friends told me that I was lucky. Blood from my arm ran so heavily down my stomach that it filled my belly button. The nurse who stitched me up also said I was lucky. Lying on that table, I thought about my unlucky mother and her unlucky brother Buster, who drank while he fished at my grandfather's camp on the Edisto River. Back at home in Orangeburg, he tripped and fell with a pan of catfish in hand. Flaming grease poured down his chest. Firemen saved the house, but doctors couldn't save Buster.

. . .

I WON ELECTION AS SOCIAL CHAIRMAN on a platform of bigger parties and better bands. Most of my brothers bought in. I started slow, booking the Plaid Camels from Auburn because they came cheap and played Violent Femmes covers. The guys in Mercyland from Athens were good for late-night Who sets and crowd dives from atop the speaker stacks. The Flat Duo Jets said yes to my offer of fifty bucks and a handle of gin.

Each semester, I enrolled in classes. Most semesters, instead of withdrawing, I quit bothering to go. When the university expelled me, my grade point average was 1.8. College was over, but my fraternity life lived on.

The plan for our spring party weekend, known as Alamo Scout, had long been to rent horses, throw hay bales into the basement, and buy a few kegs. That was our past, I told my brothers, standing before our chapter meeting in my new black-on-black uniform. Aiming to reinvent the pageant we inherited, I drew down our bank account and planned our first Woodstock weekend.

We booked 1960s cover band the Back Doors and a local act, Strawberry Elevator. Another band played Bob Dylan covers for free. We spray-painted a peace symbol on a bedsheet and hung it over the back deck. Brandt Furin pulled up in a VW microbus with a license plate that read FURTHUR, the legend Ken Kesey and the Merry Pranksters plastered on their psychedelic school bus.

Thinking of the moment Bob Dylan went electric at the Newport Folk Festival, and of the cultural shift that signaled, we printed T-shirts with a tired horse on the front and a legend beneath it that read THE TIMES THEY ARE CHANGING. I was trying to say something to my brothers who would soon return home to their turpentine fortunes and conservative politics. I was trying to change the story my fraternity told about itself. As I bottomed out, I finally embraced the change I needed to make in myself.

Atlanta with Bruce Hall, Jeff Bowie, and Garlan Barron

Chapter Four

CITY ON A HILL

I told my fraternity brothers that an all-suite hotel in Atlanta hired me into their manager training program. Truth was, I answered a want ad for a waiter trainee posted by a restaurant in that hotel. Back at the château, someone drew sunglasses onto my senior composite portrait. Timbuk 3's "The Future's So Bright, I Gotta Wear Shades" was climbing the college rock charts.

Getting to Atlanta was my goal. I still saw that city through the eyes of my childhood. From the back seat of our old Mercedes, the city had bloomed in three quick scenes: South of Atlanta, near the JCPenney outlet store, I traced the contrails of Delta jets and guessed their destinations. A couple of miles up the interstate, the blue dome of the Polaris restaurant shone like a torch atop the Hyatt. Driving toward Buckhead, we looked for the ATLANTA'S

POPULATION NOW sign, and I imagined the moment when my dream city would pass the two million mark.

About the same time I moved to Atlanta, my mother moved to Columbia, South Carolina, where her sister, Ruth Barrett, mother of my cousin Meredith, lived. She rented a two-bedroom apartment with a faux mansard roof, spray-on stucco ceilings, and hollow-core doors. Everything was there, but nothing fit. The French theater poster hung in the kitchen; silver serving pieces lined the dining room wall like coats of arms.

Showcases displayed artifacts from my childhood: locks from my first haircut, bronzed baby shoes, a service pin from Little League Baseball. In the corner stood that heirloom Confederate flag, purchased, like the poster, from Bolingbroke. Jasmine climbed the faux wrought-iron pillars on her patio.

My mother made friends with the liquor-store clerks down the street, who delivered pasteboard boxes of jugged red wine. Over breakfasts of liver pudding and grits, she charmed the waitresses at Lizard's Thicket. She ran an open tab at Applebee's. Pictures of new friends from the apartment complex littered our old coffee table, characters in the play my mother recast when our family broke apart.

One Saturday morning, my cousin Meredith called to tell me they found my mother on the floor of that apartment, laid out by a stroke. Three months later, an ambulance hauled her to Atlanta. Orderlies rolled her into a mid-rise nursing home on the edge of Buckhead, a couple of miles from the Casual Corner, where she bought her scoop-necks.

I said that I would help her recover. I joined Adult Children of Alcoholics, sat in the back of a church basement, and tried hard to listen. I read magazine articles about "the Peter Pan Principle," a pop psychology diagnosis from the mid-1980s used to describe men who refused to grow up.

My mother suffered from paranoid delusions, one doctor said. Maybe dementia, definitely alcoholism. When you bring mouthwash, a nurse told me, don't bring the brand she requests. That one has alcohol in it. I flashed back to the cabinet in the bathroom in Clinton, stocked with jugs of wine and bottles of Listerine.

I can't remember much about our visits, but I can see the clot of smokers in wheelchairs who gathered beneath the concrete overhang that passed for a porch. And I can picture the broken smile that lit my mother's face every time I stepped into that haze.

FRATERNITY CONNECTIONS WON ME CORPORATE JOBS in Atlanta. I sold processing software to payroll departments and data capacity to information technology departments. I bought a sky-blue Saab and sold credit reports to purchasing managers and a stream of news and analysis to fixed-income investors.

On my résumé, I listed my major and the year I left Athens, making a bet that my omission would not get me caught in a lie. Every time I changed jobs, I worried that my new employer would figure out that my years there didn't yield a degree. I learned to present a six-figure proposal and close a deal. I proved to my father that I could be more than a fraternity social chairman. I began to prove something to myself.

Sunday mornings, I walked from my house to the drugstore on Ponce de Leon to buy a newspaper. Passing the Plaza Theatre and the public library on my return, I held the paper across my chest like a churchgoer headed for the sanctuary with his Bible.

The country I came from didn't have art house cinemas. We

didn't even have video stores that rented films that played art houses. I loved hearing the words *art house* roll off my tongue, just as my mother loved saying *porte cochere* or *chateaubriand.* Those words spoke to who we might become if we changed who we were.

At the Plaza, I watched *Cinema Paradiso,* the Italian movie about the carnal pleasures of Sicilian life, and *Delicatessen,* the comedy about a post-apocalyptic France where food is in short supply and a butcher breaks his neighbors down into chops and roasts. Over and over again I watched *The Nasty Girl,* the West German film about a young girl's quest to write an essay, "My Town During the Third Reich."

Sonja plans to tell the story that her townspeople tell: Their forebears fought heroically against the Nazis. When she learns that her people abetted the Nazis, life turns upside down. As Sonja digs, the small lies add up to a big one. Her people tell Third Reich versions of the fictions I heard white Southerners parrot about the civil rights movement: *Our church stood up when we had to. Our family helped in quiet ways.*

In Clinton, people who looked like me told those lies: *We would love to have your Black friend over to swim, but we're cleaning the pool today. Your school was founded to serve college-bound students who lack the opportunities required.* A decade gone from Clinton, I began to realize that if I didn't dig into the history of my place and my people, that history would own me.

The books I bought at my neighborhood store showed the way. I read Walker Percy because a woman I wanted to date told me *The Moviegoer* was the first post-Southern novel. I read Kierkegaard because I was supposed to. I began to date an actress. We watched *Waiting for Godot* at a theater down the street. After North Carolina senator Jesse Helms tried to restrict NEA funding, we toured an exhibit of Andres Serrano's ethereal photographs, including *Piss Christ,* the image that pissed off Jesse.

That expansion my mother promised began. I could see my want to make change coming on the periphery. Curiosity was building. Shame and anger, too. In my head, I was already turning on the Iversons.

SMALL-TOWN SOUTHERNERS LIKE ME landed in Atlanta to escape our old homes. We came to Inman Park, the trolley-car suburb that hippies and old ladies saved from highway development, and Midtown, where RuPaul ran the streets in heels and older men picked up younger men at the Gallus.

I hadn't yet figured out my relationship to religion, but I knew that I hated everything that Jerry Falwell and Ralph Reed stood for. And I knew that I loved Doug Bell, my fraternity little brother, who came out after college. When Doug invited me to a kiss-in at a conservative Atlanta church, I showed up with a small placard that read STRAIGHT BUT NOT NARROW. Bashful and halting, I never pulled it out of my pocket.

Spectacles were everywhere: At the Star Community Bar I stomped and caterwauled to the Jody Grind and wallowed in the kiddie pool they installed for Memorial Day weekend. At a Mexican restaurant on Ponce de Leon, I watched a drag queen named Benjamin Smoke pantomime scrubbing the floor while singing "Nobody Knows the Trouble I've Seen." Across town, in another Mexican restaurant, I listened as Drivin N Cryin tore through "Straight to Hell."

My life was my neighborhood. I walked to an Ethiopian restaurant for wat and injera and bought eyeglasses from a vintage store down the block. The bar around the corner curated a foreign beer selection and made great cheese steaks. I enrolled in yoga classes, intent on bringing meaning to my life. I bought a pottery wheel at a yard sale and imagined throwing a bowl.

My passion for food blossomed, born of my father's taste for barbecue and our shared curiosity about the wider world. My college friend Greg Coleson and I began to make lunch runs to restaurants like Violette, for country pâté and brioche, and Veni Vidi Vici, for polenta with mushroom sugo. We made pilgrimages an hour south to Fresh Air Barbecue near Jackson, the 1929 vintage restaurant that inspired Old Clinton, where we ate Brunswick stew crumbled with crackers and chopped pork on white bread. "Work is what we do before and after lunch," Greg and I told each other.

To educate myself on progressive politics, I started an *Utne Reader* discussion group. Our rules required that you hold a talking stick to speak. Thinking about a return to church, I tried Unitarian services but backed off when they sang Union songs instead of hymns. (I wasn't ready to replace religion with activism.) I joined the junior donor group for the art museum, thinking I might meet a debutante.

Before I ever thought of myself as an artist, I aimed to be a patron. Instead of buying a new car, I put aside $200 a month for art. Encouraged by a beautiful gallery owner, I commissioned an encaustic painting of a grand white-tablecloth restaurant on the eve of service. A sculptor who mounted his work on the roofs of neighborhood businesses sold me a bent-steel light fixture that we hung over my dining room table like a nebula in a minor galaxy. I gave over the space under the back deck of my house to my fraternity brother David Landis, who needed a place to weld his sculptures.

Saturday nights clashed hard with Monday mornings, when I drove my Saab north to an office stuffed with salesmen's carrels, set in a mid-rise skyscraper beyond the city perimeter. I was still trying on identities. I knew that I needed to find a new way, so I tried every way.

ON THE DAY ATLANTA WON its bid to host the Centennial Olympic Games, I played hooky from work to stand in the crowd at Underground Atlanta and cheer on my city's big leap. The organ-grinder and his monkey were long gone. My mother's favorite bar had moved its fondue pots from downtown to Buckhead. Underground Atlanta was now an underground mall, a phoenix risen from the underworld to sell branded T-shirts.

One speaker proclaimed Atlanta's new status as an international city. Another said that the South was comparable in geographical size to Western Europe. Maybe I read that second bit in an Atlanta newspaper. No matter; the idea stuck. If the South contained England, France, and Italy, we contained multitudes.

I began to wonder if I knew the South at all. Magazine and newspaper writers, trying to make sense of what Atlanta was selling, documented Souths I had never considered. The roads they traced led out of Atlanta, connecting to Souths I could know. The curiosity I deferred in college began to take hold.

The South of my Georgia childhood, with its Confederate generals and battlefield memorials, figured into their narratives. So did the Gullah and Geechee South of lowcountry South Carolina and Georgia, where women wove baskets from sweetgrass and men cooked Frogmore stew with creek shrimp. Journalists reported in from Tarpon Springs, Florida, where descendants of Greek immigrants dove for sponges, and Harlan County, Kentucky, where Appalshop, a progressive group of Appalachian sons and daughters, fused front-porch storytelling and documentary filmmaking.

I planned a half dozen big trips, but I only talked my friends into taking one. I had recently read *Salvation on Sand Mountain* by Dennis Covington, a book about snake handling as a religious practice. A preacher in North Georgia agreed to meet us in the gravel lot of his cinder-block church. Hair slicked back into an almost duck, cheeks red from the summer sun, he held a heart pine box decorated with a silver cross made of hammered braids.

The energy in the low-ceilinged room popped like summer lightning on young pines. Hands withered from old bites, the preacher called his people forward. The rattler inside the box thrashed and hissed and shook, a siren made flesh. An old man with a big paunch drank from a Mason jar that sloshed with pale liquid.

Two drummers banged on snares and cymbals, sounding like gospel one minute, Sex Pistols the next. When the preacher pulled the snake out of the box, women in gingham dresses turned in circles. Men in short-sleeved dress shirts threw their heads back and hollered with joy. Kicking and bucking, they reached up and out, calling to spirits we couldn't see, speaking words we couldn't understand.

Home from that trip, I made plans to explore on my own. The corner gallery in my neighborhood displayed face jugs in the window. Black and green and misshapen, their exaggerated human features hinted of those other worlds. Enslaved Africans probably developed the American form. By the time I began collecting, white mountain people were the best-known makers. Here was the story of the banjo, an instrument with West African roots adopted by white Southerners. And here was the story of the South, a complicated and often contradictory layering of geographies and histories.

Weekends, I drove North Georgia in search of those jugs, on a path to connect with my contemporary ancestors. From Lanier Meaders at Mossy Creek I bought a squat jug with fat cheeks,

piercing eyes, and rock teeth. From Chester Hewell in Gillsville, I
bought a candelabra jug, Janus faces tattooed blue by broken milk
of magnesia bottles that melted in the kiln and streamed down
their foreheads. Moving through rural Georgia, I moved back in
time.

R.E.M. traveled the same Georgia countryside in the early
1980s to sit with Howard Finster in Summerville as he played
banjo and spoke of his visions of Elvis at age three. North of Gaines-
ville in Rabbittown, the band danced beneath metal whirligigs
cut and painted by R. A. Miller. As developers readied Atlanta for
the Olympics, Southerners like me, who heard their past and future
in the lyrics of R.E.M., became convinced that the South might
still have lessons to teach our generation. Instead of cleaving away
our past, I wanted to unpack the beliefs that swam in my head,
nagging at me to bore down, in search of truths that previous gen-
erations worked hard to bury.

MY LAST ATLANTA JOB, with a consulting firm that sold human re-
source reengineering services, showed promise. Our founders were
Princeton grads. One of my sales colleagues had earned a doctorate,
I told my mother, knowing she would appreciate the pedigree.

If an employee knows what a company expects, that employee
can align their personal growth with the growth of the company.
Or they can bug out. The idea behind BlessingWhite's training
modules sounded very Joseph Campbell, but my friends didn't buy
it. My friend Jeff Bowie played it back as *Your company helps other
companies off-load workers.*

BlessingWhite rented me a two-room office above an Indian res-
taurant that smelled of ghee and fenugreek. I took afternoon naps
there on the carpet. On Mondays I napped because I was hungover.

On Tuesdays I curled up and dug back into Thoreau: "The mass of men lead lives of quiet desperation. What is called resignation is confirmed desperation. From the desperate city you go into the desperate country, and have to console yourself with the bravery of minks and muskrats."

I wasn't sure about minks and muskrats, but I did fear quiet desperation. Nine months into my new job, I off-loaded myself. Success as a salesman in previous jobs gave me the confidence and money to go back to school. Campbell called this following your bliss.

To get ready for a second college run, I took classes at the French Consulate in Atlanta. Five-plus years in Athens, and I had passed just one of the required foreign-language credits. I also signed up for a night-school class in Southern history at Emory University. Early in the first lecture, I asked a question about Reconstruction, repeating what I learned as a boy: That ruinous experiment ruined the South.

Seated toward the back of the auditorium, legal pad in my lap, Montblanc in hand, I prefaced my question with a line from *Gone with the Wind*. Our professor redirected in a kind way that made clear I had a lot to unlearn. For the next forty-five minutes, he tore down the Lost Cause story my mother built up back in Clinton.

Reconstruction, he suggested, was a progressive effort to secure Black citizens the rights and representation they would finally begin to win a hundred years later. After sitting on the edge of my seat, I shrank into my chair. He seemed like a reasonable man. By the next morning, I came to the uneasy belief that if my question rankled him, maybe I had something to learn from him.

The next week, our class took on myths and meaning. The Old South and the New South were codependent stories, our professor said, quoting the historian C. Vann Woodward. Instead of looking to those myths, he suggested, we might find meaning by looking toward Stone Mountain, just east of the city.

Twenty years before, I had traveled there with my parents to see the new and massive carving of Robert E. Lee atop his horse, Traveller, romping a granite battlefield. In the shadow of that bas-relief carving, my professor told us, refugees from African nations began to settle in the early 1990s. They fled war and famine. With the help of relief agencies, they built new lives and told new stories from the South.

Listening, I wondered why Black people would live in the shadow of a Confederate memorial. The short answers were those jets I watched as a boy, which now connected to Ghana and Senegal. And cheap apartments, left behind by whites who moved to the exurbs. Eventually, I learned to verbalize a longer and more complex answer: All Southerners live in the long shadow of the short-lived Confederacy. Two questions followed: Where else was there to go? What else was there to do?

Audience with Howard Finster

Chapter Five

OXFORD EDUCATION

Sunday newspaper in hand, I tucked into a yellow chair on the front porch of my Atlanta bungalow to read about Oxford, Mississippi, and its many splendors, including a juke joint in the hills beyond town, where a band played drone blues against a back wall painted with a surreal beach scene.

Before I made the leap back into college, two books decorated the coffee table in my living room. Each told a story of the South I chased. A museum catalog of folk art, thick with visionaries and prophets who began their lives as field hands, showed the South I overlooked the first time. The *Encyclopedia of Southern Culture*, compiled by the Center for the Study of Southern Culture at the University of Mississippi and published with a cover montage that included a banjo, a possum, and a portrait of Martin Luther King Jr., hinted at the education I wanted to begin again.

The Center built its reputation on that book. Founded when Jimmy Carter was in the White House and the South was a cipher to figure out, the Center explained the South to itself and trained a new generation to explain the South to the world. Students earned undergraduate and master's degrees in Southern Studies and went on to careers as museum curators and history professors and documentary filmmakers.

A little digging revealed that even with a 1.8 GPA, I could get in. (Undergrads wore HARVARD OF THE SOUTH T-shirts, but Ole Miss offered what amounted to open enrollment.) Three months before I quit my job, I booked a Memphis visit with two of my BlessingWhite clients at Federal Express and added an Oxford overnight, seventy-five miles south.

The column-fronted bed-and-breakfast off the Courthouse Square included a coupon for breakfast at Smitty's. Seated in a vinyl booth, I watched regulars smear sausage biscuits with grape jelly. Novelist Tim Gautreaux, whom I recognized from his dust jacket photo, sat in the opposite corner, drinking coffee from a clunky mug, scribbling notes like an actor in a Frank Capra film about a college town.

Traffic spun around the square and the courthouse at its center, "a single cloud in the ring of the horizon." A brass plaque inscribed with that William Faulkner quote marked the south entrance. In front stood a marble plinth, a Confederate soldier on top. Sallie Murry Falkner, grandmother of the author, led the effort to raise the money. Installed in 1907, that monument, like hundreds of others on courthouse lawns across the South, cast the insurrection of 1861 as a gallant effort to defend their homeland. These soldiers faced south, I grew up saying, because that's where our allegiance lay.

Men in poplin suits walked out of the courthouse, past masonry buildings painted in sherbet pastels. Girls in sundresses drank beer and smoked cigarettes and shouted to friends from porches that hung off the fronts of those buildings. On the southwest corner stood Square Books, an auburn-colored two-story with an upstairs coffee shop and a long side gallery.

Signed author photos lined the walls of the high-ceilinged storefront. There was John Grisham, back when he lived in Oxford, his face shadowed by a half beard, and Jim Harrison, the garrulous poet and novelist who frequently came down from Michigan to eat catfish and carouse. By the time I showed up, Square Books was already a place of pilgrimage for the Southern literary set. Nobel laureate William Faulkner, who once lived and worked down the street, was part of the draw. So were contemporary writers like Larry Brown, the Oxford firefighter turned novelist, who taught himself to write by reading novels from Square Books and the local public library.

I studied the menu posted outside City Grocery, where shrimp and grits was already the money dish, and ducked into an art gallery that sold folk art crosses made from bottle caps and photographs author Eudora Welty took of county fairs and plantation ruins. *If you move here,* the owner said, *I'll give you a job.* I couldn't tell if she was serious.

The Center: That's what everyone called the redbrick building at the heart of campus, fronted by white columns and topped by three white turrets. I wore my favorite plaid suit to the interview. Bill Ferris stood from his desk in jeans and a cartoon Elvis T-shirt. Four years before I showed up, *Rolling Stone* magazine named him one of the nation's ten best college professors. Raised on a Mississippi Delta cotton farm, educated at the University of Pennsylvania, he claimed both B.B. King and Welty as friends.

Bill encouraged me to quit the corporate world. As he spoke, curly hair fell over his forehead and into his eyes. *Anything is possible with a Southern Studies degree,* Bill said. *Unconventional students thrive here,* he explained. He was probably thinking of my age. I was definitely thinking of my GPA.

He spoke of a bar owner from St. Louis who wrote a capstone paper about mythology and bourbon marketing, and a woman from New York City who planned to come south to study beauty queen culture. He quoted Black folk tales and aphorisms, like "When an old man dies, a library burns to the ground." Unspooling possibilities, Bill blinked his eyes wide and held my gaze, as if he could see a future that I couldn't see for myself.

TO RECKON WHERE I CAME FROM, I made plans to leave the world I knew. In the summer of 1995, I gave away my Big Green Egg and sold my Acura with the burled walnut dashboard. The white top on my red Valiant convertible leaked around the rear window and the back seat floor pans had rusted out, but it started most of the time and it suited the idea I turned in my head about the person I wanted to become.

To get ready for what would come next, I read the *Encyclopedia of Southern Culture* and plotted my move. Driving west out of the city that said it was too busy to hate, I would trace a path through the moments that defined the civil rights movement, past the city that turned snarling dogs on child protesters in 1963, to my new town, where rioters killed two people in 1962 during the battle to integrate my new university.

Mississippi reflects America at its worst and best: In the months before I arrived, I bought into that idea. At a time when the world began to turn its attention to Atlanta and the shiny pomp of the

Centennial Olympics, I imagined a move to what I saw as a rawer and truer South, intent to ask the 1960s questions that Mississippi still compelled three decades later: Which side was I going to be on? Past or future? And might it be possible to make a future that leveraged the best expressions of our past?

I came to Mississippi like many Americans do, newsreels flashing in my head: Fannie Lou Hamer of Ruleville, clasped purse on the table beside her, television cameras rolling, speaking to the Democratic National Convention about the brutal beatings she suffered after she helped lead a voter registration workshop. Bob Dylan in front of a cropper's cabin in Greenwood, wearing dungarees and singing freedom songs.

Emmett Till, down from Chicago for a visit, a smile on his face, reaching for the screen door on a country store in Money. Muddy Waters, who wrote the song that gave the Rolling Stones their name, teaching himself to play harmonica on the stoop of a house at Stovall Plantation near Clarksdale.

Before I left Atlanta, one of my BlessingWhite colleagues gave me a leather journal with gilt-edged pages that looked like the sort of thing a serious young man carried around to write down serious things. Planning my life in Oxford, I imagined a coffee shop on the square where I would drink espressos with frothed cream and write toward an understanding of my place in the world.

In Atlanta, I worked a weekday corporate job to subsidize weekend pleasures in my bohemian neighborhood. In Oxford, I would patch together those halves of my life to make a whole. To honor my father's belief, I would go back to school. To honor my mother's want, I would listen harder for all that was offbeat.

. . .

ON THE SUNDAY BEFORE MEMORIAL DAY, my Atlanta friends un-
loaded pasteboard boxes from the bed of a rental truck. We hauled
mattresses and box springs into a deco fourplex a block south of the
Courthouse Square. David Landis and his fiancée, Marie Baird,
loaded kitchen cabinets with bottles of gochujang and packets of
rice noodles, provisions for a life that I expected to be more barbe-
cue and less banchan. Nelson Ross, who first turned me on to
writings about the civil rights movement, connected an amp and
a turntable. And I cranked open the casement windows to blast
B.B. King into the gloam.

As the sun set on my first day in Mississippi, we drove toward
that juke joint I read about, in the kudzu-lost hills north of town.
I checked the directions in my pocket organizer. A month before, I
used that spiral notebook to track sales of employee self-assessment
programs. No one could say if Junior Kimbrough's juke joint was
going to be open. There was no number to dial, no hours posted.
Rumors about shows began to spread on Thursdays.

Crickets chirped and a thin crescent moon rose over a dark wall
of pines. Channeling the same energy I used to sell my friends on
that drive to see the snake handler, I sketched the scene, replaying
what I read in the newspaper and saw in a documentary film. Mem-
bers of the Rolling Stones once road-tripped here in search of the
blues that gave birth to rock, I told my friends. Iggy Pop and Sonic
Youth followed.

Here was my pitch: Before we hear the music, we'll see cars
parked on the shoulder of the road at the crest of a hill, then a squat
building, formerly a general store and a horse stable and a church,
maybe in that order. Two pool tables will anchor the warped ply-
wood floor. To get in the door you'll have to duck under the cue of
a player or scooch against the back wall. Men in overalls and bro-

gans will talk to women in sparkly tops and house slippers, I said, and all will pass around a plastic milk jug full of shine.

When it's cold, they light a fifty-five-gallon drum in the center of the room, feeding two-by-fours into the mouth. Sparks and cinders float toward the ceiling, I promised, twirling like fireflies. In the summer, the walls seem to leak sweat, as if the condensation that beads on the outside of a cold can of beer is running down the walls.

A painting of Oprah Winfrey, done in the style of an *Ebony* magazine cover, hangs above the scrum. When the flash of a camera lights the bar, the glitter mixed into the latex paint sparkles. Where the walls meet the ceiling, a bathing beauty will frolic and pine trees will reach toward a cerulean sky. The band plays in a kind of cubby, I told my friends, where the ceiling slopes to meet the roof and the music drawls and wanders, draping the night in slurred words and slack-chorded guitars.

We passed a scratch-and-dent grocery and a rusted trestle bridge. The white sidestep in front of us, stacked with junked washing machines, turned left. Town fell away and deep woods closed in. Tumbledown farm sheds heaved into view; so did rain-leached clay roads and rambunctious fields of kudzu.

It took two passes, but we found the rise in the road and the squat juke behind. No lights, no crowd, no glitter-speckled walls, just a man and a woman making out on the hood of a car. *Yes, this is Junior's*, the man said in a more patient tone than I might have used. *No, it won't open later tonight.*

Driving home, replaying that first day in Oxford, it made sense that I couldn't flip the switch on this scene for friends. Life in Mississippi would require that I listen for the rhythms of a different South.

...

I STUDIED TENNESSEE WILLIAMS, BORN down the road in Colum-
bus, Mississippi, with a professor named Colby Kullman, who bub-
bled with joy when we discussed the playwright's sexually charged
metaphors. We read *Twenty-Seven Wagons Full of Cotton*, the play
that became the film *Baby Doll*, and followed the text on stapled
printouts. Undergraduates in their teens and early twenties, except
for thirty-two-year-old me, we giggled as our professor broke down
the movie scene in which cockblocked Karl Malden stares through
a knothole in the door as his negligeed wife squirms in a crib.

In a drafty room with a long seminar table at its center, I puz-
zled through the business of antebellum slavery with an economist
who projected spreadsheets on the screen above and flatlined his
delivery of horrible truths. We accounted the value of the enslaved,
differentiating between men who worked the fields and women
who worked the house, factoring in how the value of field hands
decreased if they were blinded or maimed.

We talked about the gin and how that nineteenth-century tech-
nology drove the spread of cotton and the spread of enslaved labor.
No one mentioned my hometown of Clinton, where one of the
first commercially successful gins was manufactured, but we talked
about the profits that gins made possible for families like the Iver-
sons, and we traced that money from Georgia and Mississippi to
London and New York and back again.

By the time I arrived on campus, the Center was already shift-
ing its work away from folk music and folk art, toward the history
and sociology of the civil rights movement. In seminars that met up-
stairs in the main turret of Barnard Observatory, built by enslaved
laborers with bricks made by their children and embedded with
their fingerprints, students learned to define that conflict as our

signal war. True change, we learned, began with the people Martin Luther King Jr. called the "ground troops," the activists historian John Dittmer wrote about in his book *Local People.*

Students in Southern Studies made fun of history students across campus who still researched and wrote about the Civil War. In looser moments, our professors came close to doing the same. Why were they treading that old ground? We had a new war to dissect. After spending my childhood believing that the Civil War was our defining conflict and the Confederacy was a noble cause, I embraced this new way to think with a sort of fervor. Shifting the focus toward people like Fannie Lou Hamer, I gained a new lens to see my region.

Eudora Welty headlined the first Center symposium in November of 1977. The next summer, Bill Ferris began to grow the program by seeding press. In 1982 Bill appeared on the PBS television show *Firing Line* to debate "Is the South Changing?" That same year, B.B. King gifted his record collection to the university, a donation that became a talking point for Ferris and a bragging point for a school still struggling to attract Black students.

The Center published the first edition of the *Encyclopedia of Southern Culture* in 1989. In the run-up to the release, Bill became a star. He served director Steven Spielberg as a dialogue coach for the filming of *The Color Purple,* based on the Alice Walker novel. When North Carolina televangelists Jim and Tammy Faye Bakker imploded in a sex and embezzlement scandal, Bill wrote a *Los Angeles Times* op-ed that explained the roots of their evangelism and the reasons many Southerners remained devoted to them.

Graduate student enrollment spiked. Royalties from the encyclopedia drove new Center projects, including the Oxford Conference for the Book, which hosted Stephen King in its second year, Pat Conroy in its third. *Reckon,* a magazine of Southern culture, published its first issue a couple of months after Conroy took the stage. The Center became a laboratory for cultural expression, a sort of Skunk Works for a progressive South.

AS THE OPENING CEREMONY OF the 1996 Atlanta Olympics drew nearer, the South was in play again. The League of the South, founded in 1994 by a university professor from Alabama, began publishing white papers on segregation and revisiting plans for secession. William Cawthon, the onetime University of Georgia law student who fought my father over the four-laning of the highway near Clinton, became a charter member. Byron De La Beckwith finally went to jail that same year, convicted for the 1963 murder of Mississippi civil rights leader Medgar Evers.

My professors encouraged me to write about the present as well as the past. For a political science seminar that met upstairs in Barnard Observatory beneath the unused mount for a massive and powerful telescope, waylaid by the Civil War, I wrote about the return of the chain gang, revived by the Alabama legislature. Proponents claimed the punishment was color-blind, even as newspapers published photographs of shackled men, chained together in groups of five, picking up trash and trimming weeds, guarded by officers with shotguns.

To connect those contemporary scenes to enslaved work gangs of the nineteenth century, I sampled history texts and learned to source the minutes of government committee meetings. Full of research and full of myself, convinced that my witness could make a difference, I built an argument that read like a jeremiad in which I claimed that the South was better than this.

Charles Reagan Wilson, the history professor who edited the encyclopedia with Bill Ferris and Ann Abadie, associate director of the Center, led me away from judgment toward observation and analysis and reflection. To help make sense of my new place, he pointed to *Wings of Desire,* the Wim Wenders film that opens in Berlin, Germany, as a man dies on a rain-slicked roadway after a motorcycle crash. *If you want to understand how Mississippi matters,* Charles suggested, *that film is a place to start.*

Angels walk the earth in *Wings of Desire.* Their telepathy gains us access to the worries that turn in the minds of humans. We see an angel lean its head on the shoulder of a seemingly hopeless tram passenger; another listens to the interior monologue of a sex worker. Through angels, we witness the depth of human fears and aspirations.

As the man dies, his mind flashes to his reasons to live: He hasn't seen the Far East, the Great North, the Wild West. And he hasn't driven the back roads of the Mississippi Delta. Knowing Mississippi, I was beginning to learn, is essential to knowing the world.

TWO MONTHS AFTER I UNPACKED MY BOXES, writer Stanley Booth stood to address the first International Conference on Elvis Presley at the University of Mississippi. The brochure promised a Tuesday morning talk about the influence of gospel music on Presley. Booth had recently written *Rythm Oil,* a personal history of blues and rock that published with a William Eggleston photo of a neon-lit Confederate battle flag on the front and a Keith Richards blurb on the back.

I expected to hear about Elvis's formative Tupelo years and the influence of singers from the Shake Rag community, settled by Black men and women after Emancipation. Instead, Booth mumbled, teetered, and swayed. As the audience stared into the lights, trying to figure out what was going on, he buckled to the stage. An ambulance arrived and Booth exited the auditorium on a stretcher.

Booth stayed up all night drinking with Eggleston, one of my professors said in a tone that suggested he might have been with them. I wished I was with them. By that night, Booth's tumble became mythic proof of what the conference promised: The academy should take pop culture icons like Elvis seriously, but the academy didn't have to take itself too seriously. In the distance, I could almost see my mother applauding.

Vernon Chadwick, famous for teaching a "Melvis" graduate seminar that combined Elvis Presley and Herman Melville, framed the discussions, saying, "This is the first academic conference with sex appeal." Bill Ferris ducked in and out of the room to do interviews. Two hundred people registered for the conference; around one hundred registered as press.

Howard Finster, who rose to fame painting album covers for R.E.M. and the Talking Heads, cried as he talked about the vision of Elvis that told him to paint sacred art. On the stage at Fulton Chapel, Finster wore a white shirt and a tie of his own design and told us that he first saw Elvis in a smudge of paint at the end of his thumb.

That same week, El Vez, the Mexican Elvis, sang "Suspicious Minds," backed by his band, the Memphis Mariachis. Two machine-gun-carrying Elvettes, Priscillita and Gladyscita, danced and shimmied as El Vez mimicked Elvis's lyrics and added new ones. Instead of "Why can't you see / What you're doing to me," El Vez sang, "Why can't you see / Statue of Liberty," and the crowd stood and screamed, recognizing that when he mock-whispered, "They call it a trap / I can't walk out," he was talking about the promise the USA makes to immigrants.

I was in the second row when Reverend Will D. Campbell stepped onto the stage with a sheaf of papers in hand. Back in Oxford after a long absence, Campbell wore a straw hat and squinted into the lights. In 1956, he left his position here as campus chaplain, pushed by conservatives who were incensed by his views on integration. One year later, he joined Martin Luther King Jr. at the founding of the Southern Christian Leadership Conference, the only white man present.

Campbell smiled shyly that morning and started slowly. Born 250 miles south, near Liberty, Mississippi, he told the auditorium that he was happy to return home. Campbell looked wearied by the spectacle and anxious to speak. He laid down a couple of jokes, some easy banter. And then the man who faced troops with bayonets when he tried to help integrate Central High School in Little Rock loosed a blistering assault on the smug belief of many middle-class whites that racism is a working-class problem.

Judging by the posture of the crowd, many in the audience were susceptible to those beliefs. Elvis was a redneck, Campbell said, a member of a "proud and tragic people, the poor, white, rural working class of the South."

A redneck comes from people whose necks have turned red beneath the sun, people who stooped to hoe a field planted with corn or cotton. Rednecks can be bigots and racists, he suggested, and so can attorneys in pinstripes and academics in tweed. But rednecks are not necessarily bigots and racists.

Racists fuel bigotry to divide and conquer. Over the long arc of history, powerful and racist white men have pitted working people of both races against one another, he said. To gain money and power, they have preyed on people who lack both.

"I am a redneck," Campbell told the crowd. He said it with great pride and some anger. His voice rose and the papers in his hand shook. Campbell declared that his "brilliant, beautiful lesbian daughter" was a redneck, too. The crowd shifted in their seats.

At first we clapped politely. Campbell stared back at us, smiling. As his words gained purchase in our heads, we came to our feet, hooting and hollering and whistling, going as wild as a crowd at an academic conference can go.

I walked into that auditorium thinking one way, believing that prejudice in the South always broke along racial lines. I walked out knowing that my biases kept me from really seeing and hearing the South. To think in new ways: That's what I wanted to try when I left Atlanta for Mississippi. My mother first put that idea in my head back in Clinton. Here was that idea realized.

Watching and listening, I connected what the Center was doing for the South to what I tried at Sigma Nu. My efforts in Athens were grasping and immature. This time could be different. Staging new sorts of pageants, sampling what I was learning on my return to college, I told myself that I could make change in my South.

IN GRADUATE SCHOOL, I ORGANIZED my life like a syllabus, keeping a list of each book I read, transcribing notes from every lecture, telling myself that road trips were research trips. I drove Mississippi in search of stories. Everybody in the Delta seemed to talk about hot tamales, pulled from their shucks, broken into pieces, perched on saltines, and doused with hot sauce. But no one seemed to talk about how this food from Mexico came to be sold in country stores and juke joints.

For a seminar in African American Studies, I pieced together a story of the late 1800s and early 1900s, when Black workers in Delta cotton fields learned from Mexican workers how to roll tamales. My fellow students spent their time in archives, in search of historical documents, but underground economy work, like rolling tamales in home kitchens and selling them on the street, left few traces for researchers.

To begin, I tracked down the music of Arthur Collins, a vaudeville performer who recorded "The Hot Tamale Man" sometime between 1908 and 1909. The song was racist drivel, but it carried meaning: By the first decade of the twentieth century, tamales already had crossed over. What was Mexican was also Black.

My grad school friend Kerry Taylor knew Catholics kept good records. If Mexican workers came to the Delta to work cotton harvests, he guessed the church hired Spanish-speaking priests. Reading correspondence in the archives of the Catholic diocese in Jackson, I time-traveled to the years when Black workers quit cotton fields for new lives in the North and West, and white farmers in the South struggled to find workers to pull in bumper crops.

"Planters have been forced to seek Mexican labor to gather the harvest," Reverend Downing of Clarksdale wrote in 1925 to Bishop Gerow of Natchez. "Right now there are upwards of five thousand souls of this people in the Delta." Digging deeper, I found records of plantations that stocked their commissaries with masa so that Mexican workers could pat out tortillas and roll tamales.

Food history hooked me, and so did the idea that I might help tell stories that added up to a new narrative of the South. Black street vendors once sold tamales, made from pork and corn, wrapped in shucks, and kept warm in coal-fired buckets. Tamale men cried their wares. Some sang; others jangled bells. But by the time I began to wander and eat and research and write, health department regulations and new ideas about fast food had just about done them in.

When I asked questions about tamale history, people told me stories about hometown vendors. Novelist Shelby Foote spoke of two Black men who worked his hometown of Greenville, carrying lard buckets, selling half-dozen bundles. Listening to Foote, thinking about what I learned in classes about how migrations shape identities, I tracked a more diverse Mississippi.

I showed up too late to eat the tamales Isaac King of Vicksburg sold from a cart fixed with bicycle wheels, and I never caught up with the lady in Leland who sold single tamales from a walk-up window cut into the side of her house, but I did meet Darrell Moore, grandson of civil rights activist Amzie Moore, who sold bundles of six from the trunk of a car parked in front of Po' Monkey's juke joint near Merigold. He told me that tamales were a food of liberation, adopted in the years after slavery ended as Black men and women gained the freedom to start small businesses.

Oscar Orsby in Clarksdale, Mississippi, sold tamales from a pickup, parked across the street from Club Champagne. On weekends, he flipped the circuit breaker on a meter mounted to an electric pole, plugged a two-burner stove into a socket, and stretched a tarpaulin across the back of his truck.

Orsby began making tamales as a side hustle, when he worked for the Clarksdale electric department. Access to the electric meter came with the job. After he retired, Orsby kept plug-in privileges. "Be careful with those," he would yell, laughing, when drunk and hungry customers crowded the truck after the club let out. "My finger-biting insurance has run out."

In the summer of 1997, I worked the National Mall in Washington, doing interviews for Smithsonian Institution programming on the Delta. Standing behind a makeshift kitchen island, before spectators on bleachers, I talked with Gilroy Chow of Clarksdale, Mississippi, head of a large Chinese American family, about how to fry rice in a wok made from an old tractor disc.

Sally Chow, his wife, spoke in a molasses brogue of her cake-baking business and of Sunday church services and the rhythms of their household. Together, they talked about their deep family roots in the country stores of the Delta, and about how, as cotton farming mechanized, the towns that dotted the region emptied and those stores closed, leaving Black families without places to buy bologna and hoop cheese, leaving Chinese families without everyday reminders of how they began.

Robert Craig rolled his father, Lawrence Craig of DeValls Bluff, Arkansas, onto the Smithsonian stage to talk barbecue. Drippings from the pit and peelings from the apples he baked into pies made his sauce good, Lawrence said. Seated in a wheelchair, he talked about working a snag boat on the Mississippi River. *It used to be a Black man's job to do the dirty work of feeding the fire on the boat,* he told the audience. *But when all you had to do was turn a knob, they got a white man to sit down and turn that knob, and that became a white man's job.*

Like the Chows, Lawrence Craig smiled when he told these stories of home. He told me that he made his best money in the summer, when he cooked out by the highway, working a pit made from box springs and concrete blocks, set over a hole in the ground where a fire smoldered. To keep the heat in and the rain out, Lawrence topped his pit with lengths of roofing tin.

Pride lit his creased face. As he talked, I took notes. For Lawrence, those moments on stage before an audience were like U.S. Senate testimony. As he spoke, the crowd marveled. I recognized then that I could seed progress by picking up a microphone and turning it toward people I admired, people others ignored or dismissed or downplayed. By amplifying their voices, I told myself that I was changing the stories that Southerners told about their past and future.

• • •

I NEEDED A JOB TO finance my grad-school travels. If I worked the register at Square Books, I thought I might also improve my social life. To prepare for the test Square Books gives to potential clerks, I tried and failed to memorize the sequence of Faulkner's novels but learned to pronounce Yoknapatawpha, the fictional name he gave to my new home.

I arrived in Oxford fluent in Walker Percy. I could quote him on eating crawfish and sidestepping everydayness, but I felt more comfortable when the conversation turned to Flannery O'Connor. That gave me the chance to tell about the drive my mother and I made from Clinton to visit Flannery's mother at her home in nearby Milledgeville. At Andalusia, her farm just down the road from my father's favorite pitmaster, a peacock ran the yard, screeching and shitting. In Oxford, people leaned in close when I talked peacock scat.

Literature was a social pursuit in Oxford. Saturday night bonfires in the country got organized over coffee on the Square Books porch. Thursday nights at the City Grocery bar began with author signings at Off Square Books, the store's second location. Sunday mornings, I worked the downstairs register, selling newspapers to regulars who became friends. Over a soundtrack of prewar gospel, sometimes played at death-metal volume, we talked about the rise of the Republican Party in Mississippi and dogtrot architecture and primitive antiques.

Oxford was a cultural vortex in the late 1990s. *Stick around,* my new friends joked. *Everybody will eventually show up.* Warren Zevon played a Friday night show at Proud Larry's, the rock-and-roll bar across from Square Books. The crowd was sparse, as if no one believed the guy who wrote "Werewolves of London" was actually going to show at a venue that held two hundred. Zevon sang "Play It All Night Long" and leaned into the Skynyrd references.

He cranked "Mr. Bad Example" and the small crowd sang along, feeling the release that a group can share when they give voice to their worst selves.

Just short of the payoff, Zevon mugged for the crowd and shouted into the mic, "Here comes the Faulkner reference." His voice rose to a scream: "I'm Mr. Bad Example, intruder in the dirt / I like to have a good time, and I don't care who gets hurt." From the front row, drenched in rock-and-roll sweat, I could hear his voice strain to connect. Growing accustomed to the culture of my new town, I heard something else, too—Zevon's allusion to the Faulkner novel *Intruder in the Dust*.

Editors from the *Oxford American* used Square Books as a sort of reference library and break room. Sunday afternoons, founder Marc Smirnoff read proofs at a table in the corner. Between customers, I pitched him a piece about working a Lucky Dogs cart in New Orleans. He bought in, and I soon drove south with a spiral reporter's notebook and a copy of *A Confederacy of Dunces*. Between chili dogs, I planned to reread my favorite novel and act out the part of Ignatius, the flatulent and overeducated antihero of the book who turns to hot dog vending after his academic career falls apart.

In New Orleans, I worked a cart for two nights, wading Bourbon Street gutters sloshed with vomit. I sidestepped a young man dressed in black who lit books of matches and threw them at my feet, and I ducked to escape the spray of spittle on my neck from a drunk who wanted two with peppers.

By the end of the first night, a vendor adopted me. Alice taught me to fan steam from the cart toward the crowd, so customers could smell the chili. She showed me how to keep my right hand free for making dogs while rummaging in an apron for change with my left. Watching the drunks on Bourbon Street, mouths red and sticky with hurricane cocktails, I filled two notebooks with scribbles.

As the night wore on and drunks pounded their fists on the cart and Alice screamed for them to "*Shut the fuck up!*," she taught me to look past the spectacle. Alice was more than a lost soul who worked a randy job. If I turned toward her, I might learn something. On the street with Alice, on deadline for a magazine story, I began to imagine myself a writer.

Three hard edits later, Smirnoff published my first piece in the magazine. Writing for the *Oxford American,* I fell hard for my byline. In search of my next story, I fell harder for the attention I got to pay to other places and other lives.

CIVIL RIGHTS HISTORY HOOKED ME, TOO. Stories from that war were still underfoot. After a walk across campus to look for the dorm where James Meredith lived until his graduation, I met with a librarian who shared a 1962 photo of a Meredith effigy, hung from a window in his dorm. When I asked a doctor, who was an Oxford high school student during the riot, to talk about what he remembered, he pulled out a thick manila envelope of black-and-white photos and narrated National Guard movements near his family home.

On September 30, 1962, rioters opposed to Meredith's admission gathered beneath the Confederate memorial at the center of campus. Protesters drove in from across the South, joining students who walked over from fraternity houses. The mob burned cars and stole a fire truck and shot out windows in the Lyceum, the main administration building.

Paul Guihard of Agence France-Presse died that night from a bullet to the back. Ray Gunter, a jukebox repairman from nearby Abbeville, died from a shot to the forehead. Thirty thousand U.S. troops deployed to put down the insurrection. Law enforcement reported more than three hundred injuries that night, but none of the rioters earned convictions and the university expelled no students. When I enrolled three decades later, no campus marker told the story of the riot or the struggle for access that underlaid it.

I raised my hand in a folklore class, taught by Bill Ferris. We were talking about symbols and how they project meaning on a place. The University of Alabama had recently installed a temporary sculpture, marking Governor George Wallace's 1963 failure to stop the enrollment of Black students Vivian Malone and James Hood. That moment was dramatic, but no one died. I asked an earnest question that day, something like *Why doesn't our university mark the struggle for equal access to education?* Walking away from class that afternoon, Charlene Dye and a couple of other classmates asked: *Why don't we figure out how to get that done?*

Beginning in January of 1996, we posted flyers on bulletin boards for open meetings and used a new technology called email to raise money for a sculpture that told the story. Law school faculty joined us, math professors, too. Students from Southern Studies partnered with members of the Black Graduate and Professional Students Association. Second Baptist Church, Oxford's largest Black congregation, voted their support. Myrlie Evers-Williams, widow of civil rights leader Medgar Evers, appeared at our campus fundraiser.

In an early meeting with Chancellor Robert Khayat, we proposed a sculpture at the top of the circle, opposite the Lyceum, saying the artwork could be a counterbalance to the Confederate memorial then at the bottom of the circle. He didn't like that idea. Our conversation moved to aesthetics. Khayat told us that the university provost pictured two little girls, black and white, holding hands. I spoke of a recent trip to see Maya Lin's art installation at the Southern Poverty Law Center in Montgomery, a stark and abstract accounting of the people who gave their lives to the movement.

By the end of our first hour together, we found a way forward: Khayat pledged money to hire a public art consultant, we agreed to move the planned location to the ellipse, behind the Lyceum, in front of the library, and all parties decided that our student-led group would raise the money and manage the process to choose the artwork. Gloria Kellum, a vice chancellor, offered advice and support. She flew in historian Edward Linenthal, who consulted on the United States Holocaust Memorial Museum, to give a public talk and host a conversation. *This won't be easy,* he told us. *Public art is never easy.*

When our Civil Rights Commemoration Initiative announced an open call, 125 artists applied. Mary Beth Lasseter, a second-year Southern Studies graduate student, stayed up all night to organize the slideshow for the selection meeting. A jury of curators, artists, and public history leaders winnowed the field to five finalists.

Willie Birch drove up from New Orleans to present plans for a sculpture inspired by interviews with civil rights movement veterans. Despite a request that artists propose something other than a single human figure, Dennis Oppenheim shared his mock-up of a three-story bust of James Meredith with a cotton-plant-lined passageway embedded in his chest, inspired by the drive-through redwoods of California and the cash crop that Meredith picked as a boy. We hosted parties for the artists. The university museum displayed maquettes and staged a conversation about what public art could accomplish. Despite what Linenthal said, it seemed easy.

But other forces were at work. In a move to cut down on Confederate rhetoric and attract more Black students, Chancellor Robert Khayat was working to eliminate Confederate battle flags at football games. In the 1960s and 1970s, the university passed out those flags mounted on wooden sticks. Spectators waved battle flags at kickoffs and at halftimes as the Pride of the South band marched the field, trailing a monstrous version of the flag, stitched by the Home Economics Department.

The practice persisted across generations. Now that more games were televised, the optics were a problem. Khayat wanted to discourage flag-waving while steering clear of a First Amendment challenge. He banned sticks, citing safety reasons. Without sticks, it would be hard to wave flags.

Conservative white alumni and students fought back against what they saw as an assault on traditions. They draped tailgating tents with battle flags and printed cardboard flag placards, which they held up like sad airport drivers waiting on fares. They worried that the administration would soon replace Colonel Reb, the Ole Miss mascot who wore a goatee and walked the field with a cane. As their protests mounted, administration support for our effort weakened.

I KEPT RUNNING. STORY ASSIGNMENTS became excuses to try new foods. Road trips gave me chances to talk to people I wanted to know. An hour and a half southwest of Oxford, in the slanted light of a Saturday afternoon, I saw a sign for buffalo ribs. Beneath the tent in the parking lot of an old freight station in the Delta town of Drew, I thought I would find a grill stacked with charcoal and wreathed in smoke.

A woman inside worked three small fry pots connected by a long orange extension cord. Cut from big-mouthed river fish, buffalo ribs turned out to be crescents of flat bone wrapped in white flesh. Battered and fried in deep oil, tucked between white bread to make sandwiches, her buffalo tasted like wild catfish before farmers trained those bottom-feeders to surface and feed on soy pellets.

As I began to write for editors as well as professors, my curiosities defined my destinations. I took inspiration from William Eggleston, the photographer who shot seemingly banal subjects like a gleaming farmhouse sink or a blue tricycle with red grips, abandoned at the curb in front of a suburban ranch.

Eggleston talked about a "democratic way of looking around" in which "nothing was more or less important." After seeing his photographs in a local gallery and learning that he lived in Memphis, I worked the same tack.

The South seemed inexhaustible back then. Home was that place in the rearview. Each day on the road was a blacktop sprint, filtered through the worldview of a Charles Portis story: Behind the wheel by six in the morning, eat five meals, grab a cheap motel. My habits were those of a young man.

On the Sunday before the first Monday of the month I often drove an hour east from Oxford, past Blue Mountain College and Blue Mountain Dragway, to Ripley, Mississippi, where, beneath sheet-metal lean-tos, vendors sold rusted tractor parts and old Coke bottles and new bundles of tube socks. I walked red dirt aisles, eating corn dogs and washpot rinds, talking to old men with tobacco-stained beards and freckled young women in tank tops.

When I asked a man wearing a Confederate flag bandana beneath a gimme cap to tell me the story of a cast-iron skillet with an unusual lip, I earned the chance to talk to someone I might have otherwise avoided. Speaking to a woman in a pink housedress, an HO-scale locomotive from my childhood in hand, I connected.

That tack worked best in the Ripley side yards, where farmers bought and sold animals. Goats bleated and bunnies nosed against wire cages and hound dogs bayed. As I scratched the head of a feist, a man looked up to say that his grandfather raised dogs for Faulkner. The world yawned open.

...

I REPORTED FROM THE SUNDAY brass band shows at Little People's Place in New Orleans, a very small Tremé neighborhood spot run by very small women. I toured the Colonel Sanders Museum in Louisville, set in a massive faux-antebellum mansion, weaving past a display case with his original pressure cooker inside and a five-foot plastic statue donated by a Japanese franchisee.

Camera in hand, deadline negotiated, I tramped W. C. Rice's Cross Garden and trailer park in Prattville, Alabama. HELL IS HOT, HOT, HOT! read graffiti painted on the side of a junked washing machine in his front yard. Signs posted on the pine trees that rose from the scrub warned REPENT!

On a first drive through Cajun Country, Louisiana, in 1997, I ate boudin pushed from its casing like toothpaste from a tube and drank cocktails with umbrella swizzle sticks in a ruined casino. I slurped crawfish bisque scattered with stuffed crawfish heads and bunked in a railroad hotel, where the bartender let me finger the bullet hole left in the oak after a recent fight.

At nine on a Saturday morning, I pushed through the door at Fred's, a shot-and-a-beer bar on the main drag in Mamou. Donald Thibodeaux & Cajun Fever broadcast live on the local radio station. Bud in hand, I watched middle-aged couples waltz arcs around the band. Tante Sue, her face haloed by gray curls, swigged from a pint bottle of cinnamon schnapps. Bottle emptied, Fred's widow squeezed her chest in time to the music like she was playing an accordion.

During a lull, I made a run to T-Boy's Slaughter House to buy five pounds of boudin. I never got the courage to waltz the room, but I did walk the perimeter, passing links of boudin to all within reach. No one looked drunk. Everyone looked happy. These were not my people, but I wanted to belong to this place.

When our family traveled, my mother spiraled into crisis. On the road, she was joyful one moment, a mess the next. I can picture her, drunk and snoring in the back seat, in a Florida parking lot, as my father eased the car door open and the two of us crept toward the ticket booth for a mermaid show.

I willed myself to be different. Travel would be my inspiration. Seated in the back corner of an Alabama barbecue restaurant, I eavesdropped on a truck driver in coveralls and an attorney in seersucker, trying to catch snippets of what they said to each other after a waitress dropped off ribs and white bread. I stood beside a bank of fry baskets with a Florida fish cook, while he spooned hush puppy batter into oil and talked about the Minorcan origins of the peppers that floated in his clam chowder.

Previous generations of writers got the South wrong, I believed. Worse yet, they wrote like Confederate recidivists, backsliding into attitudes and vocabularies born of the Civil War and its aftermaths. Newspaper writers still wove similes inspired by the green velvet curtains Scarlett O'Hara ripped down to sew her ball gown. Novelists still called interlopers carpetbaggers.

Magazine columnists, reporting the Sunbelt economic boom, wrote, "The South will rise again!" without talking about the fall. Instead of speaking to the future, they swaddled their stories in the past, whistling by plantation graveyards to collect checks and awards. Born into a Confederate terrarium, I knew that routine. Now on the other side, I wanted to rewrite those myths.

EVERY FEW WEEKS, I DEVELOPED a crush on a different woman. We would go out on a couple of dates; sometimes we would last a few months; but my heart was never in it, until I met Blair Hobbs in the spring of 1998. To talk, I squatted beside her table toward the back of the bar above City Grocery, bouncing on my toes to tamp down my nerves.

Blair's eyes flashed through a haze of cigarette smoke. She was smart and funny. She taught writing at the university during the day and painted at night. When Blair laughed, her cheeks sparkled with the glitter she sprinkled on canvasses. I couldn't tell if she was flirting, but I believed her when she said she liked my first *Oxford American* piece. Before I rose to my feet, Blair invited me to speak to one of her classes, and I scribbled my number on a napkin.

We leaned against the side of a desk at the front of her classroom. I spoke of my time on the streets of New Orleans working that hot dog cart, and of how I came to revere Alice, the vendor who protected me from the worst of the drunks. Blair asked about my plans after grad school. I told her students that I wanted to be a different kind of food writer. I would document people and place and explore race and class. I would show the nation and the world a South unsuspected.

Reaching for a copy of the *Oxford American* to show her students, Blair and I brushed elbows. And we blushed red. Her students laughed when I quoted a vendor who yelled at passersby: "Drink up, you slobs! You know the routine. Drink! Stumble! Dance! Eat a Lucky Dog! Go home!" As they laughed, I stole sidelong glances at Blair, her eyes full of mischief and wonder.

That afternoon, Blair dropped a vase of flowers on my stoop. When she returned to class the next week, her students teased. One raised a hand to report that I was single. Despite strong suggestions from friends, I didn't have enough sense to ask Blair out, so she invited me to her thirty-fourth birthday party.

After Blair blew out her candles, she stood on a chair to recite a poem. Her eyes sparkled this time, too. "Carnation milk is the best in the land / Here I sit with a can in my hand / No tits to pull / No hay to pitch / You just punch a hole in the son of a bitch."

On my way to the bathroom, a friend asked how long we had been dating. He expected me to say something like three months. Thirty minutes, I told him. Earlier that spring, Blair dated one of my Southern Studies classmates. He still seemed interested. When my classmate announced that he was moving to Charleston, South Carolina, I helped load his rental truck. Over the next couple of years, my travel and writing entwined. Blair and I entwined, too.

INSPIRED BY THAT FIRST ELVIS conference and its mix of smart talks and wild spectacles, I pitched the Center on a conference about food culture. Ann Abadie, the associate director, made me a deal: A year before, the Center hosted the tenth anniversary celebration for Viking Range, the Greenwood, Mississippi, company that pioneered commercial-style stoves for homes. To recognize the event and support the Center's work, Viking made a donation. If I could find matching dollars, that donation would help underwrite my proposal.

We gathered for the first Southern Foodways Symposium on the first weekend of May in 1998. John Egerton, the Nashville-based writer, wore a blue button-down and gray slacks and spoke just before lunch on the first day. Less than three years before, I sat in the same room in Barnard Observatory, listening to Southern Studies 101 lectures on *A Confederacy of Dunces*. Now the man whose book *Southern Food* had become my lodestar was speaking at my request before a sold-out crowd.

Egerton praised the speakers who came before him and the ones who would follow. He told a meandering joke about time and patience and the diet of a particularly well-fed pig. He talked about Southern dualities, of the natural bounty made possible by geography and climate, and the unnatural cruelties of slavery.

And he told us the most important thing of all: When we come together to talk about food, we join a long line of people who have recognized that, like oral and written literature, like jazz and bluegrass, dishes like barbecue and fried chicken are symbols of the world we made together. Gathered at this place at this time for this purpose, he said, we held the potential to help the South realize its long-deferred promise:

"If we put aside our social and political and circumstantial differences and lose ourselves in the moment, we can begin to imagine a table spread on common ground, where the lions and the lambs, the sheep and the goats, the rich and the poor, the old and the young, the vegetarians and the carnivores, the rainbow of hues—yeah, even the neocons and the crypto-liberals—will break biscuits and cornbread together, and sip from the same bottomless cup, and party on into the night, into the future. Southern food could do that. It really could."

Egerton closed by inviting us to lunch and suggesting that we go practice what he just preached. Frank Stitt of Highlands Bar and Grill in Birmingham cooked the keynote meal that weekend. Writing the menu, he claimed a common palate for the U.S. South and the South of France. Beneath a tent in the grove at the heart of campus, we ate grilled pig ears in mustard vinaigrette, freshly dug new potatoes, and asparagus.

Those ears tasted of Provence, where Stitt cooked with his mentor Richard Olney, and they spoke of Stitt's native Alabama, where pig parts are building blocks for rich and poor dishes. Blair weaved through the crowd, working as a volunteer server, wearing a red-and-white apron, passing platters of parts and vegetables.

Before the weekend came to a close, Jessica Harris, the scholar of African American life, stepped forward to talk about foodways as a means of cultural expression. Ed Scott, the first Black man to farm catfish in the Mississippi Delta, fried filets that floated to the surface, brown and crisp and clean. Norma Jean Darden, who co-wrote *Spoonbread and Strawberry Wine,* a cookbook portrait of a Black North Carolina family told through recipes, restaged the one-woman show she debuted in New York City. At the close of the play, staged in the courtroom of our courthouse, a white member of the audience stood to confess that back in North Carolina, before the war, his people might have enslaved her people.

To celebrate the symposium's success, a crowd gathered late that Saturday night at my rental house. We drank red wine and brown whiskey. Jessica, visiting my new state for the first time, played "Mississippi Goddam" by Nina Simone over and over again, as if, attuned to the peculiar history of the state, she wanted to exorcise all demons within earshot.

John Martin Taylor, who researched and wrote about low-country foods, also played DJ that night, toggling between Simone and the album *Everybody Hollerin' Goat* by local hero Otha Turner, famous for a kind of primal fife-and-drum music. We sang along with the gusto that a baseball crowd shout-sings "Sweet Caroline." After a phone call from Jessica, Blair made an appearance. "My house looks like a majorette blew up inside," she told the crowd, explaining why her sandaled feet were covered in bright paint and brighter glitter. Everyone smiled her way.

Blair was born in Oxford, where her father, Edward Hobbs, taught political science at the university and her mother, Marleah

Kaufman Hobbs, earned a master's degree in fine art. During the 1962 crisis, her father signed a public letter in support of integration. Four years later, a local member of the state's Institutions of Higher Learning derailed his promotion to dean of the College of Liberal Arts. When Blair was three, her family moved to Auburn, Alabama.

For almost a quarter century her father served as dean of the School of Arts and Sciences at Auburn University and her mother taught art. After graduate school, Blair moved back to Mississippi. In Oxford, she joined her brother, Mit Hobbs, sixteen years older, who stayed in town for college and raised a family there after medical school. Stepping into the world that Mit and Blair made, I joined a sprawling family of brilliant people, the kind I had read about in books but never seen up close.

A year later, my father and friends from Atlanta stood beside me at our wedding in Oxford. When the preacher made his pronouncements and we were supposed to turn serious, I asked anxiously if it was time to kiss Blair. He nodded and we burst into snorts of laughter. The Tremé Brass Band, which I first heard play the year before during a New Orleans reporting trip, led a second line parade to our reception at Off Square Books. Instead of stopping, we looped the square, trumpets blaring, tuba bellowing, friends twirling parasols.

ON JULY 22, 1999, THREE WEEKS after Blair and I returned from our honeymoon, the founders of the Southern Foodways Alliance, a new organization focused on the study of food, convened a meeting in Birmingham. We gathered in a soaring atrium at the center of the Southern Progress corporate campus, inspired by the energy that came out of that first symposium I organized. The name of the parent company for *Southern Living* magazine was not lost on the thirty people who made the trek.

John Egerton, who recruited the founders along with television host and cookbook author Nathalie Dupree, spoke to "a pervasive spirit of inclusiveness that is deeply rooted in the belief that Southern food is the region's most positive and appealing symbol." To live up to that ideal, he engineered an honestly diverse group that reflected the South, even as he tried to conceal his intent, claiming that the founders coalesced without much effort.

Crescent Dragonwagon made the trek from the Ozark Mountains of Arkansas. A back-to-the-land hippie who ran a bed-and-breakfast and wrote cookbooks, she was working to turn her old space into a new writers colony. Van Sykes drove from nearby Bessemer, Alabama, where he ran Bob Sykes Bar-B-Q, founded by his father in 1957. Norma Jean Darden flew down from New York City. Jim Auchmutey, the *Atlanta Journal-Constitution* writer who would go on to describe stock-car racer Richard Petty as a "lean strip of jerky," drove in from Atlanta. Kathy Starr, a soul food cookbook author from the Mississippi Delta town of Hollandale, walked up the winding blacktop and into the room when her husband's eighteen-wheeler failed to make it up the hill.

Fifteen years later, at the height of Southern Foodways Alliance's influence and power, the organization would claim 1,500-plus members and an annual budget of more than $1.5 million. But in the summer of 1999, SFA was a wobbly idea, buoyed by Egerton's optimism. And I was a recent graduate of the Southern Studies program, living off sporadic income from freelance writing. Gathered at a U-shaped table, flanked by two flip charts, we talked for two days in Birmingham about what was being lost as ham curers and cushaw gardeners and pitmasters died. We spoke of what we might do together and of how our work could help realize a better South that seemed to stand forever on the horizon.

Seven years before, Eugene Walter of Mobile, Alabama, gave a video interview from a four-poster bed during a conference on Southern food at Seaside, Florida. Wearing a yellow guayabera, he railed about the ersatz Southern food served in New York and proclaimed the munificence of the Gulf. All the while, he purred and chortled and charmed. Sinking back into the pillows, Walter declared that oral history programs and archives should be established, before all the cooks of his generation died off. In that Birmingham conference room, we began to explore what Eugene had imagined.

Notes transcribed from flip-chart scribbles promised service projects, documentary films, and public events. Before we adjourned, the founders elected me as director, and the Center agreed to incubate the effort and furnish us with office space. Leah Chase of New Orleans, the reigning queen of Creole cuisine, was appointed to serve as president of our board of directors. After we adjourned, Pardis and Frank Stitt invited all to dine at Highlands Bar and Grill and celebrate the possibilities.

Less than a year later, Blair posed for a picture in the backyard of our new home, purchased the same month we married. Pregnant and smiling, she stands beside a mound of red dirt dug by construction workers laying in a foundation for a bigger kitchen and a new bedroom. On the afternoon of March 27, 2001, Blair gave birth to our son in Oxford. We named him Jesse Clifton Evans Edge, after my mother's father.

Willie Mae Seaton and Kerry Seaton, New Orleans

Chapter Six

SCOTCH HOUSE

In the lead-up to the publication of *Southern Belly* in 2000, a *USA Today* reporter did a ride-along with me across Alabama. Using my book about restaurants and their histories as our guide, we tracked the ghost of civil rights activist Georgia Gilmore of Montgomery, severed from her job as a cook at a downtown restaurant after she testified about the abuse she suffered on a bus ride. And we ate barbecue sandwiches of chopped pork and mustard-cut vinegar sauce at Ollie's, the Birmingham restaurant that lost its fight to segregate customers in a 1964 Supreme Court case law students still parse today.

Between meals, I tried out some of the theories I developed for Southern Foodways Alliance events and *Oxford American* columns. *All conversations about the South should center race,* I told the reporter. *Class and gender are important, too,* I said. *But race is the truth*

to confront, and writing about food is the best way to get there. I hadn't
yet seized on the more accurate idea that racism—persecution based
on perception of race and abuse of of power—was the real problem.

I talked about the need for context, too, arguing that when you
bite into a barbecue sandwich at Ollie's, you open yourself to the
story of Black Birmingham, forbidden by the white owners from
eating inside their restaurant. If an Ollie's sandwich wrapped in
white tissue is the text, I said, thinking of my graduate school
classes, then the context is the stories that swirl around that stack of
meat and bread, including the love-thy-neighbor Christianity pro-
claimed by the owners and the beliefs they carried in their heads
about so-called dirty Black bodies and pure white minds.

The writer poked gentle fun at the earnestness I wore like a
full-sleeve tattoo, replaying the lecture on transgression in liminal
spaces I gave outside a roadhouse west of Birmingham, where the
owner was known to get drunk and dance with a broom. The arti-
cle, which ran when *USA Today* was the most widely distributed
paper in the nation, called me "the country's brightest young pro-
ponent of Southern food" and connected my new book to my first,
a tribute to community cookbook recipes that I co-wrote with
Ellen Rolfes. Published the year before and nominated for a James
Beard Award, *A Gracious Plenty* paid my graduate school stipend
and funded some of the start-up costs for the Southern Foodways
Alliance.

A generation before, music writers made the same argument I
was trying to make now: To understand a people and a place, em-
phasize the stories that working people tell. During the folk revival
that peaked in the early 1960s, white college students sat at the
feet of aged bluesmen to learn how to play three-chord progressions
and mispronounce the lyrics correctly. The place to be this time was
the pit room and the sounds to listen for were the draw and crackle

of a well-laid hickory fire. Resistance to my ideas, I believed, was grounded in holdover biases that diminished people of color and the products of their work, beginning with blues and barbecue, extending to jazz and gumbo.

Back in my old college town of Athens to give a conference talk based on my master's thesis about potlikker and cornbread as cultural symbols, I spoke to a reporter for the weekly who wrote a smart article with a smarter headline: DID FOUCAULT DUNK HIS CORNPONE? His reference to the French theorist made it clear that we both took the work seriously.

As I began to publish, I became subject as well as narrator. No matter how much I talked about Georgia Gilmore and the risks she took to fuel the movement, newspaper and magazine writers asked for stories about my grandmothers. They wanted to report on my time scurrying around their kitchens, clinging to their apron hems. They wanted to know if my mother's mother cut lard or butter into her biscuit flour.

My maternal grandmother was famous for cheese waffles, but she died four years before I was born. My father's favorite childhood supper was a sleeve of crackers and a can of sardines, the filets dug from the brine with a butter knife. I rarely shared those stories. Instead, as tape recorders whirred, I told newspaper and magazine writers that my mother taught me how to fluff a pot of rice with a fork and choose the smallest and tenderest pods for fried okra. My father cooked pots of grits that spit and hissed on the stove, I told them. For company, he salt-roasted haunches of prime rib to rare and served dinner with the lights turned low to hide the pooling blood from guests who thought they wanted their beef well-done.

What I really wanted to talk about, though, were the restaurants from my childhood that I claimed as second homes. I spoke of Len Berg's, set in the alley across from my father's Macon office, where they served a summer plate of deviled eggs and cold fried chicken. I talked about the black-eyed peas that Deacon Lyndell Burton cooked to a porridge in a screen-door-fronted café near his Atlanta church, and about the time civil rights veteran John Lewis flew the deacon to Washington to fry thighs and drumsticks for a fundraiser at the Democratic National Committee Headquarters.

Telling stories about other places and other people, I draped my home in a cloak, hiding our life there from view, trying to convince magazine readers and symposium audiences that the important narratives of my life began at Old Clinton Bar-B-Q in one of those ladder-back chairs, with a vinegar-doused sandwich in hand.

Those stories were true. But they weren't the whole truth. Instead of talking of the dark woods that encircled the general's birthplace, or the dark stories that shaped my childhood, I sketched scenes of Mittie Coulter, a cumulus of gray curls atop her head, working a cleaver, weighing hashed pork on a white metal scale.

In the concrete-floored dining room of my mind, I crumble saltines into a bowl of Brunswick stew and mop the bottom with a slice of light rye. I unfold a tissue-wrapped bundle of pork and bun and inhale the vinegar updraft. I reach into the slide-top cooler for a Mountain Dew and chug half the bottle before I sit down.

I wasn't ready to say then that I claimed Old Clinton Bar-B-Q as home because death and drinking wrecked my home. I hadn't figured out how to talk about what went wrong there. I didn't see how the stories of decline and loss that united much of the white South connected to the disease that ruined my beautiful and brilliant mother. I hadn't faced down what drove me out of my childhood house to another house, where smoke swirled the eaves and cinders floated toward the sky.

...

TWO MONTHS AFTER JESS WAS BORN, the Mid-Town Farmers' Market opened in a shopping center parking lot north of the Oxford square. Earlier that spring, I had written an open letter to our newspaper, inviting farmers and eaters to gather in the courthouse, in the shadow of that Confederate statue, to talk about reviving our weekly market. We began with eight vendors. Tomatoes would not show for a month or more, so farmers sold cabbage and carrots. To fill the gaps, my friend Dorothy Howorth, whom I met when I worked the register at Square Books, pulled lettuce from her garden.

Americans then gravitated to people like Alice Waters, the Berkeley, California, chef who founded the Edible Schoolyard Project and preached the gospel of organic farming and farmers markets. They quoted her neighbor Michael Pollan, a journalist who studied broken supply chains and argued that the U.S. food system was a problem to be solved.

Friends asked if the Southern Foodways Alliance tried the same tack, organizing markets or returning honest food to public schools. I told them that I worked on our Oxford market because I wanted to shop there. SFA had different goals for the South. Instead of seeing the food system as a roster of problems, SFA saw a galaxy of people who spanned the region, with stories to tell about the role of food in their communities.

Oral history work, collecting personal stories that added up to society portraits, became our preferred tool. At first, we used *Southern Belly* as a search aid, pulling narratives from those pages as prompts. Our oral historians interviewed Delta cooks who rolled hot tamales in parchment paper and stewed them in tomato gravy. They stood in pit rooms while men stoked burn barrels and camped out in converted home kitchens where women fried chicken in skillets the size of truck tires.

Rather than build gardens as a solution, SFA worked to gather and reframe the stories on which the South built its collective identity. SFA does humanities work, we said. We play the long game, like the Federal Writers' Project did in the 1930s. Fifty years in the future, reading through our archives, the rest of the country would figure out the power of what we do. Until then, we planned to keep our heads down and let that work speak for us. The impact would show in the faces of the people whose stories we helped tell. By including people previously left out, we seeded progress. Holding up a mirror to the South, we showed our people who they really were. Progress would come slowly, but it would come.

We began our work long before the current run of food festivals, which book chefs to stand behind folding tables beneath tents, serving two-ounce tasting portions of their signature shrimp and something in cardboard boats to day drinkers looped on rosé. Chefs came to SFA symposia in search of community. Working in the City Grocery kitchens with John Currence and his crew to serve multicourse meals, they built alliances that bound Alabama to North Carolina and Charleston to Nashville. In the process, our sprawling region gained a new kind of coherence.

Regulars to their restaurants came to hang with their favorite chefs and to meet chefs from across the South and beyond. They returned home with their cell phone numbers and promises of hard-to-get reservations at Bacchanalia in Atlanta, Herbsaint in New Orleans, or Gramercy Tavern in New York City. Academics in search of audiences beyond the ivy followed, attracted by the press we earned. Writers for magazines and newspapers, trying to draw a bead on a changing region, reported stories from the annual symposia that illustrated past sins and current advances.

We modeled the South we wanted to serve. Around 25 percent of Southerners were Black, so SFA worked to book speakers at that same rate. At a time when too many nonprofits asked presenters to speak for free, we paid all and reimbursed for travel, too. The prices we charged for symposium tickets reflected our attempt at equitable treatment of all.

SFA gave no free tickets to press. We limited the tickets we gave to donors, too, arguing that every ticket we gave away translated to one less audience member. At a time when every SFA event sold out and most required that we keep waiting lists, that distinction mattered. SFA accepted money from donors who supported our mission instead of sponsors who wanted product placement. The real benefit they got was the halo effect of SFA's implicit endorsement and the chance to spend three days with the most culturally engaged audience in the world of food.

In the South we projected back to that world, all symposia participants held the same power. In the early years, speakers stood in front of the stage, down on the floor, on the same level as the audience. We removed all titles before speaker names, treating professors with doctorates the same as row-crop farmers with primary school educations. Our programming was designed to be a democratizing force.

Every detail mattered: We often sat at communal tables, according to arrangements designed to disrupt cliques. For a lunch of collards and cornbread, we played a soundtrack of songs about greens. For a dinner that celebrated kitchen labor, guests dined beneath art installations made from mopheads. When we studied pop culture, lunch came in McDonald's-inspired Pappy Meal boxes with airline bottles of the Van Winkle family's bourbon.

University of Mississippi lecture halls were our forums. Before each symposium began, I moved the Mississippi state flag, then inset with a Confederate battle flag, from its place beside the lectern to behind a curtain or potted plant. It was easy to hide a flag behind a ficus. As SFA reach expanded, we would have to work harder to make our intent clear.

I can picture the moment, at a festival in Beaufort, South Carolina. We had just screened a film about Helen Turner, the Brownsville, Tennessee, pitmaster who sold three-dollar pork sandwiches with slaw to stoop-shouldered men in dungarees and tired-eyed women in nurses' hospital scrubs. We gathered in a chapel, surrounded by wizened oaks draped with Spanish moss. A booze cruise floated the marsh. From the shore we could hear their hoots and hollers.

"Where does her pork come from?" asked a guy toward the back in a golf sweater with the insignia of his country club, probably thinking of Pollan.

There are more important things to consider, I said, in what I hoped was a kind tone. *I don't care if her shoulders come from free-range hogs fed organic grains. What matters is whether Helen can feed her family off the money she makes selling sandwiches from those shoulders. Can her customers who live paycheck to paycheck afford to eat those sandwiches? Can her barbecue feed her people?*

SFA flummoxed people like the guy in the golf sweater. We privileged stories of people who weren't privileged. We believed that our films and oral histories and events were restorative. To make our point, we quoted John Egerton, who corralled that first meeting of SFA founders. We were "paying down the debts of pleasure" owed to previous generations.

IN THE FALL OF 2002, John Egerton hauled me up from Nashville to nearby Mount Juliet for an afternoon visit with Reverend Will D. Campbell. I had heard them both speak in my first year in Oxford.

Eight months after Campbell gave that talk at the Elvis conference, Egerton drove down for the Oxford Conference for the Book. His 1994 book, *Speak Now Against the Day*, told the story of the activists and dreamers who had struggled to reimagine the South before the *Brown* decision. Standing in front of the register at Square Books, he inscribed my copy of *Southern Food*: "A little pork, a little corn, and the rest is history."

Over the next two decades, I would borrow much from Egerton. Most of all, I borrowed the idea that food and civil rights, the subjects of his two big books, had something to say to each other. We usually met at his writing office in suburban Nashville, a tight space on the other side of the carport from the ranch house he shared with his wife, Ann. As SFA grew, Egerton became the voice in my ear, challenging me to skirt petty conversations about who got credit for what and, instead, live up to the promise he talked about during that first symposium.

He did his best work at the back of a room, working a crowd like a preacher after a sermon. I picture Egerton in a sweater-vest, looking like a conservative backbencher, standing close to make a point, his eyes scrunched up and boring in, his arm around someone's neck, in a gesture of genial embrace. He would start out by saying: *This probably isn't the kind of thing you want to do. You're too busy for this. Somebody else should be doing this. But while I have you*—and he always had you—*maybe you'll hear me out?*

On the day Egerton and I arrived in Mount Juliet, we found Campbell in the backyard, beside an old hatchback car parked in front of his log cabin office. In the back seat, a baby gurgled and grinned at the kindly old man who bent over the bassinet. "You are now de-bastardized," Campbell said to the child after he married the young parents. His eyes crinkled and glinted when he smiled. The hippie couple looked down at their feet, embarrassed and happy. Notebook in hand, trying to capture the scene in my head, I laughed too loud and too long.

Near the close of our Mount Juliet visit, Campbell snapped, angry that I was taking notes instead of staying in the moment while he played "Rednecks, White Socks, and Blue Ribbon Beer" on a battered Gibson acoustic. To smooth things, Egerton passed around a jar of white dog that Campbell called the Ark of the Covenant.

If Egerton's morality reminded me of my father, Campbell, who was willing to say most anything to anyone, reminded me of the best of my mother. As I got to know him, I never grew fully comfortable in his presence. I had company: Campbell unsettled three generations of Southerners who recognized that he spoke truths about the hypocrisies that make us human. When he demanded that we join him in facing those hypocrisies down, most of us flinched or sidestepped.

Egerton told a story about Campbell touring a church that had amassed money and property. The preacher in charge wanted to hear the iconoclast talk about how to move forward in turbulent times. I remember that Egerton set his story in Dallas. Later, when I dug for corroboration, I found a similar encounter in New York City. Both versions closed with the same scene: When the preacher of the wealthy church asked what to do, Campbell said, *Sell it all. Take the money and give it to poor people.*

In *Brother to a Dragonfly,* his first memoir, Campbell wrote about the people who came before him, and about his brother, Joe, who, despite his best intentions and because of his addictions, couldn't quit making bad decisions. Campbell's brother's life read like a metaphor for the South, a place hamstrung by the bad decisions of powerful men and the people who deferred to them, from the overthrow of Reconstruction to mass resistance in the face of school integration. Those decisions, Campbell suggested, could undo a person; they could ruin a people.

Campbell's second memoir, *Forty Acres and a Goat,* retold his civil rights experience, against a backdrop of a South that was splintering into factions. In 1966, when Stokely Carmichael, the new chairman of the Student Nonviolent Coordinating Committee, told him he should work with his own people, Campbell made a bold change. White people needed the gospel, too. Especially poor white people, the rednecks of his Elvis speech from my first summer in Oxford, driven by poverty and fear to do the ugly bidding of the wealthy and powerful. "If you're going to love one, you've got to love them all," he would say, laying out his simple and radical take on Christianity.

After the Grand Dragon of North Carolina was indicted and tried for contempt of Congress, Campbell prayed with him in jail. "Prisoners are prisoners," he later told a conference audience of religious leaders. "And it is our vocation to set them free." Campbell told Klansmen the same thing he shared with that young couple he married at his cabin: "We're all bastards, but God loves us anyway."

EACH YEAR SFA EMBRACED A THEME for our research and programming. Creolization highlighted the many peoples from many places who forged what we call the South. Appalachia and the Gulf South got their due when we focused on regionality. In 2004, we marked the fortieth anniversary of the Civil Rights Act of 1964, the federal law that Ollie's in Birmingham fought with such vigor.

To frame our goals, I wrote a mission statement: "The SFA believes that racial chasms can be bridged when we recognize our common humanity across a table piled high with bowls of collard greens, platters of cornbread. We believe that food is our region's greatest shared creation. And we see food as a unifier in a diverse region, as a means by which we may address the issues that have long vexed our homeland."

Campbell made the trek to our fall symposium to deliver a homily. Diane McWhorter, who won the Pulitzer Prize for *Carry Me Home,* talked about kitchen relations in the Birmingham of her youth, tracking stories from the streets Bull Connor's men patrolled to the dining room of the Mountain Brook Club, where Black men in white jackets served a whites-only clientele. Austin Leslie, who rose to fame in 1980s New Orleans as the Black analogue to Paul Prudhomme and the inspiration for the TV show *Frank's Place,* fried chicken in the pasture across from our house and served it with a confetti of chopped pickles and garlic.

Beaten and jailed more than twenty-five times for movement work, Bernard Lafayette spoke of his time at Parchman Prison in 1961. The audience expected to hear stories of torture. Instead, they learned about the power of humanity. After police arrested students during a Freedom Riders' stop in Jackson, Mississippi, Lafayette told us, a prison trustee smuggled in pints of ice cream hidden in a mop bucket.

Before the weekend was over, I stepped to the stage with Susan Glisson, director of the William Winter Institute for Racial Reconciliation at Ole Miss, to present Campbell with a plaque that recognized him as university chaplain, the job he worked from 1954 to 1956 as resistance to the *Brown* decision mounted. Because the university no longer maintained that position, Campbell became chaplain for life.

"What took you so long?" he asked the audience. After the nervous laughter died down, Campbell turned serious. "I have received a number of so-called honors in my life," he said. "But unless one is honored by his own people, he is not honored at all. I have never forgotten that you are my people, and I have never been more honored."

You are my people. That's a strong reciprocal phrase for a Mississippian to use. Campbell spoke to the university that rejected him and the state where he came up. He spoke to all who struggle through a complicated relationship to a place and its people. We may claim otherwise, but many of us from those complicated places want to love those people. Despite their actions and beliefs, because we see ourselves in them, because those people are family, friends, wives, husbands, children. Because they are us.

Campbell's point of view ran counter to the common liberal take on my native region, in which dutiful sons and daughters claim to both love and hate the South. Faulkner wrote that refrain into his novels. So did generations of writers who followed. Campbell's take was more radical. He would not allow a straddle. We were all culpable for the South's shortcomings. We were all beneficiaries of its beauties.

ON A SUNDAY AFTERNOON IN THE FALL OF 2006, I sat with Reverend Will D. Campbell in the ellipse between the Lyceum and the library, at the center of the Ole Miss campus, to witness the unveiling of a civil rights monument. Ten years had passed since Chancellor Robert Khayat agreed that our student-led group could install an artwork here to commemorate the struggle for equal access to education. This was not that artwork.

Before us stood a bronze sculpture of James Meredith, who integrated our university in a hail of bullets and a cloud of tear gas. Crafted by Rod Moorhead, a white sculptor from Oxford, Meredith wears a suit and strides toward two limestone pillars. He walks purposefully toward the threshold, but does not breach the door. This Meredith hasn't integrated the university. Frozen in bronze, he never will.

Susan Glisson sat between Campbell and me on that day in 2006. Campbell asked us to join him for the unveiling and the chance to hear his old friend John Lewis speak. He wanted us to listen and reflect. Maybe to reconcile. When it became clear that Khayat would not mention our group's effort in his introductory remarks, Campbell grabbed me by the leg, grimaced, and grinned that same shy grin he flashed at those young parents the day we met.

Back in 2002, Terry Adkins, chair of the art department at the University of Pennsylvania, won our commission. He came to the work with a strong vita and a compelling story. In Virginia, where Adkins grew up, he integrated his grade school. Adkins presented a relatively conservative plan for two sets of archways, topped by concrete plinths, inscribed with the words "Freedom Forevermore" and "Justice Henceforth." Glass panels, printed with short aphorisms, would hang like symbolic doors from each tower: "Teach in Fear No More." "Learn in Fear No More." "Insist in Fear No More." And "Unite in Fear No More."

To understand the scale he proposed, university carpenters built a plywood version and installed it in the ellipse. A small model went on display in the student union. The university issued a press release to celebrate the moment and used a version of the artwork to publicize the fortieth anniversary of integration.

But Ed Linenthal's warning that public art always got complicated haunted us. Khayat and Adkins disagreed over changes to the placement of the work. An architect from Jackson made a case that the doors were hazardous. Conservative alumni, still upset that Ole Miss now made it hard for them to wave their Confederate battle flags at football games, suggested that Khayat scrap the project. Contractors, willing to do the work at budget, came and went. Most important, Khayat argued with Susan and me over whether Adkins's use of the word *fear* was appropriate.

In 2005, Khayat cancelled the installation of Adkins's sculpture and redirected the money to a new committee, formed to choose a quick replacement. Offered a chance to join, Susan and I declined, thinking of our decade of methodical consensus building and fund-raising. I published an open letter in the campus newspaper, in which I pushed back against his rejection of the word *fear,* when "two people were shot and killed—within sight of your office window."

"This is a day to rejoice," Lewis said on that Sunday afternoon in 2006, standing before a crowd of more than a thousand. "With the unveiling of this monument, we free ourselves from the chains of a difficult past." Lewis challenged us that day. Tough times will buffet us all, he said. "Stay with the house," he implored, stay with the cause, stay fixed on a better South. He was talking to all of us. He was talking to me. And I was struggling to hear him.

Eight years later, during Black History Month, white under-graduates looped a rope around Meredith's bronze neck. To make their point, they wrapped his chest in the old Georgia state flag, which included the Confederate battle flag.

When our group first began to host biweekly meetings in 1996, we made a decision: The art we commissioned would not depict a human figure. Recent civil rights movement scholarship steered away from great-man depictions of history. Plus, we said with mo-rose humor, if we install a sculpture of a Black man on a campus with a history of taking violent stances against Black men, someone will eventually lynch that Black man. We never wanted to be right about that.

· · ·

DURING THAT LONG STRETCH BETWEEN the beginning of our sculpture project in 1996 and its unhappy resolution in 2006, I plunged deeper into SFA work, believing that I could get more done when I had more control over the plans and processes, the images and words. We hired Amy Evans as our oral historian. Recently graduated from the Southern Studies master's program, she waded through the pluff mud near Charleston to interview oyster pickers, trying hard to capture a way of work in retreat. We began commissioning films from another graduate, Joe York, who started documenting the work of barbecue pitmasters. Joe scored his first short barbecue film with jazz, as if to say that both are great American art forms.

No matter how much oral history and film work we did in the offseason, the world came our way in the fall. SFA life revolved around the fall symposium, staged in Oxford and on campus, in which we wove together high and low, borrowing from academic research, narrative journalism, and popular culture.

We asked speakers questions that got their attention. Calvin Trillin of *The New Yorker* accepted our invitation because he never imagined any group would stage a symposium on barbecue. Olu Dara, the jazz and pop great who grew up in Natchez, played his first Mississippi show in decades. Asked why he stayed gone so long, he said, "No one asked me to come back."

From our stage, Alice Randall, a Vanderbilt professor and novelist, shared the story of famed gospel singer Mahalia Jackson's 1970s fried chicken enterprise, which began in Memphis and spread to Black communities in the South and Midwest. What seemed like a Colonel Sanders copycat, she said, was a bold experiment in inner-city job training and Black wealth development.

In a mock debate, Kim Severson of *The New York Times* and

Kat Kinsman, then of CNN, argued about how and why baked goods are cultural and emotional barometers for women. Making scripted points, occasionally diverting to playful trash talk, they answered the question "Which is more essential—cake or pie?" Half the audience screamed with laughter. The other half seemed to get the big ideas about the value of labor and the expectations of gender bound up in that moment.

Symposia were part colloquium, part carnival. Will Harris, a cattle rancher from Georgia who raised his animals on grass and called them athletes, drove to Oxford in a pickup stacked with iced-down cow heads. To make barbacoa in the Mexican American tradition, two chefs cooked those heads in a wood-fired pit. The Oxford firefighters who arrived to douse the illegal blaze put down their hoses and stayed to eat tacos de cabeza, sluiced with salsa verde and showered with cilantro.

Viking Range founder Fred Carl sent the company plane to fetch organic foods advocate Alice Waters from Berkeley to talk about the legacy of Edna Lewis, the grande dame of Southern cuisine. On her way to the stage, Waters passed through an arbor of fried bacon strips that my colleague Melissa Hall hung from denuded branches with Christmas tree hooks. I can still see Bill Smith, the chef at Crook's Corner in Chapel Hill, North Carolina, standing beneath, mouth open, trying to catch the grease that dripped onto the sidewalk. Melissa didn't build that forest from windblown branches and Walmart bacon so that Alice would pass beneath. That was just a post-symposium bonus story we got to tell.

Blair and Jess steered clear of much of it. Neither liked the way that SFA consumed me. I did much of my work on the road, meeting with donors, emceeing fundraisers, moderating conference panels. The symposium brought that work to our doorstep. The collision of my two worlds left our family off-balance. Each Sunday, though, when the weeklong sprint was almost over, we three came together to watch the final performance of the weekend.

Emotionally connected by conversations that began on Thursday, our Sunday morning audiences treated those events like secular church services. We staged a collard opera, written by Cecil Price Walden, then an undergraduate at Ole Miss, based on a book of poems from North Carolina and costumed by the designer Natalie Chanin. We hosted a ballet called *Pork Songs,* performed by dancers from Ballet Memphis, who rooted and romped across the stage as the recorded voice of Huey "Piano" Smith sang "Gimme Gimme Chitlins."

Each time we staged an SFA event, I was twenty again, dancing in the Sigma Nu basement as Dexter from the Flat Duo Jets screamed and howled, egging on the dancers to shake harder and twirl faster. Or I was twenty-one, planning our Woodstock, worrying over whether the color soak for the tie-dyed T-shirts would hold and the Doors cover band would show.

SFA at its best felt subversive like that. Propulsive, even. As if by putting the right speaker in the right room, by booking the ideal chef to cook the keynote lunch, we could conjure, for a long weekend, maybe longer, a reconciled South where all would prosper.

THE FINAL DINNER OF OUR 2002 fall symposium, the one that hooked Calvin Trillin, floats back into view. John Shelton Reed, a pioneering Southern Studies scholar, made a case for North Carolina as the cultural hearth of modern barbecue. Jack Hitt, the writer of a *New York Times Magazine* story about the role of barbecue in the fractured politics of South Carolina, spoke of Maurice Bessinger, the owner of Maurice's Piggie Park in Columbia, who ran a losing campaign for governor while sometimes wearing a white suit, riding a white horse, and distributing flyers that declared "You are white because your ancestors believed in segregation."

We heard Marcie Ferris, the scholar of Jewish foodways, report from a kosher barbecue contest run by a temple in Memphis, Tennessee, where a rack of pork ribs might as well be the coat of arms. Lolis Elie, the New Orleans–based journalist and SFA founder, explained and exploded the "natural rhythm theory" of barbecue excellence, a belief on the part of some whites that most Blacks were born to cook. Intelligence and experience were the earned roots of that genius, Lolis said, speaking in a cadence he learned from his father, a civil rights attorney and activist.

Rain fell all day as pitmasters stoked fires and heaved pigs onto oak- and hickory-fed pits. In the field across from our house, Ed Mitchell from North Carolina chopped whole hogs into brown and black threads while talking about how, on the eastern flank of the state, where he was from and where tobacco was once the dominant crop, whole-hog barbecue began as a harvest feed, cooked by Black men like him to celebrate getting bunches of tobacco leaves tied and hung in barns.

Inside our house, three men sat in club chairs, waiting for the rain to let up. Calvin Trillin of *The New Yorker* cracked sly jokes at his own expense. Johnny Apple of *The New York Times* held a spiral notebook. Blair offered a platter of cheese wafers to Otha Turner, the great fife-and-drum musician from nearby Gravel Springs who captured John Martin Taylor's attention during the Saturday night after-party near the end of that first symposium.

Turner would soon heave up from that chair and march through the crowd playing "Shimmy She Wobble" on a cane fife. Gesturing toward the round wafers, each bull's-eyed with a sliced black olive,

Blair asked, "Would you care for a kitty butthole?" Turner and Trillin howled. Apple scribbled in his notebook. And Blair went to pull another tray of buttholes from the oven.

Three days later, Apple published a report on the front page of *The New York Times*. He wrote about the change he had witnessed in Oxford, flashing back to the fight to integrate our school in 1962. And he used that moment to frame the SFA, whose board was then led by Toni Tipton-Martin, the first Black woman to edit the food page of a major U.S. newspaper.

It mattered, Apple made clear, that a Black woman was at the helm. And it mattered that we were doing this work out of the University of Mississippi. When we gathered for lunches in the grove at the heart of campus, in sight of the spot where French journalist Paul Guihard died, we were making change by changing the stories people told of this place. In that moment, we believed Oxford was the most powerful place to do that work. In that moment, we may have been right.

CELEBRATORY ACTIVISM: That's what my colleague Melissa Hall said we were attempting when SFA brought together smart people under the banner of a smart topic. Serving food and drink that drove conversations and abetted reckonings, we made a bet that SFA could pull a New South out of an Old South, like a bunny out of a hat.

I worked on instinct. Melissa, a native of eastern Kentucky who began working for SFA after volunteering for a symposium on Appalachia, wanted to actually understand why people reacted with passion to our work. As the organization grew, she became our event manager and people manager. Trained as a lawyer, she asked hard questions of our organization. As we grew and our influence spread, people outside SFA began to ask hard questions, too.

In *A More Beautiful and Terrible History,* Jeanne Theoharis writes about Martin Luther King Jr. and Rosa Parks. She says contemporary observers have stripped them of their subversive power and muted their revolutionary message. Our worshipfulness, she says, has disconnected them from their heirs. King and Parks have become "Thanksgiving parade balloons," she writes, "floating above us larger than life; unthreatening, happy patriots. Asking little of us, they bob along, proud of our progress."

Celebratory activism, Theoharis suggests, has its limits. The SFA had limits, too. Our work was too popular for academics, focused on pedagogy and tenure. Activists, who wanted us to program take-downs of agribusiness abuse, complained that our work was too subtle, more focused on historical narratives than contemporary issues. There were other limits, too, bound up in our original promise to reconcile a South torn apart by racism. We would stage more than twenty fall symposia before those limits became clear.

ON AN OCTOBER AFTERNOON IN 2005, two months after Hurricane Katrina walloped the Gulf Coast, Willie Mae Seaton stared at the water stain that ringed her corner building in New Orleans. Downed trees and storm-tossed cars blocked the sidewalk near her double shotgun in the Tremé neighborhood. The air stank of sewage, a gagging rancid funk. The place just needs a good mucking out, she thought; maybe some of the furniture might need to go.

A police cruiser pulled up, and an officer with the city's homeless task force got out. To explain herself, Willie Mae pulled a plastic bag from her purse and a bronze medal from the bag.

The medallion marked a night in New York City, five months before. Accompanied by her twenty-five-year-old great-granddaughter, Kerry Seaton, she received a James Beard Award that May for her neighborhood restaurant. Willie Mae moved slowly toward the stage that night. Each row stood to applaud as the eighty-eight-year-old woman walked the aisle.

The sparse beauty of Willie Mae's acceptance speech moved the crowd. When she said, "I'm so full, baby, I'm just so full," they cheered and whistled. They stomped and shouted and cried. At the reception afterward, Willie Mae promised well-wishers, *If you travel to New Orleans, I'll be there to cook for you.*

Evacuated to Houston as Hurricane Katrina bore down on the Gulf Coast, Willie Mae had returned to New Orleans the same morning she met the officer. Blue tarps covered roofs in the city. High winds ripped apart some; others gaped open after desperate families, trying to escape rising waters, hatcheted and chainsawed their way out of attics to wave down helicopters.

The scene at her house was far worse than Willie Mae knew. Her shotgun double took on four feet of water. In her living room, sludge soaked through the white linoleum and buckled the wall paneling. On the other side, in her restaurant kitchen, mixing bowls overflowed with muck and dislodged plaster, and cans of green beans rusted and ruptured. A refrigerator, the eggs and milk inside gone putrid, leaked what looked like pus.

In 1940, when she was twenty-four, Willie Mae and her husband moved south from Crystal Springs, Mississippi. Nothing could match the wages paid by the shipyards. L. S. Seaton found work at Higgins Industries, where men built the landing crafts for D-Day. Willie Mae drove a cab and worked for a dry cleaner. In 1957, she opened a bar where she won local fame for a cocktail of Johnnie Walker Black Label and milk. Pulled from the rubble during the rebuild, a photo from that era shows Seaton standing proud behind the bar, eyes shining bright.

Customers smelled the fried chicken and white beans that Willie Mae cooked for her family. They soon asked her to cook for them, too. No sign announced the restaurant that grew out of that bar. She didn't post a menu by the door. Before *The Times-Picayune* published an article about the Scotch House in 1999, the reporter agreed to withhold the address and phone number. Willie Mae didn't want any pictures, either. Hers was a neighborhood spot where she knew your Friday order by heart, not a tourist destination shilled by a hotel concierge.

Before the storm, Willie Mae's Scotch House ran on the barest of crews. Willie Mae Seaton usually cooked alone. Her son, a cabdriver, worked part-time, fetching supplies from the grocery store and waiting tables at lunch. After the levees gave way and dirty water filled in much of the city like a bowl, a Colorado-based group called the Heritage Conservation Network decided to rebuild Willie Mae's.

Like so many organizations that cared about New Orleans, they were looking for ways to lay hands on a smaller project wrapped up in a big American moment. They talked about the import of vernacular structures and "restoring the fabric of a neighborhood." Looking for volunteer labor, they emailed SFA. They had the skills. We just needed to bring in the labor. Only later did we realize that in addition to asking practical questions, we should have asked existential ones, like *What purpose will our work serve?* And *Who will benefit?*

AS SFA ROSE, I DID, TOO. NPR booked me as a regular commentator in 2005. Each month, Debbie Elliott, host of the weekend edition of *All Things Considered,* called to talk about whatever I obsessed over. We would speak for twenty minutes, she and her colleagues would edit me down to four or five, and a few hundred thousand people would hear me hold forth on the pleasures of hyper-aged steaks or Madeira blended and bottled to mimic the style of nineteenth-century Savannah.

I got a recurring gig on *Iron Chef.* The producers regularly flew me to New York City, where I sat on the dais to pass judgment. Bill Murray showed up to watch one of the battles I judged and stuck around to take pictures. *CBS News Sunday Morning* turned up in our Oxford backyard to watch me fry chicken in a cast-iron pot.

Gourmet magazine tapped me as a contributing editor and funded travels with what my editor Jane Lear called "walking around money." Standing before editor-in-chief Ruth Reichl's desk, I pitched an article about working a month at a Waffle House and came home, instead, with an assignment to write about Ed Mitchell, who emerged from that first barbecue symposium as a star and began working with farmers to feed hogs on sweet potatoes and peanuts instead of commodity corn and silage.

SFA didn't fund or publicize my work. My face never showed on brochures. I adopted a no-graft policy, inspired by Kathleen Purvis, a food section editor in Charlotte who helped me think through a kind of freelancer's code. If a chef would not give me a bill in a restaurant, I tipped the waiter what my dinner would have cost. I refused free trips, with rare exceptions, like when Viking Range invited me to travel Vietnam and eat my fill of bun cha and banh xeo. Even then, I paid for my airfare.

The ethos was simple: Work at SFA should not benefit me as a writer, but my work as a writer could benefit the SFA. As benefits accrued, my power grew. In 2005, I began twelve years of service on the James Beard Awards restaurant committee. For more than three years, beginning in 2009, I wrote the United Tastes series for *The New York Times*. At one point, I wrote columns for all three of the glossy magazines that covered my region: *Southern Living, Garden & Gun,* and *Oxford American.*

I wrote a 2008 article for *The Atlanta Journal-Constitution* about Taqueria del Sol that framed the Mexican-inspired Atlanta restaurant as a meat-and-three for the modern South. Afterward, the owners stepped forward to support SFA work. When I praised the bottled water menu at a Little Rock restaurant in a column that same year for US Airways' in-flight magazine, the CEO of Mountain Valley Spring Water in nearby Hot Springs called to ask about becoming a donor.

I thought of those as happy accidents; I never fished for SFA support through my writing. Sometimes my work came with complications. When I wrote a *Gourmet* article that questioned the farm-to-table narrative of newly expanded Blackberry Farm, the luxe resort in the foothills of the Great Smokies, I compromised the annual SFA benefit auction they hosted. After I toured a former Wham-O factory in Southern California and wrote a United Tastes column on a popular brand of sriracha hot sauce made there, the CEO of the company that produces Tabasco, an SFA donor, gently questioned my allegiance.

No matter how much I believed myself to be a good and fair actor, I knew that my status as SFA director benefited my writing career. SFA work gave me gravitas. Inviting speakers to step to our stage and chefs to cook our meals, I built a network of people who considered me a peer. That status drove my magazine and newspaper writing and led to book contracts. To recognize the ways that SFA benefited me, I made financial contributions to the organization through the University of Mississippi Foundation. But as the years added up, my omnipresence came with liabilities, too.

MORE THAN A HUNDRED PEOPLE signed up to work on Willie Mae Seaton's rebuild. We began in January of 2006. The Heritage Conservation Network printed a big white vinyl sign, embossed with both their logo and our Southern Foodways Alliance logo, and hung it on the front of the building: SAVING WILLIE MAE'S SCOTCH HOUSE. SFA never would have hung a sign like that. But we were glad they did, for we wanted to connect our small-scale effort to the big job of rebuilding New Orleans. If we brought this corner restaurant back, maybe the whole Tremé neighborhood could come back.

In the wake of the levee failures, we told ourselves that small neighborhood restaurants were endangered. We feared a future in which big restaurant groups flourished and mom-and-pops faltered. Two weeks in, the response to our call for workers was so strong that my SFA colleague Mary Beth Lasseter, whom I'd worked with on the civil rights sculpture project and who by then served as SFA associate director, began putting volunteers on a waiting list.

Raised Catholic in South Georgia, Mary Beth embraced this chance to serve. Four years into her work with the SFA, she was already our moral conscience. Mary Beth, also our social chair, closed emails to members with asks about their children and stayed after hours to listen to an elderly baker who called to complain that Lane Cake didn't get the respect it deserved.

Mary Beth compiled a Scotch House Survival Guide that laid out the rationale: "The city needs your time. Every hour that you clean, hammer, or paint, you rebuild New Orleans. The city needs your dollars. As you lodge in local hotels and dine at local eateries, you rebuild New Orleans. The city needs tourists. As you travel back home and encourage friends to visit, you rebuild New Orleans."

Graduate students from North Carolina drove all night. An Episcopal priest from New Mexico flew in. So did a couple who ran a bakery in Northern California. Each morning, volunteers gathered on the sidewalk outside Willie Mae's ruined restaurant, ventilation masks around their necks, foam cups of coffee in hand, waiting for assignments.

A month later, the Heritage Conservation Network stood down. The scale of the rebuild overwhelmed them, just as the scale of the destruction cowed the George W. Bush administration. John Currence, chef and owner of City Grocery in Oxford, who began serving as lead symposium chef in 2000, took over. He quickly emerged as a sort of spiritual leader and contractor.

Like nearly all the volunteers, Currence had never eaten Willie Mae's wet-batter fried chicken and white beans with pickled pork. A native of New Orleans, he grew up on the other side of town in a two-story house off a grand boulevard. Asked why he did the work, Currence said, often and elliptically, "When you have a friend in need, you help that friend."

At a time when new urbanists floated plans to turn the Lower Ninth Ward back over to marshland, our rebuild story was popular among a press corps in search of good news. *The Dallas Morning News* sent a reporter. Jim Auchmutey wrote a feature for *The Atlanta Journal-Constitution,* the cultural barometer of my Georgia boyhood. "I just have to get back in that kitchen," Willie Mae told a *USA Today* reporter.

Stationed by the front door in a blouse, pants, and a black beret, Willie Mae hugged necks and wondered where all these people came from. The debris pile mounted, reaching the same height floodwaters had reached a few months earlier. Soon the roof was off and the interior was down to studs. Willie Mae watched as we tore her restaurant apart to put it back together.

Why were we pulling out her deep fryers, she asked, when the idea was to fix the place up so she could cook again? Why did someone just toss two of her skillets on a trash heap? Didn't they know she could fix those up? How did they expect her to make good gravy without those skillets?

Mary Beth asked questions, too: Should a nonprofit, just six years old, raise money for a business? Willie Mae turned ninety during the rebuild. That prompted a new round of questions: Who is going to run this restaurant? Who is this restaurant going to serve? While I fretted, Mary Beth cut through the noise to ask the most important question of all: If this is an act of charity, shouldn't we help because we can, without expectations of payoff or appreciation?

SFA was still a fledgling organization. A consultant would have warned us away from the project. Instead of raising money for our oral histories or documentary films, we were raising money to rebuild a business in a city that some people said couldn't be rebuilt. This project made no sense on paper. But it made sense to SFA members who paid annual dues of $50 to $75 to belong to a different kind of nonprofit. As volunteers swung crowbars and we collected donation checks from Morgan Freeman and John Grisham, a restaurant rose from the ruins and the SFA came into its own.

WE PROMISED VOLUNTEERS ONE GOOD MEAL for each day worked. For lunch, we booked chefs to work in the gutter beside the restaurant. They draped tables in starched linen and lit Sternos under silver chafing dishes. The meals were ridiculous and sublime, like the effort itself. John Besh from Restaurant August rolled crawfish agnolotti. Greg Sonnier of Gabrielle Restaurant stacked slices of barbecue shrimp pie. Adolfo Garcia of RioMar served ceviche. Donald Link and Stephen Stryjewski from Herbsaint cooked bacon-and-mushroom-smothered pork chops with white bean salad.

On days when we had more people than tasks, we sent volunteers to Dooky Chase's around the corner and Angelo Brocato in Mid-City. To raise money, John Egerton sold hot pickles made by a friend of his in Kentucky. He called them SOS Sharpies, for reasons that were clear only to him. One afternoon, after a long day of hard work and a short but vigorous happy hour, Egerton prowled the bars of the French Quarter selling jars for ten bucks a pop. I followed, playing Sancho to his Quixote.

As we got closer to reopening, debts mounted. SFA sold one-hundred-dollar tickets for a Scotch House fried chicken dinner and a preview screening of *Above the Line,* the documentary Joe York made about the rebuild. Facing down the job ahead, knowing that Willie Mae was growing feeble without the centering routine of her restaurant, we told purchasers that SFA couldn't guarantee the Scotch House would redeem the coupons.

Toward the end of the rebuild we began to catch flak. Well-intentioned whites have long made problems when they step into Black worlds to fix problems. In the process, we often made the problems worse. Those stories littered New Orleans, a city flush with cultural riches but often lacking in financial resources. What good were these white people doing in this Black neighborhood? We would turn away, they said, as soon as the cameras turned away. Once we got this place back open, they asked, who was going to eat there? Would Black regulars be priced out by white tourists?

While other nonprofit-led projects in New Orleans stalled, we plunged forward. We were sometimes smug about that. I fielded a call from a staffer in the Bush White House. *No, you can't come by for a photo op,* I said, sure that they were looking for a feel-good story to divert attention from their miserable failure to provide aid. That afternoon, hacking at ruined drywall in the dining room at Dooky Chase's, I punctuated each swing of a crowbar with a shout of "FUCK BUSH!"

Bills came in higher than expected and they came in frequently. As the timetable shifted and city inspectors demanded we rebuild to code, Willie Mae grew more frail. Beyond the glare of the press coverage, outside the reach of the positive feedback loop, I began to think in new ways about my relationship to cooks like Willie Mae Seaton.

BACK IN ATHENS IN THE 1980S, Annie Johnson hummed gospel while feeding my fraternity brothers tomato soup and grilled cheese sandwiches pulled from the warming drawer by the kitchen door. I said I loved our house cook, we all did, but we paid her something like minimum wage. Later, in Atlanta, I ate lunches at Annie Keith's, a bungalow converted to a meat-and-three café, with tables scattered about the living room and the closed-in back porch. After fried pork chops and macaroni and cheese and sweet potato custard, regulars carried their dishes to the kitchen. I liked to talk then about how those two Black cooks treated me like a member of the family, but I knew better.

In kitchens run by those Black women, I seemed to belong, same as I seemed to belong in the kitchen of Elizabeth Roberson's house in Clinton. I learned in grad school that Black mothers in the South raised my generation, often serving whites at the expense of their own families, usually earning wages on which those families couldn't depend.

When I was young, I thought the ease I felt in Black spaces

spoke to my morality. As I grew older, I began to recognize that my people bought our way into those relationships, exchanging money for what felt like intimacy. For an *Oxford American* column, I developed a "booty call" theory to explain white patrons who claimed devotion to Black restaurants, in which we got what we wanted, got out, and ignored the effect of our actions. Now I was beginning to apply the insights I gained.

Before Katrina, Willie Mae's great-granddaughter Kerry Seaton earned a political science degree and studied for a master's degree in public policy. She envisioned herself as a lawyer. Her relatives warned her to avoid the restaurant business. So did her academic mentors. But when Willie Mae told her she needed help, the restaurant pulled Kerry into its orbit.

Kerry was born to the work. At five, she wrote her own menus on lined paper ripped from kindergarten notebooks: more pork chops, less green beans. Kerry stapled together order pads from scraps of paper. Weaving between table legs, she took pretend orders from judges in newsboy caps, lawyers who shot their cuffs, and young men draped in clunky gold necklaces.

When the Scotch House reopened in April of 2007, nearly two years and more than $200,000 after it flooded, John Currence ran the expo window. Ann Cashion, a Washington, D.C., chef who won a James Beard Award the year before Katrina, worked prep. John Fleer, the chef at Blackberry Farm, who would win a Beard the year after, manned the fry baskets. Willie Mae sulked in the back room, overwhelmed by the hubbub. Kerry held back, unclear of her role in this new restaurant we made from the bones of her family's old restaurant.

By the end of the first day, Willie Mae tried to sell the restaurant, first to Currence, later to Lolis Elie. They couldn't tell if she was joking. Without work to occupy her mind and body, Willie

Mae shrunk into herself. Looking into her once bright eyes, we saw that dementia was already stealing her from us.

Two days after the restaurant reopened, it closed. Volunteers called our office at the university, looking to eat fried chicken and white beans at the restaurant they helped revive. Open one day, fry baskets loaded down with thighs and drumsticks, the restaurant was locked up the next. Willie Mae moved from her renovated double shotgun to assisted living. Caught between her dreams and the expectations of others, Kerry stepped into the kitchen to shoulder a burden passed down across generations.

Fifteen years later, I texted to ask Kerry if I could buy her a happy hour cocktail. I had read about a new location of the restaurant planned for Los Angeles, and followed the press that brought hordes of tourists to her door in search of what the Food Network said was the nation's best fried chicken. Kerry seemed to have come away from the rebuild with mixed emotions and I wanted to understand her perspective.

We met for drinks in a bar near my hotel. Kerry told me that before she left the house that night, her husband asked who I was. She said, *He's the guy who made us famous for fried chicken.* She spoke kindly, connecting that moment on the Beard Foundation stage to the fundraisers SFA hosted and the banner that once hung on the side of her restaurant, helping me understand where her dreams and my drive joined, and where any friction came from, too.

As Kerry spoke with me that afternoon in the bar, I listened, playing back that two-year rebuild and those probing questions. Her recollections were generous, her outlook positive. But as she spoke, I slowly realized that Kerry never asked for our help. Following the lead of another out-of-state nonprofit, SFA stepped in to do the work we thought needed to be done. In the process, we made a new restaurant and a new role for Kerry. The aspiring lawyer was now a fried chicken cook.

SFA came into the rebuild to do something transformative in a moment that demanded boldness. We believed we took a stand that helped a neighborhood and a family recover. In the process, we forged a principled organization. We saw Willie Mae's as a symbol. Over drinks that day, listening to Kerry, I began to understand that our rebuild effort symbolized something, too.

Kevin Young at Booker's Place

Chapter Seven

RECKONING

For a 2013 summer symposium in Richmond, Virginia, SFA focused our oral histories and programming on "women at work." In search of a location, my colleague Melissa Hall went on a deep research dive and came back up with a theory that the former capital of the Confederacy was an ideal place to examine how female food entrepreneurs have shaped the South.

On Saturday night, the scholar Psyche Williams-Forson talked about fried chicken, cooked and sold by women of African descent in the years after Emancipation, as a tool of freedom. At the close of a West African dinner, cooked by an immigrant from Liberia, thirty of our guests, mostly white and middle-aged, took off on an Enslaved Peoples' Walk.

Weary after three days of talking and listening, eating and drinking, Melissa and I stayed behind to clean up. Watching our guests return and file off the bus two hours later, I knew something was wrong. Most skirted the bar and headed for the elevators. Instead of waving, they looked at the floor.

The walk began at the Manchester Docks by the James River. *Many enslaved people began trips downriver here,* Elegba Folklore Society guides told our guests. *Make a human chain by extending your arms to grab hold of the right shoulder of the person in front of you. This was the way enslaved people moved along the riverbank. Chained together, they struggled to find footing on this land, much like you are struggling now.*

In the distance, our guests heard what sounded like whip cracks. Guides lit torches to show the way. *Close your eyes and keep them closed,* they said. *Our people would have been blindfolded.*

Kate Medley, who had worked with us as a graduate student, grabbed a seat in the bar and told us why our guests, who paid $375 to join us, refused to meet our eyes. Many, including a financial planner who talked about getting taxis to pick them up by the side of the road, were angry that the SFA subjected them to what felt like abuse. Some were unsettled but inspired, like the doctor who rallied others to listen to the guides and learn what his generation refused to know. As we talked, more guests filed through the lobby, looking disconsolate. Kate told us that the whole thing was a mess. And she wondered if it might be an opportunity.

Summer events had been a part of our programming since 2001. Two to three days long, they served as grown-up versions of school field trips. By 2010, our website reached a larger audience than our events. Media was our future. But our members wanted events that showcased corners of the South that were new to them, and they wanted to stay in luxe hotels with lobby bars, where they could reconnect with friends made at previous events.

One hundred or so guests would ride in buses to visit a crawfish farm in Louisiana or an oyster-shucking house in Florida. Traveling the eastern flank of North Carolina, we played softball in a Minor League stadium with a tapped beer keg at first and third. On a tour of Buford Highway, Atlanta's international corridor, we introduced guests to catfish clay pots at a Chinese restaurant and late-night karaoke in a Vietnamese bar on the grounds of a ruined mini golf course.

Responding to sold-out fall symposia, we upgraded those annual summer field trips, adding formal talks, while keeping some of the experiential parts, like farm tours and city walks. Leading up to Richmond, SFA staff worried about our approach to events. Too many guests were white and wealthy. Summer events illustrated the problem. Members told us they built vacations around these events. But we didn't want to program adventures for foodies.

From the beginning, SFA founders and board members said that our aim was to drive honest conversations about slavery and its legacies. In a memo from 1999, Egerton declared, "Southern food has tremendous powers, as yet untapped, for social healing. The time is ripe for us to rise to the vision of a better South, and the place to start is in the kitchen and at the table."

For SFA staff, the question hung in the air: When were we going to make good on that promise? With Egerton and Will Campbell in my ear, I sometimes pushed us to act. Mostly I worried, usually in the small hours of the morning, about the disconnect between our aspirations and the everyday realities of running a nonprofit.

Rereading brochure copy for a 2004 summer event in Birmingham, with a side trip to a blues picnic at Freedom Creek near Aliceville, Alabama, I cringe at the playful copy I wrote, promising that we would be "Freedom Riders en route to Freedom Creek." But I still take pride in what we staged.

To begin, Charles Moore, the Hackleburg, Alabama, native who covered the civil rights movement for *Life* magazine, took us on a slideshow tour of his home state. He showed us photos he took, crouched on the street, pointing his camera toward the snarling police dogs that Bull Connor loosed on the children of Birmingham. He shared a close-up of a man driving down the highway, a Klan robe hanging nonchalantly from the coat hook in his sedan.

After a breakfast of sausage biscuits and grits and ambrosia, Charles McNair, father of one of the four little girls killed in the 1963 bombing of the 16th Street Baptist Church, talked about the hurt that still lived in his heart. As he spoke, he looked down at a relic, preserved for future generations: a patent leather shoe worn by his eleven-year-old daughter, Denise, when the brick walls of that church collapsed on her.

On the bus from Birmingham to Aliceville, Frye Gaillard, author of *Cradle of Freedom,* joined Colonel Stone Johnson, who led the 1960 rescue of Freedom Riders in Anniston, Alabama. We passed around a flask of white dog as the green miles unraveled. Thinking of Will Campbell, trying to conjure the spirit of his day, we called it the Ark of the Covenant. Before the crowd returned to Birmingham, John Egerton climbed onstage at Freedom Creek in a Hawaiian shirt, ball cap on his head. Full of the spirit of this day, he recited James Weldon Johnson's "Lift Every Voice and Sing," known to previous generations of Black schoolchildren as the Negro National Anthem.

SFA believed that we were bold for bringing stories from the 1960s alive in the twenty-first century. Few if any other food organizations were taking a hard look at how racism shaped our culture. We joined an immature field at a time when the United States was just beginning to embrace dining out as a cultural and social activity. SFA aimed to make a change in the hearts and minds of the people who joined us. By documenting and celebrating everyday cooks and farmers, and connecting them to stories of the everyday women and men who fueled the civil rights movement, we dreamed a new portrait of the place that made us.

Too few Southerners knew the stories that Charles Moore and Charles McNair told. SFA was here to right those wrongs. We did that work with purpose and sometimes with hubris, believing that, while organizations like the James Beard Foundation made it their primary mission to celebrate white tablecloth chefs, SFA recast the stories people told about our region.

In the years to come, that night by the docks in Richmond would play back like the beginning of a reckoning, in which the bridge between our intentions and other people's ideas about our work would collapse, demanding that my colleagues and I question who we answered to and who we served.

WOULD PEOPLE PAY $675 TO SIT in folding chairs for three days and listen to conversations about forced labor in the tomato fields of contemporary Florida? Would presentation titles like "Setting the Homeless Table" and "The Hungry South" compel chefs and writers to fly across the country or drive across the South for a long weekend in Oxford?

For 2014, we promised a fall symposium that reexamined the welcome table ideal. Fifty years after President Johnson signed the law that desegregated restaurants, we asked new questions about equity and equality. But would a hard look at the South sell?

Three minutes after we released the four hundred tickets, we got our answer when Mary Beth fielded the first calls. *Did the ticket window fail to open? Did the site crash?* She told members, some who had made Oxford pilgrimages every year for a decade, *The tickets are gone. I'll put your name on the waiting list.*

To counterbalance the challenging talks, we planned exhibits and meals. Ann Marshall and Scott Blackwell of Charleston, South Carolina, hung folk art from their collection in the dining hall for the weekend. *Hose of Birmingham,* a Bernice Sims painting of white firemen spraying down Black children, was printed on the front cover of the catalog. Bill Smith, the chef at Crook's Corner in Chapel Hill, North Carolina, served a Thursday night supper inspired by the Mexican immigrants who ran his kitchen. He began with shrimp cocktails and country ham tamales and ended with sorbets made from orange juice and Red Hots.

Bryan Petroff and Doug Quint of New York City drove their Big Gay Ice Cream truck south on a Southern Discomfort Tour. "Tighten your bible belts," they promised in a press release. "It's going to be a wild ride!" I met Bryan and Doug when I was writing a book on street food. After the *Truck Food Cookbook* published, they hosted a talk by me in the West Village and booked a drag queen named Bambi Galore as my date. When I laid out our plans for the 2014 symposium, they agreed to stage a Saturday night ice cream social in Oxford.

News crews showed to film the Big Gay boys in Raleigh and Birmingham. Crowds thronged the truck in Charleston and Atlanta. Arriving triumphant in Oxford, they sold sundaes named for Ernie Mickler, the Florida-born author of *White Trash Cooking,* and Stormé DeLarverie, the biracial Louisiana native who toured with an integrated female impersonator show and fought the police during the 1969 Stonewall Riots. The line for those sundaes stretched up the sidewalk that skirted the Mid-Town Shopping Center, past the Sears, almost to the YMCA. Inside the truck, our son, Jess, worked the ice cream spigot.

Before the James Beard Foundation refocused to train chefs as advocates for social and environmental change, before *Cherry Bombe* magazine presented its first Jubilee to celebrate women in the culinary world, the SFA symposium was the place to come if you wanted to talk about food and drink with the same gravitas as politics and art.

Ta-Nehisi Coates, who had just published a blockbuster piece in *The Atlantic* about reparations and went on to win a MacArthur "genius grant," began his 2014 keynote by saying that driving through campus that morning, he felt a kind of rage. Coates told the crowd of four hundred that he wanted to burn down the whole damn place. Giving voice to what so many inside and outside the state said under their breath, Coates marked the burdens of our history. His words also gestured to the opportunity SFA had in that moment to write a newer story of this place we call home.

Coates closed with a call for empathy in the face of distrust. That Friday night, he joined the crowd to eat catfish and drink in the street. He was easy to spot, dressed in a tomato-red MAKE CORNBREAD NOT WAR T-shirt, made by one of our donors, Billy Reid, and picked up at the registration table. Looking back, this symposium was probably the SFA's peak, which means, of course, a valley was sure to follow.

THE 2014 FALL SYMPOSIUM ENDED BIG, too, with the Sunday morning debut of *Repast,* an oratorio based on the life of waiter Booker Wright, who worked from around 1940 to 1966 at Lusco's in the Mississippi Delta town of Greenwood. Commissioned by SFA, the song cycle played Sunday morning in the same downtown theater where Coates spoke to begin the weekend. A year and a half later, *Repast* would play Carnegie Hall.

Bruce Levingston, a native of the Delta who emerged as an early champion of the project and funded some of the cost, played Nolan

Gasser's composition on piano that Sunday. Bass-baritone Justin Hopkins sang the libretto that poet Kevin Young wrote. My old colleague Debbie Elliott, reporting for NPR, was there to capture the scene, big fuzzy mic in hand.

We came to tell and hear a story that began five decades before. In 1965, an NBC documentary crew led by Frank De Felitta filmed Booker Wright as he spoke directly into the lens, telling an eventual national television audience that, to feed his family, he bucked and scraped for tips. De Felitta interviewed Wright in the front room of Booker's Place, the café and juke joint he ran before and after he served dinner at Lusco's.

That afternoon, Wright wore his Lusco's uniform of a white jacket, black pants, a white shirt, and a black bow tie. A picture of professional comportment, he draped a white napkin over his left forearm. As his wife and a waitress watched, while the camera rolled, Wright recited the Lusco's menu like he did for his customers.

He spoke in a joyful patter of shrimp cocktail, oysters on the half shell, oysters almandine, and donut-style onion rings. Before he broke out of character, he praised Lusco's broiled porterhouse steaks and fried soft-shell crabs. And then, to confess the humiliation that came with the work, he broke himself open.

In that two-minute monologue, now accessible on the Web, Wright told of why he worked at Lusco's: "I'm trying to make a living. Why? I've got three children. I want them to get an education." He spoke of the future he imagined, too: "I wasn't fortunate enough to get an education, but I want them to get it." Voice cracking, brow beaded with sweat, Wright talked of the abuse he suffered from patrons. And he explained how he had to respond:

"The meaner the man be, the more you smile. Although you're crying on the inside. Or you're wondering, *What else can I do?* Sometime he'll tip you, sometime he'll say, *I'm not going to tip that* n———, *he don't look for no tip.* Yessir, thank you. *What'd you say?* . . . Yessir, boss, I'm your n———!"

To watch that video now is to witness an act of bravery. When his monologue aired, that testimony played like self-immolation. Once he spoke his heart, Wright knew he could no longer play the role that earned him those tips. On the night *Mississippi: A Self-Portrait* premiered in April of 1966, a crowd gathered at Lusco's to watch on the black-and-white in the vestibule. Soon after, Booker Wright walked out the door.

LUSCO'S BECAME A PART OF MY LIFE in the late 1990s, after I moved to Oxford, when I went looking for a place to stare down the past. By that point, Booker Wright had been gone for more than twenty years, shot dead by a drunk patron inside his juke joint and café. The sign in front of Booker's Place was still there, but the plastic was pocked with holes and the bulbs were busted.

Lusco's, on the eve of the twenty-first century, shared a block with boarded storefronts and soon-to-be-boarded storefronts. On the opposite corner, the Likker Legger sold half pints of vodka behind bulletproof glass. Cardboard six-pack holders, soaked with dirty water, collected in the gutters. Next door to the 1933 vintage restaurant, a sign posted on the front of L.C.M.C. Mortuary Products read WE MAKE HEADSTONES. In that moment, Lusco's looked like a headstone for a lost way of life.

I came with fellow graduate students, following the lead of Jane and Michael Stern, authors of *Roadfood* and *Goodfood,* who pegged Lusco's as a "gastronomic reliquary where tradition is so enshrined that it would be sacrilegious to alter even the smallest detail. . . ." Dinner went like they promised.

A short stroll, past a wall-mounted covey of stuffed ducks, down a dim hallway, brought us to a curtain-fronted booth and a table draped in white linen. At the push of a wall-mounted buzzer, a server in a white jacket appeared, bearing a tower of onion rings and a bucket of ice for our highballs. Another buzz and a charred porterhouse followed. Before I could look up, our waiter disappeared in a rustle of chintz and deference.

Lusco's was louche and wild. So were the people who gathered there to talk of the glory days when white Greenwood was flush and cotton was the coin of the planter realm. That Delta wildness drew me in. One night a man who sold cotton combines for a living invited me to join his family and friends for dinner. I carried a notebook in my back pocket and Southern Studies classes in my head.

Midway through dinner, I asked where our host went. The woman to my left said, "Oh, he fell out." She said it in a short and sharp declarative sentence. I flashed back to our arrival, when he crossed the threshold with a clanking pasteboard box full of wine and whiskey bottles. Her words contained another promise: If time stopped here, judgment did, too.

I returned often to Lusco's, bringing friends as witnesses. Graduate school was then teaching me to define myself in ways that threatened the world that Lusco's regulars held tight. My university, with its columned buildings and defrocked Confederate mascot, seemed to depend on nostalgia. But it took a trip to the Delta to understand how the past can dominate the present. At Lusco's, I made plans to pull back the curtain, stare down that past, and get out before the fire I started licked at the baseboards.

SEATED IN ROOMS PAINTED SEAFOAM GREEN, at tables stacked with tumped-over wine bottles, we deboned pompano and mimicked regulars who flipped butter pats toward the ceiling on bent knives. Sneaking out the back door to pee on the oyster middens or stare into the blue-black sky, we breathed in the spent vapors of raucous Delta nights.

Stories of Booker Wright's 1966 television appearance still circulated in Greenwood. But no one I spoke to in the late 1990s could tell me what happened to him. And no one seemed to know if any of the footage from his television appearance had survived.

In 2003, Amy Evans, our first SFA oral historian, interviewed Lusco's co-owner Karen Pinkston for a project on the cooks of Greenwood. Karen mentioned Booker Wright. And so did a tamale maker down the street. Like all SFA oral histories, we digitized the audio and posted the transcript to our website. That's where Booker Wright's granddaughter, Yvette Johnson, found the interviews in 2007. Born a year after Wright died, Yvette didn't grow up knowing her grandfather made one of the boldest speeches of the civil rights movement.

The references in the interviews were slight, but they were the only mentions Yvette could then find. In 2011, Raymond De Felitta, son of Frank De Felitta, found a blog post that Yvette wrote about her search. He shared the long-lost television footage of her grandfather that rocked white Greenwood when it aired.

Raymond was making a documentary. He asked Yvette to collaborate. They worked together: a Black woman in search of her grandfather and a white man trying to reckon his father's responsibility to the same Black man. Their 2012 film, *Booker's Place*, tells the story of Wright's testimony and the price he paid. Yvette began writing a book, *The Song and the Silence,* about her search for her grandfather. By 2013, when SFA commissioned *Repast,* a new narrative was taking shape. With it came a new way to frame the story of a family restaurant with a complicated past and present.

· · ·

OUR SON, JESS, GREW UP in other sorts of restaurants with other lessons to teach. He was four when he ate his first barbecue sandwich at a joint near Griffin, Georgia, sixty miles north of Clinton. I can see the gray smoke that veiled the concrete-block building and the anger that lit Jess's face when he bit into the white bun, overstuffed with black and brown chunks of pork, drenched in a red sauce speckled with black pepper. His look said: *How did you think you could keep this from me?*

Before that sandwich, Jess took most of his calories from steamed spinach, which Blair formed into bite-size mounds and arranged in semicircles on a high-chair tray. She made games out of dinners. He played a green monster eating his way through a forest or a black hole devouring a galaxy. As Jess grew older, Blair shifted from role-playing to language. Asparagus were tasty snakes, strawberries raw daddies, but his hunger was already mine.

Saturday mornings we drove thirty miles to Westside Bar-B-Que in New Albany. I narrated the highway ahead. From the child seat in back, Jess talked through his order. We bought sandwiches of chopped shoulder from a counter cut in a rough-board wall and watched a model train circle on a track mounted near the ceiling. Listening for the whistle as the engine made the turn toward the bathrooms, we drank sweet tea from foam cups and ate slices of three-layer caramel cake robed in thick icing.

Ordering at new barbecue spots, Jess learned to sniff the air for smoke and check the yard for wood, much like my father taught me back in Clinton. As Jess grew older, our eating horizons expanded. Chili dogs in hand, ice cream cones in cupholders, we marveled at the people and landscapes that rushed by. Jess asked questions like "Who thought it was a good idea to open a convenience store that doubles as a tanning salon?" And "Why would a go-kart track owner close on a Saturday in the summer?"

My childhood runs to Old Clinton floated into view. Barbecue was my food as a boy. Before Jess turned eight, barbecue became his food, and traveling to eat became our bond. We planned trips and broke down routes, mapping barbecue joints by sauce types and wood sources. In a car barreling toward a house of smoke, we grew comfortable with long silences and with each other.

At Payne's in Memphis, Tennessee, set in an old filling station, we dipped potato chips in the yellow coleslaw runoff from Flora Payne's sandwiches. On a bench outside Valentina's, near Austin, Texas, we traded bites of Miguel Vidal's pork tacos, smeared with guacamole. We ate shoulder sandwiches on white bread from Jones Bar-B-Q Diner, a hundred-year-old restaurant in the Arkansas Delta town of Marianna, and brought home their thin vinegar sauce, siphoned into an Aunt Jemima bottle.

The cabin of our car was our confessional. I told Jess about the killings that haunted my childhood. He told me that the busted lip he got at church camp came from a fight, not a run-in with a tree, like he told his mother.

TEN MONTHS BEFORE *REPAST* DEBUTED, Kevin Young and I drove to Greenwood and the nearby town of Money, where a white woman accused Emmett Till of whistling at her in 1955. Now the director of the National Museum of African American History and Culture, Kevin then worked at Emory University as a professor and curator.

Snow drifted across my windshield as we raced a freight train

down a curving blacktop, passing a group of cropper cabins, retro-
fitted as a tourist camp. Out front, a small patch of cotton plants,
once thick with white bolls, swayed naked in the breeze. We trav-
eled in search of the world Booker Wright knew. And we traveled
with the ugly story in our head about how a gang of white men beat
and shot young Till, tied a cotton gin fan to his body, and sunk
his dead body in the Tallahatchie River.

Kevin had already written a draft of *Repast*. On this trip, he
wanted to gather more details about where Booker Wright lived
and worked while also tracking the story of Till, whose mangled
and bloated body floated to the surface thirty miles from Lusco's.
Larry Griggs, a deacon from Friendship Missionary Baptist Church,
met us on the other side of the tracks from Lusco's, at the front
door of the building where Wright once ran his café and juke joint.
The space was soon to become their recreation hall.

The bar from Wright's juke joint was still there, but the furni-
ture tacks he'd hammered into the vinyl to inscribe the initials for
Booker's Place were gone. Before we said our goodbyes to Larry, I
snapped a picture of Kevin behind the bar. Arms spread wide, a
colorful scarf around his neck, a big smile on his face, he looks
ready to welcome Booker Wright back home.

Driving through Baptist Town, Kevin took pictures of shot-
gun houses, tagged with graffiti, remnants of the Jim Crow world
Booker Wright knew. We moved slowly, passing a snowball truck
with flat tires and a Camaro on blocks, dodging potholes, staying
mostly silent and reverent, as if we trailed a funeral cortege that re-
mained stubbornly out of sight.

That night, in one of the curtained booths where Wright once
sing-songed the menu, Kevin and I celebrated his life. Onion rings
arrived, followed by shrimp, and a steak swimming in Worcester-
shire and butter. We poured whiskey. And we returned to the mo-

ment in 1965 when Wright stepped before the cameras to say the words that got him ostracized by his white patrons and pistol-whipped by a white police officer.

In the lobby of our hotel the next morning, Kevin handed me a draft of the oratorio. Signed in his looping cursive, it now hangs on the wall of my backyard writing shed, a marker of our time walking around inside what Kevin came to think of as a ghost story. Two years later, *The New Yorker* published a poem Kevin wrote that documented our drive and memorialized Till. When he included "Money Road" in his book *Brown*, Kevin dedicated that poem to me.

JESS WAS TEN WHEN I TOOK a magazine assignment to drive a triangle of Tennessee in search of another past in the present. The sign in front of Sam's Bar-B-Q in Humboldt showed a bald man with a cleaver chasing a white pig. At a table in the corner, we ate half chickens, smoked so long that the bones turned as soft and porous as balsa wood.

In Brownsville, Jess watched Helen Turner move through a tin-roofed shed, working two fires set in block pits. Standing in the smoke, while Helen talked to a man in a blue work shirt with a grease-blotted bag of sandwiches in hand, Jess worried about Helen. *If this makes me cough after five minutes,* he asked, *what does it do to her over eight hours?*

Garden & Gun published some of what we saw and tasted, but the most important stuff never made it into that story. In conversation over that long weekend, we became the father and son we wanted to be. SFA work too often took me away from our little family. So did my appetite for the spotlight. On trips like the ones my father and I took, Jess and I reconnected.

We drove the South, marking change over lunch in a Sikh-run dhaba in Arkansas that sold samosas in corn-dog bags, and dinner in a North Carolina joint where Degar people from Vietnam worked the barbecue pits. Too many Southerners blamed immigrants for their failure to score good jobs in a new tech and service economy. I told myself that new arrivals brought improvements. Travel gave me chances to prove that idea.

Jess was quick to adopt my latest attempt to reinvent the South. After my father and I took him to a Korean barbecue restaurant in the suburbs of Montgomery, Alabama, for seaweed salad followed by a grill-your-own galbi feast, he looked up, in search of approval. With all the gravitas he could gather, Jess told my father, "This the kind of place we take people who say the South isn't diverse and doesn't welcome everyone."

As our family gained financial footing, Jess and I ranged wider. We flew across the country, marking the crispness of hotel room-service fries and whether pool bars served ginger beers. We traveled north out of San Francisco to eat at Tomales Bay, where Jess admired the view but couldn't understand why they served his oysters with hunks of bread instead of sleeves of saltines.

Driving up the coast, we stopped at military surplus stores for him, used bookstores for me. I told myself he was learning real-time lessons in geography and history. Back in the city, I set him loose in a pinball-machine museum with a roll of quarters. Stops on our travels became the stars in our sky.

TWO YEARS AFTER JUSTIN HOPKINS took the stage in Oxford to sing *Repast*, Karen and Andy Pinkston, the owners of Lusco's, announced that the family restaurant was for sale. Two years after that, Karen said the restaurant would stay in their hands, but reduce its hours. As the family planned for an uncertain future, they faced down something new.

Ideas about Lusco's had changed, and so had the value of their reputation. When Andy and Karen took over the restaurant in 1976, they told the story of a proud Sicilian family that grew famous for the quality of their cooking and the stoutness of the hooch Papa Lusco made. A new story about Lusco's, in which Booker Wright was a more important character than Papa Lusco, gained strength in the first and second decades of the twenty-first century.

When Amy Evans interviewed Karen back in 2003, Karen said that Wright told stories to NBC cameraman Frank De Felitta for money. "And he said what they told him to say." Karen's attitude recalled the summer of 1964, when Andrew Goodman, Michael Schwerner, and James Chaney went missing near Philadelphia, Mississippi. Conservative white Mississippians then speculated that the civil rights workers went into hiding to create a press event. Forty-four days later, when the FBI dug their bodies out of an earthen dam, some of those same Mississippians made the ridiculous claim that civil rights workers did the killing because the movement needed martyrs.

Booker Wright's testimony about the Janus-faced life that Jim Crow demanded was now the story of record. The past and current owners of Lusco's were no longer unalloyed heroes who persevered across generations. Based on what we learned about how Lusco's patrons treated Wright, knowing what he dreamed of but never got to realize, the Pinkstons and their ancestors looked to some like villains.

. . .

ON A FALL DAY IN 2021, I drove south out of Oxford under lead skies raked by tines of rain, passing ranks of green cotton, white bolls showing. Afternoon lightning cut the highway, backlighting clapboard churches and rust-hollowed cotton gins. A yellow single-prop, cocked toward the dirt, whined and sputtered above, spritzing a gas carpet of boll opener.

Karen and Andy Pinkston had announced a definitive closing date for Lusco's. An advance obituary for the restaurant published in *The New York Times*. One week before they were to shutter, I came to pay my respects to the family and acknowledge my role in the new story people told about their restaurant. Staring down headlights and gas station marquees, I mouthed what I wanted to say.

When I began to write about the South, their restaurant served as a laboratory where I watched and listened and learned. I saw Lusco's as a place to prove that restaurants were theaters where Americans acted out dramas. Dinner in one of those curtained booths told a Jim Crow story that seemed to defy time, same as a back-door sandwich from Ollie's, the Birmingham barbecue joint that fought a 1964 desegregation order to the Supreme Court.

Andy and Karen were unloading their white 4Runner when I pulled up. We talked about that recent *New York Times* piece. What Booker Wright said on television in 1966 "hurt and upset" his customers, Karen told reporter Brett Anderson, "because it made them look so bad." She didn't think the treatment he talked about was evidence of racism. "It was just a thing where people think they're better than a server," she said. "That could happen to anybody."

Standing at the curb in Greenwood, Karen reminded me that her husband's family didn't fire Wright. After he spoke his mind, Wright left on his own. This distinction was important to Karen.

When I first began to tell his story, I got that detail wrong. Now her argument made sense to me.

After Wright faced down what working at Lusco's required, he couldn't work tables in a white Greenwood restaurant again. His testimony didn't indict Lusco's. Instead, he laid bare what Jim Crow life coerced. In the eyes of white Greenwood, that was his true sin. To argue today about whether he resigned or was fired was like debating the color of the drapes in a house that burned down five decades back.

Karen told me that Booker Wright and Andy were like brothers. She wanted me to see the home movies the Pinkston family shot of Wright rocking Andy in his arms. She wanted me to know that her husband's family bought Wright clothes, made sure he was fed, and gave him a job. She wanted me to know that Andy was at the hospital the night Wright died. She wanted me to understand that this wasn't about racism. I tried to tell her, in the soft tone I rehearsed in the car on the way down, that what she described sounded like paternalism, a subvariant of prejudice with a longer half-life.

As we moved inside, Andy slipped into the kitchen. Karen and I talked at the front counter. Framed articles from *Vogue, Gourmet, Southern Living,* and *Food & Wine* lined the green walls. Near the phone booth hung a framed copy of a travel article I wrote in praise of their pompano. I scanned the shelves. A photo of Emeril Lagasse in his Food Network prime hung next to a commemorative plaque from a catfish processer and a glossy signed by President George W. Bush and Laura Bush. Photos of four Black waiters hung there, too. Booker Wright was not one of them.

Toward the end of our conversation, I asked Karen if she had watched Wright's speech. "You can find it on the Web pretty easy now," I said. "Aren't you curious?" She was not. I asked why Lusco's displayed no photo of Booker Wright. She said they used to but somebody stole it. "Why not put one back up?" I asked, heart thumping in my chest. "We don't need to," she said. "Y'all are going to keep that story going for everyone else."*

* As copyedits for this book began in late 2024, a new Lusco's was being built in the Mississippi hill country community of Taylor, just south of Oxford. Furnishings that could be moved would be reinstalled. A grandson of Andy and Karen would run the kitchen. And an investor was making plans to honor Booker Wright in the new space.

My final symposium as SFA director

Chapter Eight

TWO WRECKS

I never saw the Tahoe hydroplane across the yellow line that spring morning in 2018. I can't recall the moment we slingshot backward into a muddy ditch. I didn't hear the hood of my Mini crumple or the engine drop and scrape a trench in the blacktop. I didn't see the windshield shatter or the wipers fly through the air. My brain erased what my senses took in. I remember the poof of airbags, then nothing.

My left lung collapsed. Blood spilled down my neck and pooled along my sternum. Glass confettied my hair. My friend and passenger Wright Thompson later told me he expected to see a neck and a nub where my head was. Instead, I crawled slowly out of the car. *Something's wrong with my leg,* I told the policeman.

Our crew had just wrapped our first location shoot for *True-South,* a new television series about food and culture and identity on the SEC Network and ESPN. Wright and I imagined the series over burgers at Handy Andy in Oxford. After lunch, I wrote a two-page proposal. Wright sold it, signed on as executive producer, and hired me as host.

We had spent the last three days in my old college town of Athens, following the lead of local writer André Gallant. Leaning against the counter at Polleria Pablo, a Peruvian restaurant in a gas station on the outskirts, I listened to Pablo Rivadeneyra talk about the Peru he left and the Georgia he loved. In his home of Cañete, he had worked as a car mechanic. Later, in New Jersey, Pablo learned his way around a restaurant kitchen at an Olive Garden. "I'm like a caged bird here," he told me, speaking of the ragtag Athens gas station where he did business and the threat of deportation.

At the back of that gas station, where lottery machines flashed and neighborhood kids bought Rap Snacks, I ate ceviche with corn nuts and chicken smeared with garlic, roasted on an electric spit. I talked to an immigrant activist about what it takes to make it in Georgia, and I thought about the promise of a South where Pablo could build his business and gather his people for pollo asado in salsa verde and cold cans of Inca Kola.

Rain fell as we pulled out of Pablo's and headed north to Nashville to shoot another episode. With the time change, we would get to Arnold's Country Kitchen before they closed. It was a Wednesday, which meant fried pork chops and cornbread dressing and black-eyed peas. I was set to interview musicians Jason Isbell and Amanda Shires about the legacy of meat-and-three lunches in modern Nashville. But then that big car hit my little car. And my life dimmed before it flashed bright again.

...

IN THE WEEKS AFTER THE WRECK, Blair and I hosted an open-door wake, enjoying the party that comes with a funeral without having to suffer the awkwardness of mortality. Broken leg elevated, I propped myself on the brown leather couch at the heart of our living room to read books and receive friends. Caleb Johnson, a novelist from Alabama, stopped by with a paper bag of foraged chanterelles. A box of bacon, tattooed with Allan Benton's greasy handprints, arrived from Tennessee.

Our freezer filled with bacon-wrapped quail breasts from South Carolina, a pound cake from Texas, an almond cake from Virginia. Friends in North Carolina sent a clunky brown coffee cup I still drink from most days. Frank Witherspoon from down the street baked a round of bacon sourdough. My agent, David Black, flew in from New York City and took me to dinner at Snackbar. Before we ate a couple dozen oysters, he holed up in Jess's room to edit his college admissions essay.

Each afternoon, Jess made Manhattans or boulevardiers or old-fashioneds. When he was younger, we played baseball together. But around the time he graduated from T-ball to coach pitch, Jess stepped away from baseball. He was eight before we figured out why.

Jess had a lazy eye. He couldn't follow a pitch as it arced toward the plate or track a fly ball as it lifted skyward. Jess took hits that purpled his forehead, his neck, his chest. He didn't cry from the thump of the ball. Jess cried from frustration. Baseball was my game and we both wanted it to be his.

When Jess was nineteen, I heard him tell a friend, *My father struggled to find a hobby we could share. We don't hunt or fish. Baseball was the big hope, until we found cocktails.* I wanted to steer Jess away from the abusive drinking that wrecked my mother and almost wrecked me. If I could teach him to make cocktails, he could say no to Red Bull and vodka shots. He could take a step on the path to respecting himself.

Each morning, I hobbled to the kitchen to brew coffee and wait for the rest of the house to wake. In those small quiet moments, I took stock of the world I had made through work and play, friends and family. I was now the age my father was when he divorced my mother. But life in Oxford was different from life in Clinton. My leg might be broken, but my little family was whole.

When the clock struck five, Jess reached for a jigger and a mixing glass. He muddled oranges, dashed bitters. Together at our bar, Jess standing tall, me tucked in a recliner, I offered him a glimpse of the adult world he would soon join. Jess showed me that teaching any skill, from catching a fly ball to making simple syrup for cocktails, bonds teacher and subject.

"Your body still holds the trauma of that wreck," said Gina Breedlove, a sound and spirit healer who was helping my friend Valerie Boyd, the Zora Neale Hurston biographer and professor, fight an illness. She prescribed a soak for me and Wright, saying, *A bath of lavender oil and chamomile tea will help release the toxins.* Blair stocked my bathroom with the essentials Gina prescribed, throwing in an evergreen-scented candle. And I began to imagine how Wright and I would take that bath. Two hairy middle-aged men in a tight white tub—I hated that idea, but I trusted anyone Valerie trusted.

On a phone call the next day, I asked, "So do we have to take the bath together?" Valerie laughed so hard she cried. For the next couple of years, she told that story on me. Valerie meant to show how I opened myself to new thinking, including the idea that I might shed that trauma by climbing into a soaking tub with my friend Wright, who, like me, absorbed that big crash and came away broken. She was right about my intent. I wanted to use that moment to honor life on the other side. Trauma and tragedy make us different. Making myself better was up to me.

Go hard until you feel real pain, said my nephew by marriage who runs a physical therapy clinic in Oxford, where high school football stars with scars down their legs stretch and flex next to old men with sprouted ear hair learning to walk again after strokes. At the clinic, people seemed to believe they could make progress.

I bought in: The crack I heard in my left elbow would vanish. One morning I would wake to discover the swelling in my left ankle was gone. Numb after the wreck, my left shin would tingle back to life. I got better, but I never got well. When rain falls, the cartilage in my knee stiffens. When I drive, my ankle swells against the side of my shoe. The best thing I carried away from that wreck and recuperation was a belief in the power of belief.

TO GET JESS READY FOR his college send-off, I wrote a kind of manual that included how to grill a rib eye, mix a Negroni, and haggle at a flea market. I included granular advice: "Open doors for others, but don't make a big show of it." And "When you take a cell call in a public space, walk outside."

I went deeper, too: "Think well of yourself," I wrote. "Give yourself a break. Make mistakes. Don't replay them in your head like a video game. Learn from them." I closed with a reference to the Thoreau quote my mother hung on the wall when I was far younger than Jess: March to the beat of your own drummer, "however measured or far away." I was talking to Jess. I was talking to myself.

I sat Jess down in the living room, beneath that French theater poster from Bolingbroke, amid the treasures Blair and I hauled home from travels, to tell stories about how wild and lost I went in college. I told him about the time I led a date up the concrete struts that frame the University of Georgia basketball coliseum to catch the view, and about how the cops hauled us down. I walked him through the sorority social where Brandt and I served kami-kaze shots with a bug sprayer.

I tried something similar on the eve of our marriage, telling Blair every stupid thing I could recall having done before I met her. The list included the night I jumped from a friend's car to dance in an Atlanta intersection as "Watusi Rodeo" played on the radio and a cop watched from his car. I even told her about the afternoon I made out with a married woman in the bed of a pickup in a parking garage after an art museum benefit, and about how we scrambled out when the owner banged on the tailgate and yelled, "Hey, man, get out of my truck!"

Before he left our home, I wanted Jess to understand how hard I worked to climb out of the crater I made for myself in Athens. That made me want to understand why I nose-dived in the first place, which meant going deeper into my past, explaining why I left my house and my people behind. That meant reckoning why my mother never got a funeral and why I never visited her grave.

An invitation to speak at a food conference, hosted by her alma mater in South Carolina, gave me a new chance to understand my mother better. The day before I presented my talk at what is now called Winthrop University, I stood in a patch of ivy to peer in the windows of her old dorm. And I climbed the steps of the library to thumb a yearbook from 1941.

My mother stared back from her class photo, age seventeen, precocious and confident, pale eyes shining, blond hair coaxed into tight curls. I inspected a twirler's uniform like the one she wore, and a prim school uniform, too. I studied a white staff with a ball on the end, like the one she held high while dancing across the back patio in Clinton.

I came home with a glimpse of the big dreams my mother carried to Winthrop College when she was Jess's age, and I got a hint of what might have gone wrong for her, too. According to the registrar, my mother changed roommates during her first year. Was she so wild that her roommates couldn't handle her? Many of her classmates were the daughters of farmers. For a young woman who dreamed of New York City, were the young women of Winthrop so parochial that she ran?

The registrar listed her father as a used car dealer. Had my mother, obsessed with status, quit Winthrop because she recognized a degree from that small college wouldn't land her much higher on the social ladder? Our family told the story that she returned to Orangeburg as World War Two began. That suggested she came home because the world was too much to bear. Was that true? Or did she respond to college the same way I did, by drinking hard and pretending disinterest?

I made my career writing about barbecue pitmasters and fried chicken cooks. I believed what I wrote and said about my family was comparatively unimportant. That changed when I wrote "My Mother's Catfish Stew" for the *Oxford American,* in which I used that time at Winthrop to make sense of what went right and wrong in my boyhood house and in the woods that surrounded us.

THE JAMES BEARD FOUNDATION ANNOUNCED the 2020 journalism awards on social media. The pandemic was less than three months old. Instead of gathering in New York City, nominees watched the scroll on laptops and phones. "My Mother's Catfish Stew" was up for the M.F.K. Fisher Distinguished Writing Award.

When my name popped up as the winner, I stood from the desk in my writing shed and walked into the kitchen to tell Blair. In that Covid moment, our life revolved around our Oxford backyard and the other planets in our solar system: the sidewalk that ran along our narrow street, the woods behind William Faulkner's house, and the benches on the courthouse lawn.

Generous reads of my work poured in. A friend compared me to Mary Karr, the brilliant memoirist, famous for writing hard truths about her hard childhood. The *Oxford American* announced a retrospective of my twenty-plus-year career as a columnist. The magazine had published more of my work than any other writer's, editor Eliza Borné told readers. She promised, "You would be hard-pressed to find a more compassionate and expert guide."

That afternoon, Blair, Jess, and I gathered to drink Champagne on the landing in front of our house. Blair tied a Mylar balloon shaped like a unicorn to the back of my chair. Our friend Vishwesh Bhatt delivered a couple dozen oysters from his restaurant, Snackbar. Jess and I shucked, university colleagues honked congratulations, and text messages pinged.

Emails poured in from *Oxford American* readers raised by alcoholic mothers. Neighbors stopped me on the square to talk about the violence they witnessed as children. Old friends called to tell me they loved me. Strangers wrote to say that though they lived in Texas and their mother's drug was barbiturates instead of sangria, they recognized their story in mine. A friend leaned on our porch rail to tell about his father, an alcoholic like my mother, who gifted him a camera that birthed his career.

In January of 2017, I helped send a chef friend away for psychological treatment. He was drinking to oblivion and turning on friends. When we sat him down at his kitchen table, he agreed quickly, but when it came time to drive to the airport, he hesitated. "Get your shit," another friend said. *The plane is on the tarmac,* we told him. *Your rehab bill is already paid.* The chef looked up. "Get your shit." This time we all said it.

After our friend left for the airport, our small intervention team joked. We wanted to get on the plane with him and fly west. We wanted to come clean. We needed fixing, too, physically, mentally, all of it.

TWO YEARS BEFORE OUR FRIEND the chef flew west, Chuck Reece and I sat on the back patio at Empire State South in Atlanta, watching men in polo shirts and khakis play bocce in the shadow of a skyscraper. A hawk wheeled above on that fall day as we snacked on pimento cheese and pickles and looked to the blue sky for answers.

Chuck introduced *The Bitter Southerner* in 2013. What began as a long-form narrative site morphed into a multimedia project that won an audience for stories about the progressive South. Early on, Chuck wrote a two-part profile of the SFA, built around a long interview with me and the funeral of John Egerton, who died unexpectedly that same year. In the months that followed, they published a profile of Atlanta rapper Killer Mike and a photo essay on azaleas. They were, it seemed, trying hard to get this place right.

The next year my agent, David Black, sold my history of the modern South told through food. He closed the deal fifty years to the day after President Johnson signed the Civil Rights Act of 1964 into law. *The Potlikker Papers* centered the Montgomery bus boycott as the shaper of a newer South. My book began in 1955 on the steps of Holt Street Baptist Church, on the first night of the boycott, when Rosa Parks stepped onto the stage to receive applause, Martin Luther King Jr. gave his first speech as a leader, and

Georgia Gilmore, the nurse-midwife and cook, showed up with a hamper full of bone-in fried-chicken sandwiches.

If Black citizens were going to quit the buses and set up their own transportation system, Gilmore knew they would need gas for station wagons and oil for engines. Eventually, they would need new tires and transmissions. The dollars she raised that night funded that transportation system, which is another way of saying she funded change.

I previously tried writing a history of the South that began in 1865. Nothing cohered until I recognized that the South I loved took shape as the civil rights movement ignited. To begin with Georgia Gilmore, who also figured in my book *Southern Belly*, was to begin with the big push to force the South to own up to those big American promises of freedom and equality.

That afternoon in 2015, Chuck and I talked about our ongoing work to realize that South. Chuck wanted to know what motivated me. He challenged me to talk about my vision. "Somebody's got to fix this busted-ass place," I said, summing up what I saw as our shared responsibility. Schools and restaurants were now integrated, we agreed, but other sorts of segregation remained.

The neighborhood where I lived was all white and mostly wealthy. My office at the university was mostly white and all liberal. I claimed Black friends across the South and they claimed me, but most of my friends in Oxford were white and so was our life there. What I didn't say that day was that as the Southern Foodways Alliance grew and my writing gained traction, I worried that these disconnects weren't sustainable.

In the summer of 2016, two literary scholars, one based in North Carolina, the other in Canada, announced a call for papers. They planned a book. *Against Cornbread Nationalism: How Foodways Partisans Misrepresent the South* would include "critical readings of particularly egregious foodways rhetoric" and critiques of "white grievance narratives, faithful retainer narratives, and so on . . ."

No matter their animus, they asked variations on questions that already lived in my head, turning like gerbils on a wheel: *How could SFA help fix a place that had been broken since Europeans arrived here?* And: *What good could I really do by thinking and writing about food?*

When Chuck and I talked, SFA was riding a high that didn't look like it would end. The symposium I began in graduate school sold out every year. SFA's film archive was nearing one hundred documentaries. Our oral history archive was winning awards. Our website quoted Corby Kummer of *The Atlantic.* After attending two of our Louisiana events, he wrote that the SFA was "this country's most intellectually engaged (and probably most engaging) food society."

Some part of me still believes that I have a responsibility to fix this busted-ass place. Only after a second wreck in 2020 did I see more clearly what "My Mother's Catfish Stew" revealed: If I wanted to make a fix, I would have to begin with me. And I would have to start back in Clinton, where I began.

TO MARK MY 2020 AWARD, the James Beard Foundation proposed a webinar with a panel of food writers who took complicated families seriously. Problem was, I still thought that writing about food and family was the stuff of hash-brown casserole recipes. I was after bigger stories, I said, even as I accepted an award for writing about my complicated family.

After the May 25th murder of George Floyd, an unarmed Black man killed by a white police officer, protests across the globe clogged streets and activists toppled statues. Reparations gained new advocates and new budget calculations. If there was ever a moment to prove that conversations about food should include the tolls of racism and the promise of civil disobedience, this was it. Thinking I had something to say when many smart and urgent voices strained to be heard, I suggested a more topical panel that featured me and Tunde Wey.

A few years back, I invited Tunde to share my byline and fee for an *Oxford American* piece. A Nigerian-born chef and activist, Tunde was then making a national reputation with his Blackness in an America dinner series that asked whites to listen and eat and sit with the discomfort he engineered. We had met the year before when he was running a food stall at a New Orleans market, cooking pots of ropy okra stew. Our conversation began when I returned to New Orleans for a conference and invited Tunde to join me at a restaurant for cocktails and bowls of pepper pot.

Over dinner, the idea for "Who Owns Southern Food?" arose. We decided on a call-and-response structure. He would challenge me like he did at dinner, and I would consider my privilege and responsibilities. Tunde declared that my time was up. He wrote, "You have endorsed and celebrated the appropriation of Black Southern food without consequence, and the consequences have compounded with interest." He asked, "So what will you willingly give up to ensure the Southern food narrative services properly and fully the contributions of Black Southerners?"

Tunde saw me as a colonial force who was willing to listen. He was thinking of me when he wrote, "White privilege permits a humble, folksy, and honest white boy to diligently study the canon of appropriated Black food, then receive extensive celebration in magazines, newspapers, and television programming for reviving the fortunes of Southern cuisine." Or maybe he was thinking of my friend the chef Sean Brock, a son of Appalachia who was winning national headlines for tracing the roots of lowcountry dishes back to West Africa, where Tunde claimed more immediate roots. He wrote in such a subtle and telling voice that Sean and I both recognized ourselves.

I saw Tunde as a provocateur, asking questions I avoided, pushing me toward uncomfortable stances. I welcomed those challenges. In our article, though, I pushed back when he suggested that I quit writing about Black subjects. "To walk away from writing about Black life would be to divorce myself from writing about the South," I wrote. Previous generations of white writers denied the genius of Black cooks. I was bound to correct those mistakes. "To parse my life by color," I wrote, "would be to render a syncretic culture a racial or geographical one."

Tunde and I became friends. He spoke at an SFA symposium and joined an SFA-convened group at a mountain retreat where we wrote position papers that imagined the South as an origin point for a more equitable American food culture. And I wrote a follow-up *Oxford American* article about his Blackness in America dinner series. To make clear what was at stake, I quoted an op-ed in which he wrote, "The time of dining as escape is over; the notion of food as art is finished; the era of dining as protest is now!"

FOR THE BEARD-SPONSORED WEBINAR, I proposed that Tunde and I take up the questions about the role of food in media and society that we left dangling in our shared article. Jamila Robinson, then a *Philadelphia Inquirer* editor, now editor-in-chief of *Bon Appétit*, would moderate our discussion about what food writing can achieve in a fractured moment. I told myself that this American moment required the sort of bold reckoning I could bring to a conversation. I could not have been more wrong. My decision to not talk about family would soon take a toll on my family.

To get ready, I thought back to a speech I gave at a literary conference in Charlotte. The SFA was two years old and I was full of myself, buoyed by the promise of our work. "I write about food," I said to the crowd, dropping into a confessional register. "And I have a chip on my shoulder."

I wanted to upend the standard set by Lewis Grizzard. At the height of his 1980s popularity, four hundred newspapers published his rants against feminists fighting for their rights and gay men leaving their cloistered small towns for Atlanta. As a boy, I loved him. Grizzard published books with titles that sounded funny, like *I Haven't Understood Anything Since 1962 and Other Nekkid Truths.* Like Alfred Iverson, he once confirmed my knowledge of the South that made me.

My other foil was recipe writers. "I rage against the sentimental pap that many people pass off as food writing," I told the audience that night in Charlotte. I explained that I don't write caramel cake recipes. I leverage our common interest in food so that readers face down what was really at stake on February 1, 1960, when four freshmen at the Agricultural and Technical College of North Carolina walked into an F. W. Woolworth Company store in Greensboro and ordered coffee and donuts.

"I write about issues that have long vexed our region," I said. "My work corrects decades of whitewashed stories unworthy of the South and its people." I told them about Ed Scott, the catfish farmer we showcased at SFA's first symposium. In 1965, he marched across the Edmund Pettus Bridge with Martin Luther King Jr. One year later, after James Meredith took a gunshot in the back on his March Against Fear, Scott fed the men and women who stepped in to finish the march. I told the audience that Scott's work to open the first Black-owned catfish farm and processing facility in the Mississippi Delta suggested how food work could achieve change.

On the afternoon of June 17, three weeks after George Floyd died, as protests in response to his murder spread to include other injustices and other time periods, the webinar went live. Our question was "What is food writing's role in a divided nation?" I planned to say that one of the steps we could take would be to stop all this chef worship. Idolatry based on media, reflected in the terms *star chef* and *celebrity chef*, stratified the field, causing harm to women and people of color, who were often overlooked.

To talk about the power a cook could wield, I was ready to tell a story from *The Potlikker Papers* about "Big Daddy" John Bishop, founder of Dreamland Bar-B-Que in Tuscaloosa, Alabama: In 1956, after the Klan burned a cross in his yard and burned down the wood-frame building where he cooked, Bishop used profits from selling ribs to build a new brick building the Klan couldn't burn down.

I planned to dismiss gradualism, reminding our audience how that approach was used as a delaying tactic during the civil rights movement. Instead, I told the world that I supported that approach and forgot all about John Bishop. I'm still not quite sure why. Did I misspeak? Or did the pace of change in that moment briefly torque the belief system I worked to develop since I left Clinton? Asked for a solution to that moment, when Black men were dying in the streets, and protesters were making plans to topple statues of Thomas Jefferson and Christopher Columbus, I called for a return to the table. Even as I said those words, I recognized how weak and pat they sounded.

Tunde sounded smart and articulate at the beginning of our

fifty-five minutes, smart and disgusted by the close. I came off sounding out of step. And I acted self-destructive, as if I aimed to take a fall. At minute forty-seven, I started to fall apart. At minute fifty-two, Tunde asked when I was going to resign my job at the SFA. Instead of talking about the role food writing could play in that pitched American moment, or speaking to what makes a good story in any moment, I became the story.

After twenty-plus years on what I believed to be the right side of progress, I planted myself on the wrong side of history. Hubris— a belief that this was the time to show the world how a progressive white man could lead—undid me. Centuries of racism and sexism fed the rage that came for me. That rage was always righteous and sometimes indiscriminate, burning hotter every day, fueled by its own locomotion, boosted by its own exhaust.

My conversation with Tunde catalyzed a broader conversation about the role of white men in food. But the purposeful call for my resignation from SFA came from inside the house I helped build. Five days after our panel, a friend dialed to say that Ronni Lundy, an SFA founder, was circulating a letter to SFA members and colleagues that demanded I give my job up to a Black woman.

The plan was, my friend explained, to collect signatures, convince our board to vote "No confidence," and convince the university to fire me. Momentum built. Two days after I learned about Lundy's effort, journalist Kathleen Purvis, who, early in my writing career helped me figure out that no-graft policy, rejoined the SFA. The idea, I believe, was to use her renewed membership to gain access to the SFA roster and secure more signatures.

When I got on the phone with Lundy, she talked about the long history of prejudice against people of color and women that intersected in this moment. She told me that I built an organization to benefit myself. She told me it was time for me to step down. I told her that she might kill off the organization she helped bring to life. She said, "If the SFA can't exist without this particular white man in charge, it doesn't deserve to exist."

BACK IN 2017, *THE NEW YORK TIMES* published a profile that labeled me a power broker and kingmaker: "With not much more than a few kind words over a bourbon," Kim Severson wrote, he "can fill seats in a restaurant, snag media attention for a promising chef, or jump-start the academic future of a bright acolyte." Timed to coincide with the publication of *The Potlikker Papers,* the article also suggested that I was a problem to be solved.

Severson quoted Scott Romine, one of the scholars who railed against "cornbread nationalism" and accused me of looking past the violence Black Southerners endured to celebrate the beauty of the fried chicken they cooked. Instead of reminding people of the films we recently produced on the struggle to integrate restaurants in Southern cities, or pledging to do more and better work, I said the scholar wasn't paying close enough attention to what SFA attempted.

Now in 2020, lots of people were paying unwelcome attention. As Ronni Lundy talked, I listened. Headphones on, I typed notes, trying to make sense of what was happening. Did I need an attorney? Would I have to sue to protect my job and my family? Early in our conversation, she diverted from a critique of the role I played and the organization I directed. Even as she said this wasn't personal, she made clear that it was. Lundy told me that despite her success, she struggled to live comfortably. She said men like me, who soaked up too much recognition and pay, were responsible. She reminded me that when she won a Beard award, I did not publicly congratulate her.

Over the course of the conversation, Lundy mentioned that the letter she wrote would soon be in the hands of Kim Severson at *The New York Times*. Or maybe it was already there. I begged Lundy to not send it. She said that it was too late. I cried at my desk. I stepped into the backyard and screamed into the bricked-up window of our neighbor's garage. And then I walked inside to tell Blair.

In a stream of emails and texts and phone calls, this wreck came for me in slow motion. My critics said I had been in my job too long. In posts on Instagram and Twitter and Facebook, they said I controlled stories that were not mine to tell.

I fought my worst and weakest self to listen. Critiques are hard to bear, especially when they're aimed at an organization you helped build. My critics made good points. I controlled an organization that annually spent more than a million dollars on stories about the South, distributed via a podcast, a journal, and a website, plus documentary films, oral histories, and events.

We told the right stories. From our platform, civil rights leader Shirley Sherrod, who ran a five-thousand-plus-acre collective farm near Albany, Georgia, explained how institutional racism worked. When she and her husband requested an emergency loan during a multiyear drought, a government supervisor said they would get it "over [his] dead body." We hosted the right meals, too. Mashama Bailey, chef and co-owner of the Grey in Savannah, collaborated with Zora Neale Hurston biographer Valerie Boyd to imagine a symposium lunch. She cooked red rice and stewed okra, fried whiting and grits, and greens with ham hocks, inspired by Hurston, the famed Alabama-born anthropologist and novelist who chronicled Black life in the South.

But our organization was mostly run by whites. And here I was, a fifty-seven-year-old white man who controlled stories about people of color.

My fiercest critics extended that idea, casting me as a white overseer who profited from Black labor. SFA put writers and chefs on pedestals, but we owned the pedestals and the klieg lights that shone on those pedestals. In the summer of 2020, my beliefs about the role I played in the South began to crumble beneath the weight of their accusations.

Jessica Harris, who spoke at that first symposium and read at our wedding a year later, asked me who needed to hear those stories and eat those meals. "Black Southerners lived them," she said. "SFA exists to serve and educate whites." She told me that the best way to take stock would be for me to think about how much white SFA staffers profited from our work and compare that to how much Black SFA founders profited.

SFA rose to prominence by challenging audiences to take a hard look at their beliefs about the South. Here was my chance to take a hard look at my actions. I worked for more than twenty years to rethink and subvert the lies and myths that shaped my world. Now I had to examine whether new takes on those old lies and myths shaped the way I led the SFA.

As the week unfolded and the critiques mounted, about a third of my critics bore down on systemic issues. But the rest wanted to take me down. "Good trouble," Amy Evans, the former SFA oral historian, declared, claiming the moral high ground of civil rights movement leader John Lewis.

Osayi Endolyn, who had worked for SFA as an editor, circulated a letter that accused me of profiting from her work without giving credit. To try to prove her case, Endolyn made it sound like I stole her ideas. Speaking of my role managing SFA, she accused me of "innuendo, back-room scheming, and outright lies." She mailed the letter to chefs across the South and she emailed it to media outlets across the nation, including the *Oxford American*.

On a Friday afternoon, nine days after the webinar with Tunde, the magazine fired me. Twice during my tenure, the magazine paused production, and I forgave or reduced my fee to help out. Twenty-plus years after I published my first column, *Oxford American* editor Eliza Borné delivered the news to me via email.

ESPN and the SEC Network were sticking by me, Wright Thompson called to report. Dave DiBenedetto from *Garden & Gun* emailed to say they believed in me, too. The Center for the Study of Southern Culture, our parent organization, wasn't so sure. At the end of the summer, the Center called for a change in leadership. The document cited "recent and long-standing critiques" and specifically referenced the term *gradualism*, which I used in the Beard conversation.

WHEN THE *NEW YORK TIMES* STORY PUBLISHED, I asked Pete Wells, then the restaurant critic for the newspaper, to mail a print copy to Oxford. A decade back, when he edited the food section, I wrote a monthly United Tastes column for him. To document the rapidly diversifying American food scene, I filed copy from Bosnian bakeries in St. Louis, Somali-owned teriyaki restaurants in Seattle, and Levantine sandwich shops in Jacksonville.

Pete called back because he couldn't find the article in the food section. That was because it landed in the national section. Nearly a full page, it dwarfed the story beneath about Elijah McClain, a young Black man in Aurora, Colorado, who died after police restrained him with an illegal choke hold. The story spoke to a deeply troubled moment in the United States, and it didn't speak well of me.

"You are a prop in what felt like a dog-and-pony show," Atlanta chef Asha Gomez told Kim Severson, referring to my work as moderator at an event where she spoke. "I feel he is most interested, more than anything, in perpetuating and protecting his role as a kingmaker," Osayi Endolyn said. "If you stop being the person who is the collector of the shiny brown things, who are you really?"

This wake came with familiar gifts: A caramel cake landed on our porch. A pound cake, too. A university colleague brought a vase of wildflowers. Our neighbor Michael Koury drove me around in his pickup. Kathy Knight from down the street left a pink shoebox, lined with paper towels, stacked with fried peach pies. Richard Howorth, co-owner of Square Books and once our two-term mayor, dropped a bottle of bourbon on our doormat. Twenty-five years after I moved to town, I deeply loved Oxford. And Oxford loved me.

Wright Thompson dropped off bottles of bourbon, vermouth, and Campari, the makings for boulevardiers. Earlier that spring, after the pandemic descended and my father's long-term care facility closed to visitors, we began to drink virtual boulevardiers. As my father and I drank, I heard the rattle of ice in his glass and the tremor in his voice. He sounded scared. Now I was, too.

I JOINED THE RESTAURANT AWARDS COMMITTEE of the James Beard Foundation in 2005 just after an embezzlement scandal flared, when Beard revealed that it raised almost $5 million the previous year but spent only $29,500 on scholarships. Brett Anderson, the New Orleans writer who recruited me to the committee, said Beard was worth saving.

By the time I stepped down from Beard in 2018, public relations reps who promoted chefs regularly packed SFA events, critics claimed that a Southern mafia controlled the awards, and SFA detractors and faithful both saw me as its boss. But in the early days, when Pete Wells served on the Beard committee with me, we argued about restaurants with a kind of earnest, almost naïve intent. After meetings, over cocktails, we wondered when writers would take the food beat seriously.

Too few asked hard questions about the role restaurants could play in a progressive society. To write about food and drink, we said, you have to write about race and gender and class. You have to engage all the senses and take on all the issues that trouble and uplift American life.

By the late 2010s, a new generation of writers began to own up to that promise. Reading their work, I recognized a difference. When I wrote about the civil rights movement, distance from the violence of that era made some of my work read like an affirmation of the progress my generation made. Wrongs had been made right, I suggested. While I chafed against food writing that merely entertained, this new generation worked to overturn the interlocked systems that paid for and distributed that work.

Reading Tunde Wey on financial inequities and access to capital, or Soleil Ho on why immigrant restaurateurs continue to struggle under the burdens of colonial ideas, I recognized that while they bore down on contemporary sins, I still worked the celebratory activism beat. Their arguments made readers uncomfortable. Sit with that discomfort, they said, and then work to understand how and why you feel that way.

When Tunde and like-minded writers came for me in the summer of 2020, I tried hard to listen. It took a while to recognize that they had long been ready to push me aside, in the way a new generation always comes for the one that came before, in the way I came for Lewis Grizzard acolytes and recipe writers. It took longer to recognize that they were trying what Pete and I imagined when we gathered to talk about a future when writers took the food beat seriously.

SOON AFTER MY FATHER MOVED to Oxford, his doctor diagnosed him as legally blind. Daddy suffered from macular degeneration. Instead of faces, he saw shapes. He recognized me by voice, or by the purr of my car's muffler as I pulled in front of his porch. To arrest the progress of the disease, he received monthly shots in both of his eyes.

My father subscribed to large-print magazines and tried to read them with a magnifying glass. He still couldn't discern the words. Books stacked his coffee table in the summer of 2020: a biography of Jimmy Carter, three tell-alls by Donald Trump cronies, and *Brown* by Kevin Young, which included that "Money Road" poem. My father couldn't read those books, but he still bought them. Most afternoons, his girlfriend, Martha, read aloud to him.

A couple of weeks after my second wreck, my father asked me to read that *New York Times* article to him. I delayed as long as I could. When I did read it to him, I skipped some parts, including quotes from old friends whose names he might recognize. I also corrected errors and omissions that the *Times* refused to acknowledge. Even with my edits, the article landed hard. My father's silence told me he heard every word, including the ones I left out.

HOME FOR THE PANDEMIC, Blair and I sat before the television like Archie and Edith Bunker in their Astoria living room, TV trays stacked with mail, our dog, Lurleen, curled beneath, our lives a remake of *All in the Family.* Early in our marriage, Blair returned home between classes to watch soap operas like her mother and father. Now we gathered on our couch to watch *Cheers* reruns and brace for what came next.

As we ate gas-station chicken salad on sourdough baked by a friend, an ad for a 1-800 trial attorney flashed on the screen: *Have you been injured in a car crash?* "Yes!" I shouted at the television, my volume rising to match the screech of the man with the silver hair and the serious black suit. I meant to be playful, but what came from my mouth sounded hard and frightened.

My voice cracked. Thinking of that wreck in 2018, my spirit did, too. I still carry that car wreck in my body. *Slow down,* my body tells me. *Be thankful.* The screen flashed again. The attorney asked, "Have you been injured in a car crash?" Blair and I turned to each other. A pause followed, then smiles. "This feels like that," we said, our voices rising. This wreck, like the one that derailed the civil rights sculpture on the Ole Miss campus, I carry in my head.

Blair put me in a therapist's chair the same week the *New York Times* piece put me in the news. My therapist and I met in a brick bungalow behind a drugstore on the strip-mall end of Oxford. The light was low. A scented candle burned on his desk. We talked about power struggles and the gut punches of betrayals. I told him that this moment reminded me of the worst of my time in Athens.

After a big night out in college, people told me that I had done things I couldn't recall. Sometimes I wondered if they made that stuff up. This was like that, I told him. Now people posted to social media that they always suspected I was a racist. They said I collected Black collaborators like tchotchkes. They claimed to have been calling for my resignation for more than a decade. My therapist said, *The plural of anecdote is not data.*

Fifteen days separated the *Times* article that portrayed me as a statue to be removed from the actual removal of the Confederate statue at the heart of our campus. My friend Andy Harper captured a shot of the moment that gray marble soldier achieved liftoff, left arm raised in salute, right hand on his rifle. Wrapped in yellow nylon straps, tied at the chest into a sort of corsage, the sculpture diminished as it came free from its base. Soon, Andy's photo suggested, the sculpture would, like a minotaur returning to the maze, disappear into the green boughs of the surrounding oaks. With it would go the ugly rhetoric on which that ugly story depended.

After the *Times* story published, older white men who glimpsed their future downfall in mine wrote long letters in strong and steady voices. Younger white men, trying to prove their relevance in a moment when attention was turning away from them, wrote emails that condemned me and revealed their fears of being the next person called to account. In the noise of the moment, friends called, knowing I was confused and hurting, just to hear the sound of my voice and ask if I was okay.

The right wing approached often. Some guy who called himself Billy the Impaler wrote on Twitter, "So at what time do #whitemales report to the boxcars?" When a reporter for a news nonprofit criticized me, someone who posted as Roland D. LeBay responded, "Thank you for your courage, white savior." Matt Taibbi, an investigative reporter who sometimes writes about liberal overreach, pitched a story about my plight. I declined to participate, wrongly believing that the storm would soon pass. The day after the *Times* story ran, a group led by onetime SFA oral historian Amy Evans posted an open letter, signed by dozens of former collaborators, calling for my resignation.

The conversation I helped start had overtaken me. There was a bigger, more philosophical problem, too. I was no longer writing against a fossilized story of Southern food. In the eyes of a new generation of thinkers and writers, I was now a fossil myself, working for an establishment organization, reducing complicated ongoing issues to celebrations of past racism overcome, trying to lead people who didn't accept me as a member of their tribe, much less as their leader.

BACK IN THE FALL OF 2019, I watched author Kiese Laymon step onto the brick side porch of William Faulkner's Rowan Oak on the opening night of our SFA fall symposium. Beneath a canopy of stringed lights and a rope-hung chandelier, on the edge of the deep woods, a mostly white audience sat in white folding chairs. I was proud that my invitation landed Kiese there. He had a reputation for speaking with frankness. Kiese's presence in our midst was bold, I told myself.

The symposium that year revolved around labor. We paid tribute to the people who did the work to put food on our tables. Earlier on that October night, our group wandered the front lawn of Faulkner's home, eating oysters on the half shell beneath tilted cedars. After Kiese's talk, we gathered in the pasture alongside to drink wine and slurp bowls of oyster stew.

Before Kiese spoke about Callie Barr, the Black woman who worked for the white Nobel Prize winner and lived in a cabin in his backyard, he pointed his phone toward the trees and took a picture of a bright chandelier that hung from the boughs. As he spoke, Kiese gestured toward Barr's cabin, connecting her undervalued labor to the undervalued labor of his grandmother, who worked a Mississippi chicken processing line, slitting bellies and pulling out guts. If Faulkner loved Barr, Kiese seemed to ask, how could he let her live like she did?

How could Faulkner look away from what the white South demanded of her? How could we, gathered in those chairs beneath that rope-hung chandelier, look away from that question in the year 2019? Looking away led to the "moral annihilation" of white people, Kiese said. He talked about recent immigration service raids of chicken plants downstate, where his grandmother lived. And he talked about the love and respect he carries for the people who work in those plants. Kiese closed by saying, "If you can afford to come to this symposium, you can afford to do more to free the land of our region. Please do it."

Some in the audience shifted uncomfortably in their chairs. Many stood to applaud. Instead of inviting questions, I asked guests to sit with what Kiese said. In the pause, I took a photo to memorialize the moment: Turned toward me, Kiese is saying something I can't recall. He is smiling. To my eyes, the lights strung from the trees give off the look of a small-town carnival.

Walking toward the Courthouse Square after dinner, I joined a group of friends who gossiped about what went on that night across town. At about the same time Kiese spoke from Faulkner's side porch, Donald Trump Jr. stood in front of a tractor shed across town and said that the North was brainwashing Southern children with "liberal crap." He claimed Democrats wanted a communist government. And he cracked "Me Too" jokes at the expense of his girlfriend, who stood by his side.

When I learned that the two events had neatly overlapped, I pumped my fist in the air like the high school football player I once was. *Somebody ought to write about what those two moments illustrate,* I told myself.

More than a year passed before I saw the photograph Kiese took that night from the porch at Rowan Oak. By then, my comeuppance had come. And plenty of people had weighed in on what my fall illustrated. In the image Kiese captured that night, the smiling white faces in the audience appear ghoulish and the light from those chandelier bulbs distorts.

High in the boughs, the chandelier looks like the ghost of a body, suspended by ropes, given up for dead. SFA didn't string that rope. Another group left the lights behind after another party, but there that chandelier hung.

For a while Kiese used that photo as his Twitter profile picture. He didn't include commentary, but the message was clear to me: Threats of violence forever remain here. With those threats come reminders of who belongs and who doesn't, markers of the thin scrim that separates past and present.

I would think of that image often in the years to come. If I could try to see the world through the eyes of people who saw a ghost in those trees, I stood to gain, even if that knowledge challenged my ideas of where I belonged and for whom I spoke and what good I could do.

SIX WEEKS AFTER THE *TIMES* STORY RAN, a driver hooked my new Mini to the back of a rock-and-roll tour bus, and we hit the road. A Covid vaccine was still four months away. Colleges canceled games for the fall. Without live sports, we worried the SEC Network would fail and ESPN would tank.

Our crew of eight tested negative to get on the bus, making a bet that we could get season three of *TrueSouth* done in the gap between the threat of comorbidities and the chance we took each time we masked up and stepped off. What no one said, at least to me, was that we also took to the road so that I could get my life back in gear.

On the way out of Oxford, we looped the square twice so the drone above could capture our exit. Our first stop was Brownsville, Tennessee, for buffalo fish, one of the first foods I obsessed over after moving to Oxford. And pork shoulder sandwiches capped with slaw, served by Jess's favorite pitmaster, Helen Turner.

The last shoot was scheduled for my mother's birthplace of Bowman, South Carolina. Instead of our usual formula of two restaurants in one town, set in conversation to talk about some bigger issue, we planned to tell the story of my family with a recipe. Just two months had passed since I told the Beard Foundation that I wanted to talk about serious stuff, like race relations, not frivolous things, like family relations.

When we made the call to break our show formula and use reporting and realizations from "My Mother's Catfish Stew" to make an episode, I broke myself open. Among the casualties were my ideas about what purpose family recipes and family stories can serve.

WHEN MY MOTHER PASSED BACK IN MARCH OF 2001, Blair was on bed rest before the birth of Jess. Beginning that January, I flinched every time the phone rang. Was my mother going or was our son coming? Eleven days separated her exit and his entrance. End-stage dementia and malnutrition took her. That's what her death certificate says, but the previous two decades did damage that an autopsy might not show.

Her newspaper obituary said the service would be private. In truth, there was none. Later that summer, as Jess began to sleep through the night, my father drove to Bowman with her headstone in the trunk of his Buick. In the loam of a suburban graveyard, he set the small rectangle inscribed with her name alongside her mother and father and brother.

In the years since, I drove through Orangeburg County on the way to and from Charleston for lunches that began with sturgeon caviar and dinners that ended with chess pie. Each time I traveled to the city my mother loved more than any other, I was less than an hour's drive from Bowman Memorial Cemetery. But I never visited the grave of Mary Beverly Evans Edge until I traveled that way with a television crew.

We made our headquarters in a house near Bowman that was everything my mother hated. The columns out front were tin. Where pocket doors once slid in and out of the walls, hollow-core doors hung. The furniture was overwrought, manufactured in a style I once heard described as Rococola. THESE TOWELS ARE FOR DISPLAY ONLY, read the sign posted in the bathroom above an assemblage of yellow and white terry, elaborately wrapped in silver cords.

Working with ladders and drapes, the crew made a kind of interrogation theater out of the living room. Wright sat opposite me, behind a black curtain, notebook in hand. Three cameras stared back at me. The crew installed one on top of a tall wooden ladder. If that camera fell, it would hit the sofa cushion laid at my feet.

I mixed a fat boulevardier and took my seat. Wright asked blunt questions like "In what ways did your mother damage you?" I told him that her lies robbed me of trust in myself, my family, the South. He said things like "Tell me about the fake suicide attempts." And I said things like "Shit" and "Fuck you." I talked, despite and because of the audience that would tune in. Here was another chance to understand how much my family story could mean to others, an opportunity to understand how much my family story meant to me.

On the way to the cemetery, Wright and I passed beneath oaks that sagged with Spanish moss, a drag strip that hosted motorcycle races, and a metal sign, posted beneath a falling-apart timber-and-

tin spaceship, that read UFO WELCOME CENTER. Killing time while
the crew set up cameras among the tombstones, Wright and I
stopped for boiled peanuts at Quick Pantry #3, where R. J. Patel
sells bags packed by the Hindu temple in nearby Orangeburg.

As we got closer to showtime, Wright and the crew began to
worry if they were going too far. At the cemetery, cars lined the nar-
row asphalt lanes, like they do at real funerals. As I stepped from
the Mini to find the place where my mother lay, Wright said, "I
love you."

I dropped to one knee at the foot of my mother's grave. All
week, knowing where we were headed, I feared that I would not
feel anything. I worried that I had pushed my love for Momma
down so far that I couldn't pull it back up. I should not have wor-
ried. I cried heaving, wracking sobs. The cameras caught it all and I
felt it all.

I told her I was sorry that it took so long for me to get there. I
talked about her grandson's big goofy grin and the kindness with
which he moves through the world. I recounted all the good things
that happened after she left us. I told her about the house Blair and
I made together and the dinner parties she would love. I begged her
to take me back.

It was quiet there in the cemetery, and then it wasn't. To give
my mother the funeral she never got, our director, Tim Horgan,
brought a Grammy-winning band. Born of her beloved low-
country, Ranky Tanky played beneath a shade tree while our cam-
eras rolled. A trumpet sounded, upright bass and guitar followed.
Reaching for the heavens, Quiana Parler sang, "Oh, death, won't
you spare me over 'til another year."

The next day, as the crew packed their vans for the drive to the
Charleston airport, our bus driver loaded my Mini back onto the
trailer. Only Wright and I climbed aboard the bus this time. As we

pulled down the lane, beneath an allée of oak and palmetto trees, bound for the highway and home, Tim stood at attention, hat in hand, beating his chest. For the second time since Wright asked those hard questions, I knew what it felt like to be loved.

IN OCTOBER OF 2021, a week before Blair and I threw a goodbye party for my SFA colleagues, I walked out of Barnard Observatory with my last box of file folders. The next week, I donated a couple hundred books to the Ole Miss library.

Twenty-six boxes went down our front stairs and into the back of an SUV. The food studies collection now shelved under my name in the library includes books I helped edit, like a study of urban food economies in the Jim Crow South, and a biography of Ed Scott, the catfish farmer and activist who cooked for the first SFA symposium.

For the goodbye party, I met each of my colleagues at the door of our house, a flute in one hand, a bottle of Veuve Clicquot in the other. Blair walked the crowd, handing out cheese wafers, this time without sliced black-olive rounds in the center.

In the weeks that followed, we leaned into ceremony as a way to memorialize the break. Blair pulled *Oxford American* cover blow-ups from issues I guest-edited off our living room wall and hung them in the laundry room above our cat's litter box. In our back-yard firepit, I burned a cookbook by Ronni Lundy and a painting Amy Evans made for my fortieth birthday. White cinders floated across a gray sky.

No person or group forced me to leave the SFA. My prompt came from within. Critics said I had stayed too long in my job. They said the world in which I worked was too white. If I believed in myself enough to imagine a new job, I couldn't argue with that first complaint. If I believed in a South that would someday free itself from the choke holds of racism and its inheritances, I couldn't argue with the second.

By the time I left, more than a year had passed since that webinar with Tunde. In the breach, I worked with my colleagues and our board to plan a transition. After that censure from the Center, I didn't want my job anymore. With those books gone, a gap opened in the shelves that line my bedroom. With my job at the SFA gone, a gap opened in my life.

Back where I began

Chapter Nine

RECONSTRUCTION

"[H]e must have felt and heard the design—house,
position, posterity and all—come down like it had been
built out of smoke."

—William Faulkner, *Absalom, Absalom!*

My people left forty years back, but the legend on the map near
the courthouse site in Clinton still marks the Iverson-Edge house.
Same as it does on the brochures the Old Clinton Historical Soci-
ety first printed in 1974, when my parents believed our town would
become a Colonial Williamsburg for the Deep South. The society
markets Clinton as "The Town That Time Forgot." Color photos
have replaced line drawings. But the words on these new brochures
still speak to old ideas about the town where I grew up.

Instead of the Civil War, the society often refers to the War Be-
tween the States, just as it does on the marker they installed near
the center of town. That language seems dated, born of a time when

white Southerners rationalized secession by claiming that our nation was merely a loose confederation of independent states, until you hear U.S. Representative Marjorie Taylor Greene of Georgia argue that our nation needs a national divorce. The war fought by soldiers may have ended, but the war of words and the ideas bound up in them continues.

For our Bowman, South Carolina, episode of *TrueSouth,* our crew also made a trip to Clinton. To capture B-roll, we stood on the gravel driveway on the outside of a red cattle gate and turned our cameras on my old house. I didn't know then who owned it, but I already knew that I wanted to tramp those woods again. I needed to stand at the back door and hold that iron burglar bar in my hand to test its weight.

After the episode aired, a friend introduced me to Chuck Johnson, the current owner of our old house. When I called to schedule a visit, Chuck picked up on the second ring. I heard kindness in his voice and curiosity about the house and history we shared.

That red gate was open when I returned in 2021. At the top of our old drive, Chuck met me at my car, a sweet and hesitant smile on his face. I liked him instantly. "Want to walk the land?" he asked, his voice fluttering with excitement. Cedars and black walnut trees curtained the road. The privet my mother loathed and the nandina she loved grew rambunctiously. As we walked, a blue heeler named Dixie followed.

Scampering across my old backyard like a billy goat, Chuck plunged down into the gulley at the back of the property. We threaded stands of bamboo. He showed me where foxes dug a den into a red clay bank. Using an old photo on my phone as our guide, we looked for the site of my mother's rock garden. Gone was the cedar arbor, where she ran into the night with a gun in her hand.

The pole for that second historical marker lay in the bushes at the foot of an oak tree.

Where we kept the washpot I climbed atop to speak of Iverson, Chuck parked a military surplus trailer. He told me that he worked as a sutler and called his business Rum Creek Sutler, named for a nearby body of water. Sutlers traditionally followed troops, supplying them with clothes and tents and canteens. Now they also follow reenactors, who follow the troop patterns of the Civil War toward fates they already know.

Chuck planned to convert the old jail kitchen into a store. Where my mother wanted to sell pedigreed artifacts, he would sell gray wool uniforms and blue felt kepis. Like my father, Chuck worried over maintaining that old building. As we passed azaleas and palmettos, he narrated his fight to keep the squirrels out, fearful they would chew through the electrical wires and start a fire.

Chuck brimmed with enthusiasm for the mysteries this land holds. Born a year and six days after me, he reminded me of my young self. In his knowledge of munitions and his beliefs in the Confederate South, I heard where I might have ended up, had I not tried and failed and tried again to step from the dark woods and outrun the long shadow of Alfred Iverson.

Walking toward our old home, Chuck showed where the Iverson kitchen probably stood, back when kitchens often burned down and homeowners built them detached. He spoke of relics he found near the goldfish pond my mother's father dug and stocked with Japanese carp.

As Chuck talked, I caught sight of my father, a ghost in the morning light, moving through the clearing, a bucket of mineral spirits in hand and a plan in his head to restore the latest treasures my mother hauled home.

Back inside my boyhood home for the second time since I helped my mother load the truck for Columbia, I followed Chuck as he walked from the back hall to what we called the red room, accounting his own treasures. Chuck showed me a terrine and told me that Varina Davis used the same pattern in the Confederate White House. Passing a display case lined with glass jars and ceramic jugs, sidestepping a wooden drum wrapped in white rope, we talked about the evolution of the house, from a simple dogtrot to a foursquare with a paneled wood dado in the formal living room. "I'm a caretaker," Chuck said. "The idea is to not let this thing go down on my watch."

Books were everywhere: *Lee's Lieutenants,* the three-volume series by Douglas Southall Freeman, stood next to a taped-together edition of *The Railroads of the Confederacy. Echoes of Glory* sat atop *Civil War Heavy Explosive Ordnance* and *A Southern View of the Invasion of the Southern United States and War of 1861–65.*

Chuck talked about flats, the thin buttons sewn onto civilian clothing. He cradled the tip of a bayonet scabbard, pulled from the yard. And he told me about the precision of his metal detector and Gray Ghost brand headphones, embossed with a portrait of a Confederate soldier.

Music played from the kitchen. The sound was staticky, like it was coming from that box radio I listened to as a boy. As I drew closer, the sound grew clear: "Blinded by the Light," piped directly from 1973. I turned eleven that year. Walking toward the kitchen, I was eleven again.

In the hall, a taxidermied squirrel stood on hind legs beneath a replica flag from the 3rd Confederate Infantry Regiment, inscribed with the names of battles they fought: Farmington, Chickamauga, and Ringgold Gap, a roll call of loss and death. Wearing a tiny hat on his tiny head, the squirrel held a rifle in the crook of his right arm. His left paw gripped a wood staff topped by a Confederate battle flag. My mother would have called it tacky. My eleven-year-old self loved it.

As I said goodbye, Chuck and a friend panned that metal detector across a bank of centipede in the shadow of my old tree house. They found a Mercury dime and handed it to me, a good luck charm for the ride home. At the bottom of the drive, as I pulled even with that historical marker, embossed with the script that shaped my childhood, my cell phone dinged. Blair had texted to say that the episode about my mother was playing on ESPN. Her funeral was about to start.

WHEN I LEFT GEORGIA, I left behind the Civil War. But I got drawn back in as the 150th anniversary of Gettysburg approached in 2013, and historians and journalists took another look at the stories the United States tells itself about what caused the war, who won the war, and what price our nation paid. A Tony Horwitz article published in *The Atlantic* that June asked, "Should we consecrate a war that killed and maimed over a million Americans?"

To illustrate the horror, Horwitz used my boyhood hero Alfred Iverson and his performance on the first day of the Battle of Gettysburg. The marker in front of our house name-checked Gettysburg. When I was a boy, knowing that Iverson participated in that battle was all I needed. Horwitz demanded that I look again.

He quoted a soldier under Iverson's command who got sprayed by the brains of another. He panned a row of seventy-nine North Carolina troops, killed by a single volley. He described a soldier shot between his eye and ear, a soldier who lost his left arm, and a soldier who lost his left thigh. Horwitz wrote of the shallow pits where the men who survived Iverson's charge buried the men who died. If I stared down the truth about Iverson, I wondered, what other truths could I reveal about my South and myself?

At home in Oxford, I flashed to my childhood, asking old questions with a new urgency. As a boy, I never saw my Black teammates take seats in those ladder-back chairs at Old Clinton Bar-B-Q. What role did they play in that pageant? And what happened around back? Did Black men in blue work shirts unload pickup trucks swaybacked with hickory? Did they shovel soot from the pit into ash middens and haul trash to the burn pile?

In the 1960s, Black customers ordered from a window on the side of the restaurant. Not much had changed by the 1970s, when I became a regular. Black people in Jones County lived in the shadows that white lives cast. Most whites seemed to look past the Black men who worked barbecue pits, same as we ignored the Black women who washed and fed our children. When I was a boy, all I wanted out of the Civil War were stories that lifted up my place and my people. And all I wanted out of Old Clinton Bar-B-Q was a sandwich and a stew.

In my twenties, as my mother declined and my father made a new life in Macon, I tried to leave my family. Thanksgiving meant New Orleans road trips for oyster po'boys at Dooky Chase's and shrimp in chili sauce at Uglesich's. Christmas translated as day trips from Atlanta to Macon, down in the morning for sausage biscuits and presents, back home by night for a cheese steak and a pint at my neighborhood bar.

But I never quit my hometown barbecue joint. The sound of tires on gravel, the sight of those cedar pillars, catapulted me back to a time before my mother's disease robbed her brilliance, before two deaths stole my innocence.

Each generation thinks they're making a new way. What we mostly do is cover up what came before, following the same paths our people traced. That goes for the roads my grandfather tore up and laid down when he worked that grading crew, and that goes for the stories I used to tell and retell of the South that made and nearly unmade me.

When I began to write about the South, I told everyone that Old Clinton Bar-B-Q was my second home. In my mind, Mittie Coulter forever stood before me, chopping auburn hams into fatty chunks beneath the glare of a tube fluorescent. From the front porch, I stared through the screened door, watching her wrap vinegar-drenched sandwiches in tissue bundles and spear each with a toothpick. Woodsmoke wreathed her boll of gray hair; pork skin and meat arced through the air.

In grad school, I returned to Clinton with a tape recorder and new ideas about that old place. Mittie Coulter and Wayne Coulter and I sat in the kitchen of her small white house, across the gravel lot from the restaurant. We talked about her father, who taught her husband, Big Roy, to cook. We spoke of the poured-concrete pit where Wayne and his helpers worked, and about how they patterned that pit after Fresh Air Barbecue near Jackson, Georgia.

I pledged allegiance to Old Clinton in the first edition of *Southern Belly*. While I was away, though, something changed. About the time Mittie Coulter died in 1996, Old Clinton pulled out that dogleg-shaped pit. An Illinois-founded company named Southern Pride installed a machine. Smoke still curled from the chimney at Old Clinton Bar-B-Q, but it pains me to say that I could no longer taste the combusted ghost of hickory and oak in their chopped pork.

Something changed in me, too. If memory is a weave of sights, sounds, and smells stitched together to reveal the past that lives in the present, then Old Clinton Bar-B-Q was a quilt I could drape across my shoulders and disappear into my childhood.

Now I saw through the smoke. If I wanted to become the reconciled man that life in Mississippi demanded, I had deeper work to do back in Georgia. Now that I knew Iverson wasn't truly a hero, it was time to dig up the taproot of the lies I learned to tell as a boy.

WHEN WE JOINED HOUSES IN 1999, Blair and I fought over what to sell or toss. A decade of post-college acquisitions were in the balance. Out went my black leather armchair; in came her side chairs decorated with carved devil heads. Early one morning, I staged a sale in the front yard. All went well until Blair walked outside to check the progress and discovered that I was selling her Revere Ware pots and pans.

We merged our art with more ease. Our walls now tell the story of our lives together, including a wooden mask from a Oaxaca trip, a golden scarab we bought in London, a friend's color-saturated photograph of a shuttered corner store, and a portrait of a gothic farmhouse, painted by Blair's mother.

The scarab, which has a habit of falling from its perch, is glued together and wrapped with wire. Pulled from a junk shop, the mask shows just the right patina of dirt. All of the objects telegraph that they were born of another time. Pairing them with treasures my mother collected, Blair weaved our families together across time.

Blair didn't set out to design a living room my mother would have loved. But that's what happened as she hung artwork and mementos, making a narrative with that French theater poster from Bolingbroke at the center. Within the frame, children leap and

bound through the ruins of a village. Bombed out shells of build-
ings loom. Boys wear pointy helmets, presumably pulled from dead
Germans. Girls look wan and stare toward the horizon. Amid the
ruins, they pretend a new world.

I've sold or abandoned many of the odd and lovely things my
mother bought on her antique hunts, including the brass spittoons
she hauled from the Jones County courthouse and a glass front she
pulled from an old slot machine. But that French theater poster
made every move, from apartment to apartment in my twenties,
and from house to house to home in my thirties. Mounted on our
living room wall, it reminds me of what ruins can yield.

A few years back, Blair gave me two prints by Jerry Siegel, a
photographer born in Selma, Alabama, where Blair's father was
born. Both hang above my favorite reading chair. One shows a
Black girl at a county fair, pointing a toy gun at a stack of red and
blue and yellow cans. Think like a photographer and you see the
shapes that caught his eye. Seen together, they look like a color-field
painting.

In the background you see what Siegel missed until he devel-
oped the print: The stars and bars of a Confederate battle flag show
from the back of the booth. Look again and the photo reads like a
metaphor. Today, symbols of that insurrection remain in the frame.
We don't always see them, but they're always there and they always
have something to say.

A PORTRAIT OF UNION GENERAL GEORGE STONEMAN hangs today
opposite those Siegel prints. The scene is from July of 1864, when
Stoneman moved through Middle Georgia, on orders to destroy the
railroad near Macon and liberate Federals from the Confederate

prison camp at Andersonville. Stoneman marched with 2,100 men, believing that he would trounce the Confederates in his path. Instead, just down the road from Clinton, at the Battle of Sunshine Church, memorialized on that marker in front of my boyhood home, Iverson's force of 1,300 tricked Stoneman into thinking he was surrounded. Five hundred men from Sherman's ranks were soon on their way to Andersonville.

In the painting by F. Scott Hess, the battle has just ended and the Union general sits on the back porch of our house, near where my father installed our washer and dryer, at about the spot where our dog Lilliput liked to nap. I was nearing the end of my research for *The Potlikker Papers* when Mark Sloan, a museum curator from South Carolina, shipped me a copy of *The Paternal Suit*, a catalog of art and relics created by Hess, a great-grandson of Brigadier General Iverson.

For an exhibition tour that began in my mother's beloved Charleston, Hess sampled stories that cut across his family and connected to mine, making social and political points about the burdens we humans carry. In my copy of his book, he wrote, "Bound not by blood but by memory."

Hess based some of the art on footnoted research. Other works were exaggerations, including a battlefield rendering of Iverson at Gettysburg, binoculars in his left hand, a bottle of whiskey in his right. His poster for *The Stoneman Raid,* a so-called lost movie from the Jim Crow South, offers a more direct clue of intent. "The many inaccuracies make the film a poor substitute for historical fact," Hess wrote, implying that the same is often true of the stories we tell about our wars and our families.

The year after Hess and I connected, Blair bought me a print of that Stoneman painting and hung it above the couch where our dog, Lurleen, pounces to bark at passersby, next to a print of a family tree that traces the Hobbs branch of her family back to colonial New England. In the foreground, a Confederate soldier leads his black horse away as the Union general sobs into his hands.

Beside Stoneman stands a Confederate officer, likely Iverson, or maybe young Colonel Cruise. In at least one account of the Battle of Sunshine Church, Cruise led the charge that won Iverson the battle. The clapboard wall on the southwest side of our old house frames the horse. If the blinds weren't drawn on the window Hess painted at the center of that wall, viewers could have seen into my old bedroom, where that Thoreau poster hung opposite portraits of Confederates Jeb Stuart and Stonewall Jackson.

Blair's present gave me something new to figure out: Why would an image from the aftermath of a Confederate victory in the last phase of the Civil War earn a place of honor in the home of a man who, long gone from the Confederate terrarium in which he grew up, now says that he gives less than one fuck about the guys in gray?

Back in Clinton, a map of Georgia Civil War campaigns hung over the white paneled mantel in our den, Federal routes traced in blue, Confederate in gray. At the base of the black frame my mother fixed a small brass plaque that memorialized Iverson's birth. A kind of heraldic crest for the stories we told about the valor of our adopted family, that map seems to show in every third picture from my childhood.

When my mother moved to Columbia, she hung the map in that mansard-roofed apartment she overstuffed with her prized camelback sofa and a pair of Staffordshire dogs that now crouch on our mantel in Oxford. After she died, that map became mine.

Iverson wasn't really part of my family, and he certainly didn't belong to the family Blair and I would make together. So after we settled in, I hauled that map to the attic and leaned it against the upper reaches of our capped chimney, next to a plywood Frosty the Snowman I bought in an Athens junk store.

Up the ladder a few years later, stepping from rafter to rafter to retrieve a box of notebooks, an insight bloomed into view: That map remains at the center of our home. Perched against the back side of our chimney, it stands out of sight but never out of mind, like those stories of Iverson and the valiant men in gray I once unspooled and now was trying hard to reel back in.

AFTER I TOOK THAT TOUR of our old house in Clinton in 2021, I drove the road that ran behind it, past the field where my friend Dwight Bohler and I played tackle football, toward the woods where the Stanleys lived. A man sat on his porch reading a Bible. Late-afternoon sun shone on his face. I stopped to ask about Chester Stanley, saying we knew each other when we were young. I said the Stanley I was looking for got into some trouble a while back. The man nodded, put down his book, and pointed across the road. "He cuts grass for a living," the man said.

No one was home when I knocked so I left my card in his door. Medical bills were scattered across the porch. Around the side, a riding mower and a couple of push mowers leaned against the clapboard. A black pit bull yelped and strained at his leash and a brown Ford pickup reared back on concrete blocks.

Earlier that summer, I went looking for ways to reconnect with the Roberson family. I was too late to connect with Clinton, who died in 2013. His mother, Elizabeth, was gone, too. Over the phone, his little sister, Senesta, told me that the family buried her at Cedar Ridge Cemetery near Clinton United Methodist Church.

Thinking about the deep loss Elizabeth Roberson suffered in our old house, I placed a bouquet of roses and carnations in front of her headstone.

Chester Stanley called that afternoon as I drove toward my hotel in Macon. His voice sounded throaty, like he was tired. I reminded him about the burglaries, I told him they had scared me, and I spoke of the patch of burned road that haunted me. I didn't summon the courage to ask if his attacks on our house were some sort of mislaid revenge for Charles Roberson's death, but I did ask what he was thinking when he robbed us. "I can't tell you much about that," he said, his voice going soft.

The next day, I dug back into the *Jones County News,* hoping I could find a paper trail for the two deaths, believing I could make better sense of why I divorced myself from Jones County and why I was now compelled to return. I did the microfilm scroll work on a machine at the library, but one answer was just a Google search away.

A hit for Chester Stanley yielded a January 2014 article about the five-year sentence he received for threatening to chop off the head of a family member with a machete on Christmas Eve. Three and a half years before, Stanley entered a guilty plea for possession of drugs, driving under the influence, and driving with a suspended license. According to the article, his probation for both convictions ended eleven months before I knocked on his door.

Charles Roberson proved harder to track. The county coroner told me that a flood soaked and ruined the records of his predecessor. The Jones County sheriff had already tossed files from the 1970s. On the suggestion of Senesta, I drove to nearby Sparta, to look for his grave at the family plot behind a redbrick AME church.

Walking sandy lanes through the cemetery, I came upon a large pine-needle-covered slab, inscribed with the family name, and a dirt plot marked by a rectangular headstone with a pebble finish but no name. When I texted a picture of the grave to Senesta, asking if that was where the family buried her brother Charles, she wrote back, "I was too young to remember." And I wished that I was, too.

EACH TIME I RETURNED TO CLINTON, I traced a path across the sawdust-covered porch that fronted my childhood barbecue joint. Trying to get in touch with the current owner, I left my card with the clerk a couple of times. This time, I bought a sandwich and a couple of bottles of sauce, and took a cell phone picture of my tray.

The sandwich looked like ones Mittie Coulter made in the 1970s when I was a twice-a-week regular. But the pork lacked the smoke and savor, and the sauce tasted thinner. After, I sat there for a good long while, staring into the middle distance. The guys at the next table had to think I was praying.

Everything was there. The cash registers Wayne collected still lined the walls. Ceramic butter churns with tobacco-spit glaze stood on the floor. A photo collection, mounted near the door, brought the family I knew back into focus. There was Wayne, walking the dining room, keys jangling. And Little Roy, watching his cowboys fight the Indians. And Mittie Coulter weighing a pit-cooked ham gone black in the pit.

Staring into their faces, swiveling to look at the interior wall that now covered the spot where the pit once pulsed with smoke, I thought about the price men pay when we go back home with new ideas about our past.

. . .

THE TEXT ON THE HISTORICAL MARKER in front of our house was my childhood scripture. Embossed into iron seven years before I was born, the words spoke to a boy on a search for heroes. Looking at a photograph of that marker in 2021, though, I saw an error in the first line: "Brig. Gen. Alfred Iverson, C.S.A., son of Senator Alfred Iverson, also a Brig. Gen., and Caroline Goode Holt, was born here February 14, 1829."

The date was right, but the titles were off. A year before, on a trip to Columbus, Georgia, I read through the archives at Columbus State University, looking for details of the elder Iverson's life. Thumbing the notes I brought home, I realized that he turned sixty before the war began. That seemed late to serve, even in a war that strapped both sides for troops. So I called Aubrey Newby, a Jones County friend who shares my curiosities. He texted a local historian, who confirmed the mistake. The elder Iverson never served as an officer, much less a brigadier general.

When the state historical commission installed that marker, they ascribed the grandest possible lives to both of the Iversons. The words on that green field were born of exaggeration. They matched my childhood want to believe that the house where I grew up was a place of great import. They echoed the stories my family told about our place in the world, reflecting the want of much of the white South to believe that the men of the Confederacy were heroes. If facts didn't support those beliefs, the stories they told would.

TO FIGURE OUT THE IVERSONS, I dove into the library at Emory University in Atlanta, less than three miles from my old house in Little Five Points, working to connect one Alfred to another. Surrounded by pasteboard boxes, the text for that historical marker in my head, I followed the documents back in time.

The father fell first. Educated at what is now Princeton University, the elder Alfred Iverson won election as a state legislator from Jones County in 1827. His wife died in 1830, less than a year after giving birth to their son, also named Alfred. In late 1830 or early 1831, Iverson moved the family west to Columbus. It's difficult to track which of the twenty-six enslaved people he purchased while in Clinton came with the family to Columbus, but he may have brought a woman named Easter and a boy named Moses.

In Columbus, Alfred Iverson managed federal government contracts to relocate Native Americans from Georgia and Alabama, working with anodyne-sounding companies that did terrible things. As a lawyer for the Alabama Emigrating Company, Iverson accepted cash payments from the federal government to remove Creeks west along what came to be known as the Trail of Tears. On the forced march, thousands of Native peoples died. His Columbus Land Company defrauded Creeks out of more than one million acres. In the process, Iverson purposely fouled up the paperwork so that no one could disentangle it.

Even in an age when many whites characterized Native peoples as savages, Iverson's cruelty and greed stood out. The *Montgomery Advertiser* called Iverson and his colleagues "blood suckers." Their work was "a base and diabolical scheme devised by interested men to keep an ignorant race of people from maintaining their just rights and to deprive them of their small remaining pittance."

The elder Iverson made his fortune off the federal government. By 1855, he rose through the political ranks to win election as a U.S. senator. But Iverson soon wanted the federal government out of the South. Standing before Senate colleagues in 1859, he predicted the inevitability of secession. On a January morning in 1861, after waiting through last-minute petitions to save the Union, Iverson promised secession.

His voice rose that day in the Senate. So did his bile. Money from the cotton trade will win over the North, he said. Speaking of Northern abolitionists, Iverson proposed, "Let us feed them and fatten them and gorge them out of the public crib, until, like young vultures, they vomit in our faces; let us smother their fanaticism with masses of gold and silver; and then, perhaps, they will let us keep our n———!"

Iverson gained momentum as he imagined what might happen in the aftermath of the war he wanted. He seemed to already know that the Confederacy would fail. "You may whip us, but we will not stay whipped," Iverson told his fellow senators. Sounding a rallying cry that would reverberate across generations, he declared, "We will rise again and again to vindicate our right to liberty, and throw off your oppressive and accursed yoke, and never cease the mortal strife until our whole white race is extinguished and our fair land given over to desolation."

"The South will rise again!" As a boy I heard that threat in an ironic away, usually coupled with the phrase "Save your Confederate money, boys." No one seemed to take it seriously. I was almost fifty before I realized that Iverson popularized that threat. Back in 2009, Ole Miss chancellor Dan Jones asked our band to quit playing "From Dixie with Love" during football games. The real problem wasn't the song. As the band played the final notes, students shouted Iverson's threat: "The South will rise again!"

IN MARCH OF 1855, the younger Alfred Iverson received a commission as a lieutenant in the U.S. Cavalry from his father's friend, U.S. secretary of war Jefferson Davis. He was twenty-six. His father took office the next day as a U.S. senator. In March of 1861, seventeen days after Abraham Lincoln became president, the younger Iverson resigned from the U.S. Army. Elected president of the Confederacy, Davis pushed his new army to commission the senator's son as a captain. For the rest of his life, calls of nepotism trailed the younger Iverson.

Before his troops fired a single shot, Iverson's twenty-four-year-old wife, Harriet Harris Hutchins Iverson, died back in Georgia. Like his father before him, young Alfred was now widowed with two children. During the war, he kept Harriet's picture in his breast pocket, tucked inside his journal. The poetry Iverson wrote during that time reeked of loss. "My lips no more her loving kisses draw," he wrote in 1862. "Her heaving bosom to mine no longer strain . . ."

In one of those file boxes at Emory, I found photostats from the journal in which he wrote that terrible poetry and a copy of that picture he carried of his wife. Her image moved me more than I expected. Wearing a ruffled dress, she looks dour and frightened, as if she can see in the ghostly reflection of the glass plate negative all the darkness soon to settle over her country and her family. As if she already knows that her husband, eager to give hell to the Yankees, will fail spectacularly under the pressures of war.

PORING OVER FIELD REPORTS IN the archives at Emory, scribbling notes on a yellow legal pad like my father used, I was a boy again, holed up in the genealogy room at the Macon public library, reading to confirm my beliefs. This time, I read to learn. Battles came into gory focus. At Gaines' Mill near Richmond in June of 1862, Confederates suffered around eight thousand casualties, including Iverson, who took a bullet to the hip and earned praise for his bravery. Scarred by that moment, Iverson never led from the front again.

Three months later at the Battle of South Mountain, his men ran for their lives over rugged terrain, leaping from boulder to boulder. Three days later at Sharpsburg, his troops ran again. Rumors spread that Iverson would be demoted. Instead, he was formally appointed brigadier general. When Iverson chose a Virginian as colonel, some of his North Carolina troops spoke of mutiny. In a fight supposedly built on states' rights, Iverson was challenged by men who wanted the right to be led by a man from their state.

Iverson's 1863 march into Pennsylvania began well. On June 22, his brigade of four North Carolina regiments crossed the state line, the first Confederate troops of the war to clear what they considered a national border.

Nine days later, on the first day of what came to be called the Battle of Gettysburg, they marched across a ripening hayfield beneath a cloudy sky. Thirteen hundred Confederates bounded forward, eyes on bluecoats in the distance, headed toward a stone wall on an oak-lined ridge north of town. Flags at front, guns at right shoulders, the Confederates moved "as if on parade," a captain later recalled.

Eighty yards out, Union soldiers hidden behind that wall rose and fired. Balls hissed and cut through gray lines. Smoke billowed across the field, so dense that neither side could see ten feet distant. A Confederate marching in the second rank got pelted with the brains of a man in the first.

Unable to advance or retreat, many in Iverson's brigade lay down in a hollow to return fire. An hour later, all ran out of ammunition. Found clutching his rifle, one of Iverson's men took five shots through the head before he hit the turf. Blood ran over the field in a stream. This was the gore Horwitz wanted me to see.

Trapped men raised handkerchiefs to beg for mercy or placed

their hats or boots on their bayonets. Troops ran toward enemy lines to surrender, crossing the field while holding hands.

As his troops fell or surrendered, Iverson shouted them down, calling them cowards. Fewer than five hundred of his men answered roll call the next day.

That morning, Colonel Christie, leader of the North Carolina 23rd, met with survivors. Gathered on the porch of a farmhouse, surrounded by the men who survived Iverson's charge, Christie, close to death, lifted himself from a stretcher to say that, though he would not live to lead them again, the "imbecile Iverson never should."

Theories of why Iverson performed so poorly circulated before Gettysburg was over. Was he still drunk from drinking with colleagues the night before? Or did that day expose him as a son of privilege who used his privilege to win a commission that helped lose a war? A colonel under his command complained that he was "devoid of that energy and vim essentially prerequisite to a commanding officer." Still grieving his wife, did Iverson suffer from depression?

A year and a month after Gettysburg, Iverson won the Battle of Sunshine Church. But over the decades to come, as the mothers of North Carolina recounted the deaths of their sons on a battlefield in Pennsylvania, his name became an epithet.

In 1910, a photographer took a portrait of the younger Iverson on the front porch of a cypress cabin at Shingle Creek near Kissimmee, Florida. Iverson wears frayed work pants, a white shirt, and a dark vest. He leans back in a chair, a newspaper in his lap. His gray beard is well trimmed. He wears wire-rim glasses. Iverson looks sad, as if his eyes reflect the losses he'd suffered. To his left, a hound dog sits.

It's a common photograph, found easily through a Google search. Thumbing a vertical file at Emory, though, I found a print with some writing on the back. The text was new to me. From the writer, I learned that Iverson posed for the photo a little more than a year before he died in 1911, and that he called the dog Nig.

At home with Blair

Chapter Ten

HOME FOR GOOD

On the first morning of War Days in 2023, I ate breakfast at a Waffle House, across the parking lot from a motel in Gray. I expected to find men with hollow eyes wearing butternut trousers that smelled of mildew. Instead, I met a man named Bart in a white T-shirt and red shorts, just off an overnight shift. He was going fishing later. After I told him what I planned, Bart paid his bill and told me to have a blessed day.

A mile closer to my old home in Clinton, a man in a gray wool getup too tight for his body rode the highway in an E-Z-GO golf cart with a Confederate battle flag on the front bumper. Threading through the early crowd on this May day, a bluecoat at his side, he nodded like a pasha. The dull sky above threatened rain.

In the camp, among a rank of white canvas tents, a mother braided a daughter's brown hair. A father reclined on a blanket as his son played checkers on an iPad. Down the hill, I met Louis from nearby Sandersville. "I'll spend sixty bucks for powder and caps for my rifle this weekend," he told me. "In the war, they would stuff the gun with powder and top that with the ball and then ram-rod it down. Here we don't do the ramming because people have left the ramrod in the rifle and shot it like an arrow."

Louis fights for both Georgia and Wisconsin. On this day he would fight for Wisconsin. Louis also serves as the company cook. He gestured toward a blue enamel pot, stacked with biscuits. I asked about technique. "They're canned," he said. I asked which brand is best. "It doesn't really matter."

In the yard where the old jail kitchen stood before my father hauled it to our land, blue and gray troops moved in halting forma-tions to face a flagpole. A boy of maybe fourteen, wearing a buck-skin hat, his face a mask of freckles and acne, dropped his rifle. The guy in gray who looked to be in charge whispered something in his ear. "I'm a doo-doo head," the boy chanted as he ran in circles. "I'm a doo-doo head, I'm a doo-doo head."

In 1982, the Old Clinton Historical Society began restaging Iverson's victory over Stoneman at the Battle of Sunshine Church. Brochures for War Days promised the "crackle of musketry, the thunder of cannon fire, and the pounding of hoofbeats." My mother and father imagined the society as a means to preserve early Geor-gia architecture and foster pride in place. They aimed to train the spotlight through history tours and architectural pilgrimages. But then came the fight over the highway. The society splintered. Grant applications failed to bring in big money. To raise awareness and funds, the society announced, "Confederate Clinton calls you to the Defense of Middle Georgia."

I spoke to my mother before the first reenactment. This was before she left Clinton, when she still held court in that bentwood rocker, in the room where Brigadier General Alfred Iverson took his first breath. When my mother called War Days tacky, she was talking about more than aesthetics.

In her head, tacky was the opposite of genteel. Alfred Iverson, writing poetry by a campfire before leading troops into battle, was genteel. Wearing the old colors, waving a battle flag like a high school cheerleader, was tacky. "War Days is tacky," she said, in the same tone she used when talking about our neighbors who wrapped their floral-print couches in protective vinyl.

War Days worked, though, raising money for restoration efforts, including a plan to excavate the old tanyard pits where my father and I dug for relics of the days when Clinton thrived. Each May for forty years, with a pause for Covid, the blue and gray have fired their muskets in the field below the old jail site. But I never heeded the call. Reading the brochure for the 2023 event, I recognized that something more than my mother's chagrin turned me away.

As a child, I obsessed over Confederate stories. I memorized the names of the major generals. I knew the names of their horses, too. War Days reminded me of the boy I used to be, who swallowed the stories he was fed, divided the world into the South and everybody else, and called enemies carpetbaggers and scalawags. Their pageant reminded me of a time when I believed that claptrap about the terrors of Reconstruction and liked to say that a Yankee was anyone who didn't have the good sense to live south of the line mapped by Mason and Dixon. I didn't want to be that boy.

Colonel J. C. Nobles stepped from the crowd to welcome all on behalf of the Old Clinton Historical Society and the 16th Georgia Infantry. He wore a green hat, cocked at a jaunty angle, and what looked like a long housecoat, trimmed in cardinal selvage. Twirling a walking cane, relishing his time in the spotlight, he spoke in flourishes and exclamations. My first thought was: *This guy's doing drag.*

Back home in Oxford, the seventh annual Pride Parade would round the square in a couple of hours. For the first parade in 2016, I wore a JOHN QUEER T-shirt, printed by a farm in Arkansas to stake a claim to gay rural life, and drove the grand marshal through town in my convertible. The theme for 2023 would be Long Live the Queens. The parade would honor the late Colby Kullman, who taught me Tennessee Williams plays and cackled over that Karl Malden scene in *Baby Doll.*

My Instagram feed soon filled with gay women friends wearing rainbow flower tiaras. Wrapped in feather boas, they smiled big for the camera. Straight male neighbors, wearing dollar-store crowns, marched past the sign in front of the Episcopal Church that read JESUS LOVES YOU. But I never posted the photos I took in Clinton to social media. This drag was harder to share.

Troops stood on opposite sides of that flagpole. The colonel handed out ribbons to families who had lost loved ones since they last gathered. He paid tribute to a charter member of the Old Clinton Historical Society and a teenage reenactor killed in a car wreck. He showed care. He prayed for their families. He was funny. "If you're a heathen and you want to step out of the ranks," he said before a prayer, "I won't chastise you publicly."

As the colonel spoke, I followed a guy wearing a khaki suit with a pleated back and an off-white hat. He had a kind, soft face. Before I realized it was Chuck Johnson, the new owner of my old house, I thought, *I could wear that.* When I walked up to reintroduce myself, Chuck invited me to stop by his sutler tent before I left.

...

MOVING THROUGH THE STREETS of my old town, I thought about what to buy. Boiled peanuts, yes. Dream catchers with the slogan "Sweet Southern Breeze," no. Creamed honey from local bees, maybe. A gray wool overcoat with brass buttons, no. A five-dollar pair of Yankee reenactor socks, slightly used, definitely. Historians tell us that we now perform our identities as consumers. To connect with a shared regional identity that is in retreat, Southerners buy stilted reminders of what we left behind.

Dora's Soul Food did business in a tent catercorner from the Sons of Confederate Veterans headquarters. She and her children fried chicken that day. Collard greens, black-eyed peas, and sweet potatoes, too, kept warm in three Crock-Pots daisy-chained together. I watched a Confederate reenactor step up to buy a foam cup of sweet tea. I watched a black hand take green bills from a white hand.

Waiting for their orders of hot-water cornbread, three ladies in period dress joined me. Each carried a campstool, so they could sit and watch the battle. They loved Dora's fried chicken. "It's real old-timey," one said. They lived somewhere near Athens. I told her I went to school in Athens. "We went to school in Stone Mountain," she said, back when Stone Mountain was nice. "It's a war zone now," another said.

I thought of my late friend Valerie Boyd, the kind and fierce author and professor who lived in the shadow of Stone Mountain, beneath that bas-relief of Robert E. Lee on his horse, Traveller. And I thought of that Emory professor from way back who asked me to think about Stone Mountain in new ways.

I met a woman who called herself an ice angel. Lillian wore her blond hair in a tight bun and carried a canvas bag, loaded with cubed ice and Gatorades. Reenactors in wool needed to stay hydrated. To keep up period appearances, she placed a cloth napkin on top to hide the bottles. Rachel, who stood beside her, served as chief medical officer for the battle. In real life she was a nurse practitioner. Rachel talked about the first time she witnessed a skirmish, of how she smelled gunpowder that day and held a cannonball.

"That gunpowder is in my blood," she said. "So is the spirit of my ancestors." Rachel spoke of the Civil War, before quickly correcting herself to say the War Between the States. I asked why. "That was not a civil war," she said. "It was secession, which the Southern states had a right to do." Anticipating my next question, she said, "Slavery was one of the causes for the war." She paused. "I'd say it was in the top ten."

Back on the battlefield, Colonel Nobles laid down the law: "When the barn-burning, chicken-stealing, white-trash Yankees come through, you can't shoot." He said something else about protocols and keeping a full canteen. The rest was lost on me. I sat on the highway shoulder to listen. As he began talking about Iverson, the sun burned through the clouds. "He lived just a half mile from here," the colonel said. I turned to look.

When a cannon fired, a gasp rippled through the crowd. I felt a thud in my stomach. Leaves shook in the trees. A dog barked, and smoke drifted across the field. The colonel did a kind of play-by-play. Another cannon fired, and he yelled, "That's twenty-five dollars right there!" adding up the cost of gunpowder. I watched Confederate troops sneak through the woods as Union wounded dropped face down in the grass.

I spotted a man who wore a blue canvas vest, with patches on the flanks. The slogan AMERICAN BY BIRTH, SOUTHERN BY THE GRACE OF GOD wrapped around a battle flag. He wore a blue palmetto, symbol of my mother's native South Carolina, atop a small rectangle stitched with the words: I AM THE MONUMENT.

I thought of nights in the summer of 2020, when Blair and I sat before our television in Oxford, watching work crews dismantle Confederate monuments, so surprised by what was happening that we giggled. And I thought of my friend Caroline Randall Williams, an author and professor from Nashville who, in that moment, wrote about the "rape-colored skin" she inherited from her white ancestors for a newspaper essay "You Want a Confederate Monument? My Body Is a Confederate Monument."

Toward the end of the day, I met a young man named Ben who lived in Macon and worked as a computer software engineer. His parents met at a reenactment and now he did it, too. "I love to die in an impressive fashion," he said. Ben asked what I thought about all this.

I told him that I expected to see more overt racism. "People were nice," I said. "Even when they suspected I thought differently than they did." He looked up at me and said, "I think differently, too." At the close of our conversation, he asked if I wanted my picture taken with his reproduction rifle. Gripping the barrel of his gun in my right hand, I grinned like a goofball. He said, "No smiling in the Civil War."

Before I left for Oxford, I stopped by Chuck's sutler tent. He was hammering a new sole onto an old boot, so I had time to look around. I passed a rack of Confederate action figures, next to a stack of toy rifles, alongside a row of vinyl Confederate flags. Chuck sold blue and gray dress coats, blue and gray kepis, and coffee mugs with Alfred Iverson's bearded face on them.

Back at home, I had folded a red-and-white Confederate flag into a square, tucked it into a plastic bag, and written Chuck's name on it. As a boy, I saw great value in the stories that flag could tell. Now, on the backside of my search, I saw the lies woven into the fabric. I wanted to put those lies in their place. When I handed the flag to Chuck, I told him about the estate sale north of Macon in Bolingbroke, where my mother bought that French theater poster and this flag, too. I told him that my mother thought of it as an heirloom.

"I used to believe this flag was really old," I said. "But before I packed it up, I took another look at the stitching. Whoever made that flag stitched the panels together with a machine. This flag once hung in my house," I said, gesturing over my shoulder toward the house where Alfred Iverson was born and I lived for seventeen years. Embarrassed, I corrected myself: "It hung in your house."

AFTER A WEEKNIGHT DINNER IN OXFORD, Blair and I talked in the kitchen. Face jugs from my Atlanta days, purchased on road trips through North Georgia, showing rock teeth and kiln-melted eyes, line the back wall. Above the sink hangs a plywood Howard Finster portrait of Elvis, cut into the shape of a winged angel, based on that dream I heard him talk about the summer I moved to town.

"We display few family pictures," I said to Blair, unpacking the guilt I carry for shutting my mother out. "Her style has gone missing from my life," I worried, remembering her love of well-cut clothes and stiffly poured drinks. "To make a new life, I cut her from the stories I tell about myself."

As I rambled, an image came into view. My mother lies on the floor of our den, arms and legs extended, feet planted against my belly. I fly above her, grasping her hands for balance, playing airplane, thinking of the Delta jets that soared above us each time we drove into Atlanta. Suspended there, I feel safe, knowing she will never let me fall.

None of the bad stuff has happened yet. No drunken rants in the back hall, no gunshots in the yard, no dead boy in the bedroom, no thieves in the woods, no dead preacher burned to bone on the road. Decades will pass before she dies alone in a hospital bed two states away from me. I let go of her hands, arc my back, and make the zoom and whoosh sounds I think that jets make.

That night, Blair reached for a piece of silver that passed to us when my mother died. Engraved with the words WINTHROP COL- LEGE, the spoon was a souvenir of her short time there, when she marched in the band and twirled that wooden baton. I traced the letters with my finger, rubbing the handle like a genie lamp.

Blair gestured to a fish plate from Clinton, displayed in a glass-fronted cabinet. She nodded toward a framed copy of my mother's catfish stew recipe, inspired by her father's fish camp on the Edisto River. I leaned in to read the recipe, with its calls for streak o' lean and catfish bones. Gently, patiently, Blair reminded me that although she adapted that recipe, using a modern one from chefs Scott Peacock and Edna Lewis, the reason we serve catfish stew for every third dinner party is that we made a decision to remember my mother that way.

We served it to Kiese Laymon when he moved back home from New York to Mississippi. Blair cooked it for Rosalyn Durant, ESPN executive vice president, before she green-lit our television show. My father ate that stew at our dining room table and told Blair that her version tasted better than the one my mother's father cooked.

Blair didn't have to say what I already knew: My written voice, my visual style, my want to step into the spotlight, my tendency toward maximalism—all were born of my mother's deferred hopes. The worst of her is forever in me. The best is, too.

That stew reminds us that recipes are inheritances. Passed down from my grandfather to my mother and now to my wife, that stew gestures to where my family came from and to the progress we've made across decades and generations. Blair cooks that stew because it's flat-out delicious, and she cooks it to remind us both that my Georgia past doesn't have to topple our Mississippi present.

Mississippi is hard on a soul. Mississippi is just plain hard for many. It's a broken place, in the slow and fitful act of mending. That's why it feels like home. Twice, after I stepped into conversations about slavery and its aftermaths, I paid a price. Once, I went down on principle. The second time, I went down in flames.

In Mississippi, I've learned lessons about how to listen and how to love. Here, I've owned up to the power I have to help tell the stories of others. That knowledge has made me more aware of the change I can make as I rewrite my own story. Oxford is the site of my ongoing reconstruction. After years of running from my Georgia home, I now run toward my home in Mississippi.

Momma would've loved the catfish stew Blair cooks in our galley kitchen. Instead of the gelatin from fish backbones, Blair thickens hers with potatoes. She uses bacon from our friend Allan Benton in Tennessee instead of streak o' lean from the Red & White store in Gray. For company, Blair spoons stew into the bowls with handles my mother bought at that Bolingbroke sale. *If a bowl has handles,* my mother would say, *you have permission to drink from it.*

My mother wanted out of her small town. She didn't see herself living in a bungalow next to the railroad tracks. In my mother's head, her father didn't run a filling station and her mother didn't sell flowers from a stand in the front yard. Our life here in Oxford, in which I write books and Blair makes art, has made good on my mother's wildest dreams. She would've flourished at our table. And she would've loved to know how we use the things she collected.

One winter afternoon, as I poured an old-fashioned for a friend, I reached for a glass cocktail stirrer, wondering about the paddle at the end with the small divot. It looked more than decorative. A week later, another friend sent us a tin of caviar to celebrate the new year. I went looking for a mother-of-pearl spoon. Surely, my mother collected one of those.

Rummaging kitchen drawers, I flashed to that cocktail stirrer. At the edge of my comprehension, I heard my mother say, *Glass can be an acceptable substitute for mother-of-pearl.* The divot was the tell. What was now my cocktail stirrer was once her caviar spoon.

Blair and I have rooted our lives here, but Oxford's geographical and social contours do not limit us. We make our home here because we choose to stay. I can picture my mother now, reaching for that caviar spoon, talking about the South Carolina that birthed her, reveling in what Mississippi has made possible for us.

Three generations

PASSAGES

In 2021, two years before I went back to Clinton, we moved Jess into his dorm at Belmont University on a sunny August afternoon. The next morning, before Blair woke in our Nashville hotel room, I drove east twenty miles to Mount Juliet, Tennessee. I had recently been talking with Reverend Will D. Campbell's family about moving his writing cabin, vacant since he passed in 2013, to Mississippi, where the preacher and writer and activist was born and raised.

Dragonfly sculptures, donated by admirers of his first memoir, dotted the yard. The knocker plate on the front door of the squat log building read THAR HE, a gesture to the brave words Moses Wright spoke to identify one of Emmett Till's killers. Inside, black-and-white photos told the story of Brother Will's civil rights work.

In the runup to my new job, developing programs to seed

creativity across my university, those conversations with the Campbell family gained traction. We made plans to restore and move the cabin to Greenfield Farm, a writers residency I'm helping develop outside Oxford on a ridgeline where William Faulkner once ran a mule and cotton farm.

After I paced off the length and width of the cabin and took close-ups of the foundation, I drove back to Nashville, where our little family ate chili-cheeseburgers and talked about the promise of college. Jess chose Belmont University after a false start at American University in Washington, D.C., and a pandemic year at Ole Miss. Early on, I feared he might wallow in the ditch like me. But Jess takes after my father.

We walked the campus after lunch, weaving between gazebos where tie-dyed kids played guitars, past a baroque new business school with soaring columns. Showing off his new campus, Jess beamed, as if he could already see the home he would make there. On my phone, I now keep a picture of our family, taken later in that first Belmont semester, in which Jess, taller than both of us, smiles big and drapes his arms across our shoulders, as if to say, *Thanks for making the home that made me.*

One year after we dropped Jess at Belmont, my father died in Oxford on the morning of his ninety-sixth birthday. As cancer took him, we listened to Johnny Cash sing his favorite song, "Folsom Prison Blues." When I was a young man, my father worried over me. Would alcoholism take me, like that disease took my mother? Would the ghosts from our days in Clinton haunt me all my days? That worry ate at him. I could see it in his eyes.

Back in 2016, after he moved to Oxford, Daddy began to laugh more. Watching him grow older, I saw him change. He smiled often. His eyes flashed and crinkled when he laughed. Too many people seem to grow more fearful as they age. Too often, that fear curdles into bitterness. It took me a while to figure out why my father went the other way.

Living two miles from us, he got a chance to see my world, to belong in our home. He came to love Blair and marvel at her art and her cooking. He got to witness the grace and intelligence that Jess shows. That meant, I think, that he knew I was going to be okay. He could quit worrying, and so could I.

Blair's Catfish Stew

J esse Clifton Evans cooked a version of this stew at his fish camp on the Edisto River near Orangeburg, South Carolina. His daughter, my mother, Mary Beverly Evans Edge, memorialized his method in a recipe. Elaborated, rewritten, and cooked by my wife, Blair Hobbs, this version of that recipe now connects our family across generations. My hope is that what I've written about my people helps you connect with yours. My belief is that a pot of catfish stew might help, too.

Serves 8

2 tablespoons butter

2 strips good bacon, chopped (we love Benton's)

3 celery stalks, sliced

1 big onion, chopped

4 garlic cloves, minced

2 teaspoons dried thyme

1 teaspoon dried basil

Salt and pepper, to taste

6 to 8 red new potatoes, half-inch dice

3 big carrots, peeled and sliced

1 (14-ounce) can diced tomatoes

1 cup dry white wine

6 to 7 cups water

3 chicken bouillon cubes

4 green onions, green parts only, chopped

2 pounds catfish filets (we love Simmons Farm-Raised)

1 to 2 tablespoons honey

½ bunch Italian parsley, chopped

Tabasco

In a Dutch oven (we use Lodge), heat the butter and the bacon over medium high heat. Cook the bacon until it begins to brown, about 7 minutes.

Add the celery, onion, garlic, thyme, and basil. Season with a few pinches of salt. Stir, picking up any browned bits, until the mix sputters, releases its water, then cooks off and sizzles and the onions are translucent, about 10 minutes.

Add the potatoes, carrots, and tomatoes. Stir and bring to a boil.

Add the wine, water, and bouillon cubes. Season to taste with salt and pepper and bring back to a boil.

Stir in the green onions. Turn the heat down to a simmer, cover with a lid (leaving a crack for steam), and cook until the potatoes are tender, 15 to 20 minutes.

Lightly salt and pepper the catfish filets; cut them in half if needed to help fit in the pot without crowding. Gently lay them in the pot and cook for 3 to 4 minutes. Flip them and cook another 3 or 4 minutes, or until you can cut them into chunks with the side of your spoon. Do not overcook or the chunks of catfish will turn to feathers.

Season one final time as needed with salt and pepper, and add honey to taste.

Serve in bowls (preferably with handles), garnish with parsley, and splash with Tabasco, as needed.

Bookshelf

House of Smoke began as scenes in my head. Reading these books (plus one album, one thesis, one law enforcement report, one speech, and a few digital sources), I gathered the inspiration and borrowed the techniques needed to turn those scenes into a story.

Chapters nine and ten utilize some research and writing for the *Oxford American,* originally published as "Getting the Look" and "My Mother's Catfish Stew."

MEMOIR

These authors helped me understand what memoirs demand of writers and promise to readers. Most are contemporary. The three exceptions—by Will D. Campbell, Harry Crews, and Willie Morris—are classics from white Southern men who grappled with their inheritances and responsibilities as they tried to make a way forward. I attempted here to follow in their giant footsteps. Some craft books are listed separately at the end. The Birkerts and Gornick books were especially helpful when I was figuring out where to situate myself in this story.

Brother to a Dragonfly, by Will D. Campbell (1977)

A Childhood, by Harry Crews (1978)

Elephant in the Room, by Tommy Tomlinson (2019)

Fire Shut Up in My Bones, by Charles M. Blow (2014)

Half-Life of a Secret, by Emily Strasser (2023)

Heating & Cooling, by Beth Ann Fennelly (2017)

Heavy, by Kiese Laymon (2018)

House of Prayer No. 2, by Mark Richard (2011)

In the New World, by Lawrence Wright (1987)

Lost & Found, by Kathryn Schulz (2022)

Low County, by J. Nicole Jones (2021)

Memorial Drive, by Natasha Trethewey (2020)

My Father, the Pornographer, by Chris Offutt (2016)

Night of the Gun, by David Carr (2008)

North Toward Home, by Willie Morris (1967)

The Yellow House, by Sarah M. Broom (2019)

The Art of Memoir, by Mary Karr (2015)

The Art of Time in Memoir, by Sven Birkerts (2007)

The Situation and the Story, by Vivian Gornick (2001)

Writing About Your Life, by William Zinsser (2004)

CLINTON AND THE CIVIL WAR

As a boy, I wondered why no one had written a book about my hero, Brigadier General Alfred Iverson. My wish has now been twice granted. *The Rashness of That Hour* focuses on Iverson's failure at Gettysburg. *The Paternal Suit,* a catalog of artwork and essays inspired in part by the Iverson line of F. Scott Hess's family, asks a question: "Where does personal story end and national history begin?" That question is also at the heart of the book you hold in your hands.

The Cawthon work is a thesis. To read it, contact the Hargrett Library at the University of Georgia. To read work from the latter phase of Cawthon's career, look up his articles in the *Southern Partisan* and other publications monitored by the Southern Poverty Law Center.

> *Clinton: County Seat on the Georgia Frontier 1808–1821,* by
>   William Lamar Cawthon Jr. (1984)
> *The Paternal Suit,* by F. Scott Hess (2012)
> *The Rashness of That Hour,* by Robert J. Wynstra (2010)
> *Robert E. Lee and Me,* by Ty Seidule (2021)
> *Troubled Commemoration,* by Robert J. Cook (2007)

ATHENS AND ATLANTA

An earlier version of this book included a long digression about Deacon Lunchbox, the alter ego of Tim Ruttenber, a self-described "socially conscious redneck poet." Deacon played Atlanta music clubs in the 1980s and 1990s. The first time I saw him read, Deacon wore a flower muumuu and a cowboy hat and revved a chain saw until purple smoke clouded the stage. The next time, he strapped a pair of plastic boobies across his chest and strummed them like a frottoir. At parties, I still like to quote from his 1989 book of poetry, *Some Different Kinds of Songs*: "They got dope-sniffing dogs at Dollywood / My vacation plans are ruined."

The Complete Lunchbox, by Tim Ruttenber, edited by
   Robert Sean Roarty (1994)
Cool Town, by Grace Elizabeth Hale (2020)
New Georgia Encyclopedia website, by Georgia
   Humanities, University of Georgia Press (ongoing)
The Tom Patterson Years, by Tom Patterson (2021)

Oxford and Mississippi

"To understand the world, you must first understand a place like Mississippi." Despite the T-shirts and dish towels you might see for sale in Oxford, William Faulkner didn't write or say those words. More than likely Willie Morris wrote those words and passed them off as Faulkner's. That's the theory W. Ralph Eubanks advances in one of the following books. No matter, those words sound true.

One quick note on the University of Mississippi nickname, Ole Miss. For the longest time, I avoided that term, because I knew that it referenced the mistress of the plantation and was born of the years before Emancipation. More recently, I've begun to refer to my alma mater and employer as Ole Miss, taking into account my affection for the university I know and arguments made by some Black faculty, who say the term reflects the history of the institution.

Absalom, Absalom!, by William Faulkner (1936)
The Barn, by Wright Thompson (2024)
Heritage and Hate, by Stephen M. Monroe (2021)
Mississippi: An American Journey, by Anthony Walton
   (1996)
The Other Mississippi, by David Sansing (2018)
A Place Like Mississippi, by W. Ralph Eubanks (2021)
The Price of Defiance, by Charles W. Eagles (2009)

Remembering Emmett Till, by Dave Tell (2019)
The Song and the Silence, by Yvette Johnson (2017)
The Statue and the Fury, by Jim Dees (2016)

THE SOUTH

Good Old Boys is the lone album in this roster. Randy Newman's song cycle promised "glimpses into the collective mind and past of a maligned, neglected, and vital portion of America." I'll speak more directly: That album is a masterpiece, one of the very best attempts, by any artist in any medium, to reckon with my home region.

The American South, by Charles Reagan Wilson (2021)
Away Down South, by James C. Cobb (2005)
"Elvis as Redneck," by Will D. Campbell, presented
     August 7, 1995, at the University of Mississippi*
     (included in *In Search of Elvis,* edited by Vernon
     Chadwick [1997])
Encyclopedia of Southern Culture, edited by Charles Reagan
     Wilson, William Ferris, and Ann J. Abadie (1989,
     updated editions available)
Forty Acres and a Goat, by Will D. Campbell (1986)
Good Old Boys, by Randy Newman (1974)
A Mind to Stay Here, by John Egerton (1970)
A More Beautiful and Terrible History, by Jeanne Theoharis
     (2018)
Notes from No Man's Land, by Eula Biss (2009)

---

*   In the printed copy of the speech, given to me by Campbell, he does not
    refer to his daughter as a redneck. In my notes from the speech, he did.

South to America, by Imani Perry (2022)
The Southern Way of Life, by Charles Reagan Wilson (2022)

SOUTHERN FOODWAYS

Nearly a decade after *The Potlikker Papers* published, I still take great pride in that book. I wrote it to push forward the conversation that John Egerton began with *Southern Food.* If you don't know the Ribbat book, translated from the German, it's a brilliant social history of the restaurant as idea and reality, told in narrative form.

The Edible South, by Marcie Cohen Ferris (2014)
Gravy podcast, Southern Foodways Alliance, via your
     favorite app
Gravy quarterly journal, Southern Foodways Alliance,
     published by Hub City Press
In the Restaurant, by Christoph Ribbat (2018)
Joe York films, via southernfoodways.org
The Potlikker Papers, by John T. Edge (2017)
Southern Food, by John Egerton (1987)

TRUESOUTH

Writing and hosting this show is a joy. New episodes premiere in the fall on the SEC Network. Episodes re-air on ESPN and the SEC Network. All episodes stream on ESPN+, Disney+, and Hulu+.

Thanks

My debts are as deep and wide as the big river that runs along the western edge of my adopted state. Meredith Berry, my first cousin, gifted the framed recipe of my mother's catfish stew that prompted this book. (Yes, the same Meredith who took me to see *Animal House*.)

Beth Ann Fennelly, a great Oxford friend and a great writer, helped me see the promise of this manuscript. Jan Winburn, my MFA program colleague at UGA, cut away the flab and straightened out the curves to help me find the power of the book within. Katie Carter King, who also worked with me on *The Potlikker Papers*, dug for research, checked my facts, and called my bluffs.

Brett Anderson, Meredith Berry, Rosalind Bentley, Rebecca Cleary, Brandt Furin, Melissa Booth Hall, David Landis, Debbie Lurie-Smith, Sam McNair, Stephen Monroe, Aubrey Newby,

Melany Robinson, Dave Tell, Wright Thompson, and Charles Reagan Wilson read manuscript versions of this book and offered insights, corrections, and amplifications. Thanks to y'all, this book is a whole lot better than the manuscript you read.

In 2022, I founded the Mississippi Lab, a new program at the University of Mississippi. That same year, I began serving the Department of Writing and Rhetoric as writer-in-residence. Noel Wilkin, Stephen Monroe, Mary Conaway, LaToya Faulk, Julie Glasco, Andrea Jekabsons, Glenn Schove, and Afton Thomas are a few of the UM colleagues who inspire me. I'm also thankful to Dawn Denham for convening our department's Wednesday morning writing crew.

Since 2015, I've taught in the low-residency MFA program in narrative nonfiction at the University of Georgia's Grady College of Journalism and Mass Communication, founded by Valerie Boyd and now directed by Monimala Basu. This book really began when Valerie invited me to join the faculty. Her love and trust fueled a belief that my experience and my story could serve others. Teaching in that program, working with dedicated mentors and smart students, I've become a better writer.

Also in Athens, Kat Stein, director of the Hargrett Rare Book and Manuscript Library at the University of Georgia, shared William Cawthon's thesis on Clinton, Georgia, and his accompanying papers.

My old Atlanta friend Howard Pousner helped me understand the role of my birth state in the rise of folk art. In Macon, Bob Long and Dan Lanford shared insights about my father's work. Kelly Crow and Sam McNair, pledge brothers in Sigma Nu, recalled the Athens music scene.

Curator Mark Sloan gifted me a copy of the catalog for artist F. Scott Hess's exhibit *The Paternal Suit*. In an effort to understand both Alfred Iversons, I relied on Hess, an Iverson descendant. Civil War battlefield guide Gary Kross also helped. I often turned to the research and writing of Robert J. Wynstra. And I benefited from the stewardship of Kathy Shoemaker of the Stuart A. Rose Manuscript, Archives, and Rare Book Library, part of Robert W. Woodruff Library at Emory University.

Back in Jones County and Macon, these kind folk shared stories, cooked dinners, and poured cocktails: Gordon and Josephine Bennett, Tavia Mellard and Jeffrey Henderson, Charlie and Terri Newberry, Aubrey and Jennifer Newby, Frances and Jimmy Roberts, Durette Childs, Richie Jones, Sara Roberts, Mike Seekins, Katherine Walden, and Bob Woodcock.

Leigh Sloan of the Jones County public library shared knowledge of my old backyard. Earlene Hamilton, president of the Old Clinton Historical Society, cracked open a door to my past. Cecil Ethridge helped with Clinton connections. Special thanks to Dwight Bohler for our eggs-and-grits reunion breakfast. Researching this book resurfaced a terrible moment in the Roberson family's history. Senesta Roberson, long gone from my life, still welcomed me back into hers. Senesta, I'm genuinely sorry that my inquiries triggered old traumas.

To make sense of my time in Oxford, I talked to Susan Glisson, who helped lead our effort to commemorate the struggle for equal access to education, and to Dave Tell, who is writing about how James Meredith is remembered. Sheri Castle, LeeAnne Gault, Melissa Hall, John Kessler, Mary Beth Lasseter, Elizabeth Sims, and other friends from my SFA days helped me gain perspective. Though I left the SFA in late 2021, I'm immensely proud of the work we did together, and I follow closely the good work SFA continues to do. To learn more, point your browser to southern foodways.org.

Writing *House of Smoke,* I hopscotched the South in search of quiet places to work. The Writers' Colony at Dairy Hollow in Arkansas fed and watered me for ten days. The Art Farm at Serenbe, Georgia, was the site of two full-manuscript rewrites. The Hambidge Center for the Creative Arts and Sciences in Rabun Gap, Georgia, awarded me a two-week stay and a Wisebram Culinary Distinguished Fellowship. Waylaid in New York City by a cancelled flight, I wrote the prologue in the Chelsea Hotel. (RIP, Leonard Cohen.)

Friends and friends of friends also offered spaces to bunker, including Rinne Allen of Athens, Milton Lovell and Erin Pate of Memphis, and, over in Texas, the Dalgleish Family of Frio Cañon, Anne and J. R. Carter of Frio Cañon, and Julia Gabriel and Morgan Weber of Rio Frio.

I've worked with my agent, David Black, since 2001. He's as kind a man as I know. He's also fierce and clever as a wombat. David closed the deal for this book when I was on the road, filming season three of *TrueSouth.*

When this book published, the SEC Network was airing season eight and we were planning season nine. Thanks for taking a chance on me, Rosalyn Durant, Michael Thompson, Joe Disney, and a host of other SEC Network and ESPN colleagues past and present. Next plate of keftedes at Johnny's in Homewood is on me, Greg Sankey and Charlie Hussey.

I've learned so damn much about the power of narrative while working with our Bluefoot Entertainment location crew of Stephen Allmendiger, Jeremy Davis, Tim Horgan, Hillary Horgan, Thom McCallum, Matt Furuta, Santiago Garcia, Vin Guglielmina, Annie Hayes, Angie Pierandri, Nicole Pugliese, Shane Pugliese, Kaline Schounce, and Matt Spear. Our executive producer, Wright Thompson, helped me recover from two wrecks and inspires me to move through the world with as much grace and kindness as I can muster.

Francis Lam was the ideal editor for this project. At every step of the way, he asked good questions that made this a better book. Some of those questions made me a better person. His colleagues at Crown were kind and smart and joyful collaborators. Thank you, Darian Keels, Amani Shakrah, Patricia Shaw, Dianna Stirpe, Chris Tanigawa, and Heather Williamson. All hail publicists Tammy Blake and Josie McRoberts, marketers Kimberly Lew and Dyana Messina, creative director Chris Brand, and art director Anna Kochman. It was a great pleasure to consult with Melany Robinson of Sprouthouse on communications for this book.

My wife, Blair Hobbs, is my best reader and my best friend. Her art surprises and delights and gives me new ways to see. We laugh a lot. Sometimes we snort when we laugh. The home we make together sustains and inspires me. Our son, Jess, is proof that generational success is possible. He also stirs a mean boulevardier.